WITHDRAWN FROM THE LIBRARY UNIVERSITY OF WINCHESTER

Contemporary Diplomacy

Representation and Communication
in a Globalized World

D0434358

Contemporary Diplomacy

Representation and Communication in a Globalized World

GEOFFREY ALLEN PIGMAN

polity

UNIVERSITY OF WINCHESTER
LIBRARY

Copyright © Geoffrey Allen Pigman 2010

The right of Geoffrey Allen Pigman to be identified as Author of this Work has been asserted in accordance with the UK Copyright, Designs and Patents Act 1988.

First published in 2010 by Polity Press

Polity Press
65 Bridge Street
Cambridge CB2 1UR, UK

Polity Press
350 Main Street
Malden, MA 02148, USA

All rights reserved. Except for the quotation of short passages for the purpose of criticism and review, no part of this publication may be reproduced, stored in a retrieval system, or transmitted, in any form or by any means, electronic, mechanical, photocopying, recording or otherwise, without the prior permission of the publisher.

ISBN-13: 978-0-7456-4279-6
ISBN-13: 978-0-7456-4280-2(pb)

A catalogue record for this book is available from the British Library.

Typeset in 11.25 on 13 pt Dante
by Toppan Best-set Premedia Limited
Printed and bound in Great Britain by MPG Books Group, Bodmin, Cornwall

The publisher has used its best endeavours to ensure that the URLs for external websites referred to in this book are correct and active at the time of going to press. However, the publisher has no responsibility for the websites and can make no guarantee that a site will remain live or that the content is or will remain appropriate.

Every effort has been made to trace all copyright holders, but if any have been inadvertently overlooked the publisher will be pleased to include any necessary credits in any subsequent reprint or edition.

For further information on Polity, visit our website: www.politybooks.com

UNIVERSITY OF WINCHESTER

In memory of Agnes M. Thomas (1918–2004), who encouraged me over so many years in all of my endeavours, and who loved the giant pandas of Washington.

Contents

Acknowledgements   *page* viii

List of abbreviations   x

1. Introduction: Understanding Global Interactions Through
    Diplomacy   1

Section One Actors and Venues   **15**

2. The Changing Landscape of Diplomatic Actors and Venues   17

3. Nation–state Governments, Sub-national and Local
    Governments   31

4. Multilateral Institutions, Supranational Polities and
    Regional Bodies   49

5. Global and Transnational Firms   70

6. Civil Society Organizations and Eminent Person Diplomats   88

Section Two Processes and Functions   **107**

7. Technological Change and Diplomatic Process   109

8. Public Diplomacy   121

9. Managing Economic Diplomacy   138

10. Managing Military and Security Diplomacy   161

11. Managing Cultural Diplomacy   180

12. Conclusions: Contemporary Diplomatic Practice
    and Theory Looking Ahead   200

Notes   213

Bibliography   224

Index   235

Acknowledgements

So many people have provided assistance to me in the production of this book in countless large and small ways. I am grateful to everyone whose lives have touched mine during this time for their support and help. To those whom I have omitted to mention by name in this space, please accept my heartfelt apologies, and know that you are not forgotten. In particular I would like to thank Richard Langhorne for all his advice and good counsel throughout all stages of the writing process, including extensive detailed and thoughtful reading of the draft text. I would also like to thank Jodie Lewinsohn, Paul Blackburn and two anonymous readers for Polity Press, each of whom provided invaluable insight and comment on the draft chapters. I want to express huge thanks to my research assistants: Chris Broadfoot for producing the index to this volume and providing a key reading of the text, and Anthony Deos for his collaborative work on public diplomacy. For helping me to shape my theoretical perspective, which has informed the structure and narrative of this volume, I would especially like to thank James Der Derian, Costas Constantinou, Donna Lee and Kathy Fitzpatrick. For their ideas about diplomacy and general intellectual inspiration, I would like to thank Jan Melissen, Paul Sharp, Brian Hocking, Dominic Kelly, Daryl Copeland, Evan Potter, Kishan Rana, Erik Goldstein, Stuart Croft, David Dunn, Geoff Wiseman and Bishop Geoffrey Rowell. I would like to thank all the students of my Contemporary Economic Diplomacy classes since 2003 at the University of Kent's Brussels School of International Studies and at Bennington College for being co-developers of my theoretical and practical approach to the study of diplomacy. For crucial administrative support without which this project could not have been completed I would like to thank Charlene James and Amy Kuzmicki at Bennington College. For institutional support, including research funding, accommodation and vital access to documentation, I would like to thank Bennington College, St John's College Oxford, the Bodleian Library, the British Library, the New York Public Library at Bryant Park, and Oxford University's Social Science Library. To my grandfather,

Augustus Penn Pigman, who taught history in secondary school in New York City for much of his career, I give thanks for inspiring my early love of and appreciation for the discipline of history. To my mother, Nancy Sweatland Pigman, for her endless love and support for this project and for me and my career from its start up to the present, thank you.

The publishers would like to thank the following for permission to reproduce the images in this book:

Page 8, © A.S.A.P./ Rex Features; 18, World Economic Forum; 37, © the author; 61, © Sipa Press/ Rex Features; 74, © Rex Features; 87, © Sipa Press/ Rex Features; 131, © Rex Features; 140, © Richard Jones/ Rex Features; 168 © KPA/ Zuma/ Rex Features; 182, © Rex Features.

List of abbreviations

ABM	anti-ballistic missile
ACP	African, Caribbean and Pacific
AFS	American Field Service
AIDS	Acquired Immune Deficiency Syndrome
AML	anti-money laundering
ANZUS	Australia, New Zealand, United States Security Treaty
APEC	Asia-Pacific Economic Cooperation Council
ASB	Accounting Standards Board (South Africa)
ASEAN	Association of Southeast Asian Nations
AU	African Union
BCCI	Bank of Credit and Commerce International
BDA	Business for Diplomatic Action
BIS	Bank for International Settlements
BSE	bovine spongiform encephalopathy
BSIS	Brussels School of International Studies (University of Kent)
CA	Computer Associates
CBW	chemical and biological warfare
CEO	Chief Executive Officer
CFE	Conventional Armed Forces in Europe
CFSP	Common Foreign and Security Policy
CGI	Clinton Global Initiative
CII	Confederation of Indian Industry
CIS	Commonwealth of Independent States
CNN	Cable News Network
CSCE	Conference on Security and Cooperation in Europe
CSO	civil society organization
CSTO	Collective Security Treaty Organization
DATA	Debt, AIDS, Trade, Africa
DG	Directorate General
DRC	Democratic Republic of Congo (formerly Zaïre)
DVD	digital video disc

EAPC	Euro-Atlantic Partnership Council
EBRD	European Bank for Reconstruction and Development
ECOWAS	Economic Community of West African States
EMP	electromagnetic pulse
ESDP	European Security and Defence Policy
ESU	English-Speaking Union
EU	European Union
FAO	United Nations Food and Agriculture Organization
FASB	Federal Accounting Standards Board (United States)
FATF	Financial Action Task Force on Money Laundering
FCO	Foreign and Commonwealth Office (United Kingdom)
FIFA	Fédération Internationale de Football Association
FIS	Fédération Internationale du Ski
FTAA	Free Trade of the Americas Agreement
G7	Group of Seven
G8	Group of Eight
GAAP	Generally Accepted Accounting Principles
GATT	General Agreement on Tariffs and Trade
GCC	Gulf Cooperation Council
HIPCs	Highly Indebted Poor Countries
HIV	Human Immunodeficiency Virus
HSBC	Hongkong and Shanghai Banking Corporation
HSTC	Harmonized System of Tariff Classification
IADB	Inter-American Development Bank
IAIS	International Association of Insurance Supervisors
IAS	International Accounting Standards
IASB	International Accounting Standards Board
IBEF	India Brand Equity Foundation
ICBM	Intercontinental Ballistic Missile
ICC	International Chamber of Commerce *or* International Cricket Council
ICRC	International Committee of the Red Cross
IDA	International Development Association
IFC	International Finance Corporation
ILO	International Labour Organization
IMF	International Monetary Fund
IOC	International Olympic Committee
IOM	International Organization for Migration
IOSCO	International Organization of Securities Commissions
IPU	Inter-Parliamentary Union

IRB	International Rugby Board
ISAF	International Security Assistance Force (Afghanistan)
ITF	International Tennis Federation
MAI	Multilateral Agreement on Investment
MFA	Ministry of Foreign Affairs
MIGA	Multilateral Investment Guarantee Agency
MIRV	Multiple, Independent Re-entry Vehicle
MONUC	United Nations Mission Democratic Republic of Congo
MP	Member of Parliament
MSF	Médécins Sans Frontières
NAC	North Atlantic Council
NACC	North Atlantic Consultative Council
NAFTA	North American Free Trade Agreement
NATO	North Atlantic Treaty Organization
NGO	non-governmental organization
NRC	NATO–Russia Council
NYSE	New York Stock Exchange
OAS	Organization of American States
ODA	Official Development Assistance
OECD	Organization for Economic Cooperation and Development
ORSAS	Overseas Research Students Awards Scheme
OSCE	Organization for Security and Cooperation in Europe
OTM	organization employing terrorist methods
PD	public diplomacy
PfP	Partnership for Peace
PJC	Permanent Joint Council
PSC	Political and Security Committee
S&DT	special and differential treatment
SACEUR	Strategic Allied Commander Europe
SADC	Southern African Development Council
SAIS	School of Advanced International Studies (The Johns Hopkins University)
SALT	Strategic Arms Limitation Treaty
SARS	Severe Acute Respiratory Syndrome
SCO	Shanghai Cooperation Organization
SORT	Strategic Offensive Reductions Treaty
START	Strategic Arms Reduction Treaty
TB	tuberculosis
TCO	transnational criminal organization
TRIMs	Trade-Related Investment Measures

UK	United Kingdom of Great Britain and Northern Ireland
US	United States
UN	United Nations
UNCTAD	United Nations Council on Trade and Development
UNDP	United Nations Development Programme
UNESCO	United Nations Educational, Scientific and Cultural Organization
UNHCR	UN High Commissioner for Refugees
UNICEF	United Nations International Children's Emergency Fund
USAID	US Agency for International Development
USIA	United States Information Agency
USTR	Office of the United States Trade Representative
VCR	videocassette recorder
WIPO	World Intellectual Property Organization
WSF	World Social Forum
WTO	World Trade Organization

Introduction: Understanding Global Interactions Through Diplomacy

Talking to Dictators: An Argument About Diplomacy

In the summer of 2007, two candidates for the 2008 Democratic Party's nomination for President of the United States had a very public disagreement about whether the American President should communicate directly to heads of government of nations perceived as hostile to US interests. At a candidates' debate in Charleston, South Carolina, hosted by major television and internet media channels CNN and YouTube on 23 July 2007, the two then-front-running candidates gave very different responses to a question from a viewer about whether, as President, they would be willing to talk directly to dictators without preconditions. Senator Hillary Rodham Clinton (New York) stated that she would be willing to speak directly to any dictator, provided that certain preconditions were met. Senator Barack Obama (Illinois) replied that he was willing to speak to any dictator without any preconditions at all. Based on her experience in making foreign policy in the US Senate and as First Lady in her husband Bill Clinton's presidential administration, Clinton argued that it was important to US foreign policy objectives to establish dialogue, but not at the expense of allowing foreign leaders to exploit high-level meetings with US officials for their own purposes. Obama averred that he would bring a wholly new and different approach to the problem of communication between the United States and perceived hostile states, which he argued had been lacking during the administration of President George W. Bush. In the days following the debate, both candidates expanded upon and amplified their positions to full court press in an otherwise slow news week. Clinton supporters, seeking to differentiate their candidate from the relatively less experienced Senator Obama, emphasized her ability to respond to the question in a nuanced way. Obama supporters portrayed their candidate as possessing the capacity to get past traditional Washington 'business as usual' and pursue diplomacy in a genuinely different way. A year later, Obama was elected President of the United States. He then appointed Clinton to be

Secretary of State, the chief US diplomatic representative to the rest of the world.

Why is this seemingly minor vignette important? It occurred within the domestic political process of a country seen by the rest of the world in 2007 as inward-looking and not sufficiently concerned about the perceptions of other peoples and other nations. Its significance lies in that it was an argument, in which tens of millions of Americans engaged through the media, about how to practise diplomacy. The initial question was submitted for inclusion in the debate by a would-be voter over the internet in the format of a YouTube video and selected through online voting by other viewers. The query embodied a concern that US officials should be representing themselves to and communicating with the leaders of all states, those potentially hostile as well as those friendly. The question's thrust revealed a US public more self-consciously aware of and concerned about how diplomacy is practised than perhaps has been the case for a very long time. The responses of the two candidates were equally revealing. Clinton's response was indicative of the value placed by practitioners of diplomacy upon experience and skill, subtlety and nuance to achieve objectives. Obama's response reflected the frequent perceptions by those outside the diplomatic community of diplomacy's shortcomings and the desire to reject or reinvent traditional diplomacy to create a better mechanism. This debate has been going on among diplomatists for over two centuries. The candidates' debate took place against the backdrop of the terror attacks of 11 September 2001 and thereafter and the widely perceived failures of diplomacy leading up to and during the Anglo-American invasion of Iraq in 2003. The Clinton–Obama *contretemps* over talking to dictators highlights the importance of understanding what contemporary diplomacy is and how it works. It emphasizes why it is a crucial undertaking to theorize diplomacy and, in so doing, imagine how we might do a better job of practising it in future.

Why Study Diplomacy?

Of the numerous reasons to study diplomacy, the most dominant motivation has risen and evolved over the past few centuries in tandem with the evolution of modern diplomacy itself. A second significant reason has come to the fore in more recent times. The most important traditional reason to study diplomacy has been the professional one: as a means to prepare to practise in the field. Early significant modern writings on diplomacy, such as Wicquefort's *L'Ambassadeur et ses fonctions* (1681) and De Caillères's *De la manière de négocier* (1697) were intended to give readers the historical and empirical background they needed to become effective negotiators.[1] As the modern nation–states system has evolved since the sixteenth century, and with it the concurrent need for diplomatic relations between states (and, later, other actors), the demand for trained professional diplomats to staff ministries of foreign affairs has grown steadily. Numerous texts on negotiation, the original core of diplomatic practice, have followed. In his landmark *Diplomacy: Theory and Practice*, Geoff Berridge devotes the first half of the text to the art of negotiation.[2]

The second and more recent of the major reasons to study diplomacy is at once both more academic and more general than the first. Beginning in the first half of the twentieth century, diplomacy came to be understood in a broader sense than that of the practical art of representing one's sovereign and conducting negotiations on his or her behalf. Scholars in the first half of the century began to study diplomacy as a vehicle or lens for understanding what at the time was becoming known as international relations: the relationships between nation–states in the international system, and the characteristics of the international system of nation–states itself. This occurred in part because of a need felt by scholars to understand the causes of the First World War (the Great War) and the subsequent pitfall-strewn processes of creation of international structures and institutions designed to prevent a repeat of the ruinous consequences of the 'war to end all wars'. Could a scholarly understanding of diplomatic actors and processes in the international system help to prevent errors of diplomacy, and in so doing reduce the likelihood of future wars? Perhaps. But at the same time that academic interest in diplomacy increased, giving birth to a sub-discipline now known as diplomatic studies, the interest in diplomacy of the citizens of nation–states whose fates were influenced by their diplomats – with increasingly dramatic consequences as the age of weapons of mass destruction dawned – began to grow as well. This occurred as a direct consequence of broad-based transformations such as democratization of the domestic politics of nation–states and the emergence of technologies of mass communication. Governments and their diplomats increasingly had to come to terms with the need to communicate with publics, both foreign and domestic, in addition to communicating with their official counterparts in other nation–states.

The contemporary period has seen a further transformation of this second and more general reason to study diplomacy, in that academic and popular interest in the subject have converged. After a forty-year period of relative stability of the international system resulting from the nuclear rivalry and diplomacy between two superpowers, the end of the Cold War and dissolution of the Soviet Union at the beginning of the 1990s ushered in a new era of uncertainty for a system now populated not only by nation–states, but increasingly by powerful multilateral institutions, large transnational firms and global civil society organizations. The first great crisis of the post-Cold War global order, the 2001 terror attacks and the subsequent invasion of Iraq, has focused the interest of the public and of scholars on diplomacy much as the Great War of a century earlier had done. Yet in the internet age of instant global communication, in which the fall of Baghdad could be covered live in real time by embedded journalists on CNN and the hanging of Saddam Hussein captured on home video and distributed to the world nearly as fast, public perceptions of a lack of employment of diplomacy by governments and of failures of diplomatic initiatives and projects undertaken have arguably reached a level hitherto not imagined. The objective of this book is to help the reader to be able to use diplomacy, in both practical and theoretical ways, as a vehicle for understanding global interactions between the broad range of actors that inhabit the post-Cold War, communication-intensive world environment.[3]

What Diplomacy Is, and What It Is Not

The question of why to study diplomacy is inseparable from the broader question of what diplomacy is. What we understand diplomacy to be is important not only for its intrinsic significance, but also because to give a definition of diplomacy is to define the bounds of the field of diplomatic studies: what counts as part of diplomatic studies, and thus by extension what does not. As noted above, early modern usages of diplomacy were largely concerned with a process: the art of negotiation, and how to use negotiating effectively to achieve objectives of state. But by the twentieth century, it had become clear that not only processes of negotiation but the actors doing the negotiating – nation–states and their representatives – were crucial objects of the study of diplomacy. Senior British diplomat Sir Harold Nicolson, a founder of the modern academic disciplinary area known as diplomatic studies, in his core 1939 text *Diplomacy* endorsed the *Oxford English Dictionary* definition of diplomacy as 'the management of international relations by negotiation; the method by which these relations are adjusted by ambassadors and envoys; the business or art of the diplomatist'.[4] Nicolson's definition acknowledged a broader range of diplomatic processes than only negotiations, as well as the rôle of the practitioners: the ambassadors, envoys and other professional diplomats. Another senior British diplomat, Adam Watson, who turned to scholarship of diplomacy in the second half of the twentieth century after retiring from the Diplomatic Service, in 1982 characterized diplomacy more generally as 'the dialogue between states',[5] a definition encapsulating the balance between diplomatic actors – states – and processes. Since the end of the Cold War and its overweening global focus on the balance of nuclear and conventional force between two superpowers, an awareness has grown amongst scholars and the general public alike that perhaps the prevailing understanding of diplomacy was still too restrictive. In this 'postmodern' age in which an increasing share of global economic activity is involved in cross-border flows of goods, services, capital, labour, knowledge, ideas and culture, and in which technological advances have made a growing share of global communications immediate, a wider range of actors than governments of nation–states can be seen to be engaging in diplomacy through an even broader range of processes than those envisioned specifically by Nicolson and Watson. For example, transnational firms such as Gazprom, Citigroup and Toyota represent themselves to and negotiate with governments much in the way that other governments do. Multilateral institutions such as the World Trade Organization have created ongoing venues and special multilateral conferences for particular types of diplomacy, in this case the agreement and implementation of rules for international trade.

As this book addresses both the changes and continuities reflected in the practice of diplomacy since the end of the Cold War, it seeks to build on Nicolson's and Watson's balance between actors and processes by considering both notions in a broader and more dynamic context. Another way to think about diplomatic actors and processes is to understand diplomacy as consisting of two core functions or activities: representation and communication. Representation begins with the notion of the diplomatic actor itself, but asks how the actor represents itself to others with whom it wishes to establish and maintain a relationship or dialogue. Does a sovereign ruler represent him- or herself at a negotiation directly, in person? Does he or she appoint a special envoy to undertake a diplomatic mission? Does the sovereign appoint a permanent representative or ambassador to reside at the location where he or she wishes to be represented? Does he or she establish mechanisms for regular or emergency communications using technology, such as a weekly video-conference meeting or a telephone 'hotline'? How do these choices differ if sovereignty resides not in the government, but in the nation itself? How do they vary if the sovereign is not the head of government of a nation–state, but instead the Chief Executive Officer of a large global firm like Microsoft, the head of a civil society organization such as the International Committee of the Red Cross, or the Secretary-General of an international organization such as the United Nations?[6]

Going beyond this layer of questions about representation, when an actor represents itself to others, it raises questions of how the actor represents itself to itself: the problem of identity. Choices about how, and to whom, to represent oneself play a direct rôle in who one is, or who one becomes. They form part of the social construction of one's identity and one's interests. By deciding to join the World Trade Organization in December 2001, the government of the People's Republic of China chose to subject itself to a set of multilateral norms of international trade favouring open markets and less government intervention, as well as to an established set of procedures for resolving disputes and for further liberalizing trade. Joining the WTO would have consequences for China's own trade policy process that the Chinese government was not necessarily able to foresee. Joining the organization strengthened the economic position of those interests within China favouring WTO membership, such as large exporting manufacturing firms and financial institutions, even whilst weakening opponents, such as heavily subsidized industries. This shifted the domestic balance of political power within China on trade policy making. Even more significantly, by deciding to sign the Conference on Security and Cooperation in Europe's Helsinki Final Act in 1975 with the objective of gaining international legitimation for its post-World War II territorial gains, the government of the Soviet Union created within its own population for the first time an expectation that the Soviet government would adhere to international norms of human rights, which contributed in turn to the eventual fall from power of the ruling Communist Party.[7]

The other core diplomatic function or activity, communication, is distinct, although inseparable, from representation. Communication by its nature must take place not between collective or aggregate entities such as nation–states, multilateral organizations or global firms, but between the individuals entrusted with representing or speaking for them. The contemporary media, through their unparalleled power and reach, have complicated processes of communication greatly through their ability to convey large quantities of information, accurate or not, with or without context, to huge segments of the global public. 'Diplomacy is bargaining', as Thomas Schelling wrote in 1966; '. . . it seeks outcomes that, although not ideal for either party, are better for both than some of the alternatives.'[8] The idea of communication as a core diplomatic function begins with this original understanding of diplomacy as the art of negotiation, but it recognizes that diplomacy comprises a much broader range of communications than those that would strictly be considered negotiations. An ambassador presenting credentials to a head of state upon arrival at a new post, a President hosting a state dinner for a visiting Queen, or a commerce minister giving the CEO of a global software firm a tour of a new technology park and export processing zone are examples of the building and maintenance of diplomatic relationships that are no less important as diplomatic communications than a high-level negotiation over the release of hostages or a trade and investment treaty. A government–business partnership to promote a country as an investment destination through a multimedia website, a government-funded cultural foundation hosting an exchange of performances by local dance troupes, or an airdrop of information leaflets aimed at a population of a hostile state during a military conflict are examples of communication for the purpose of public diplomacy, a type of diplomatic communication that has always been practised but in the current era of technology-enabled connectivity has assumed a new significance.[9] Another form of diplomatic communication, as old as high-level negotiation itself, has been consular communication. Consuls originally were sent abroad to adjudicate disputes between citizens of one country residing in another, but the consular function in diplomacy has evolved to encompass all of the 'routine' business communications between two governments: the issuing of visas, providing services to home-country nationals travelling abroad, and trade facilitation, among other things.[10]

The power of communication, in all its guises, as a core function of diplomacy lies in its ability not only to achieve its primary objectives – resolving a conflict, maintaining a relationship, promoting social and economic exchange – but also in so doing to modify the interests and even the identity of the actors communicating with one another. Communication between Egypt and Israel is a particularly vivid example of the transformative power of diplomatic communication at all levels. When Egyptian President Anwar el-Sadat flew from Cairo to Jerusalem in October 1977 to meet Israeli Prime Minister Menachem Begin and address the Israeli Knesset, he transformed the Egypt–Israel relationship from one of enemies of thirty years since the founding of Israel into one of peace and (albeit limited) commerce. But in negotiating and signing a bilateral peace treaty, Sadat and Begin re-prioritized their states' respective interests: Israel sacrificed its occupation and 'settlement' of the Sinai peninsula in return for a

Anwar el-Sadat, Jimmy Carter and Menachem Begin at the White House for the signing of the Israel–Egypt peace treaty, March 1979

peace agreement with an Arab state, whilst Egypt sacrificed solidarity with its Arab neighbours in return for repossession of its Sinai territory, financial gain from the ability to reopen the Suez Canal, huge foreign aid transfers from the United States and enhanced security flowing from peace with Israel. Beyond modifying their respective interest preference orderings, however, Egypt and Israel altered their identities as nation–states. Israel abandoned its expansionist Zionist identity for that of a state willing and able to trade land for peace with its neighbours. Egypt gave up its identification with pan-Arabism and the destruction of Israel for the relative economic and political gains of being a state at peace with its neighbours.

Given the transformative power of communication over the actors and their representatives doing the communicating that the Egypt–Israel case displays so effectively, one might be tempted to think of communication, an updated and broadened proxy for negotiation, as encompassing all of the core activities of diplomacy. What acts of representation, it has been asked, are not in themselves communicative acts?[11] For example, is not the opening of a permanent mission or embassy itself a communication to the receiving state? Whilst it may well be true that every act of representation embodies a communicative component, it does not make sense to reduce the study of diplomacy to a subset of the study of communication, to see it as just a set of signals. As the study of diplomacy focuses on how actors interact with one another through their representatives, the primary function of many diplomatic activities is more primarily representative than communicative in nature. Choosing a trade minister to appoint, selecting a menu and a seating plan for a state dinner, reallocating duties between a ministry of foreign affairs and a trade ministry are all examples of diplomatic activities whose primary function is representative rather than communicative. Such primarily representative activities often involve choices and decisions, made within the political or administrative structure of a government, firm, civil society organization or other diplomatic actor, that affect how the actor constructs its own identity. These types of decisions are at the core of interest to scholars of diplomacy, whereas they may be of peripheral interest at best to students of communication.

Understanding what the study of diplomacy encompasses requires not only a clear sense of the objects of study, but also a solid sense of what diplomacy is not. If we understand diplomacy as one distinct lens or prism through which to understand global interactions more broadly, we can distinguish between viewing those interactions through that particular lens and viewing the same interactions through another sort of lens, such as that of foreign policy analysis or other approaches to the study of international relations. Of particular importance is the distinction between diplomatic studies and foreign policy analysis. The study of diplomacy differs from the study of foreign policy significantly, in the sense that foreign policy is generally analysed from the perspective of the state or other actor engaged in making and executing it. The student of foreign policy asks empirical questions: what is Russia's policy towards the United States, or towards the World Trade Organization? Normative and prudential questions may be asked, such as does the European Union have an ethical obligation to deploy troops to defend human rights in Kosovo or Darfur, or which among several US policies for ending violence in Afghanistan is most likely to be successful? Policies adopted and executed are then evaluated: which Australian approaches to achieving agricultural trade liberalization in the WTO Doha Development Round have succeeded, which have failed, and why? Students of foreign policy may be studying the same issues and events as students of diplomacy, but the focus for diplomatic studies is different. Like foreign policy analysis (and unlike some other approaches to international relations), diplomatic studies emphasizes the link between individual agents – representatives – and the collective actors

– states, multilateral organizations, firms – that they represent, or on whose behalf they take decisions. But even as they ask similar sorts of empirical and analytical or evaluative questions about these relationships, scholars of diplomacy tend to focus on the interactions between the actors rather than on particular actors for their own sake. How do Russia and the United States represent themselves to one another? How do they communicate, and how effective is their communication at achieving their respective objectives? Normative questions are also asked, both ethical and instrumental, but they tend to be asked about the prevailing system and practices of diplomacy and the structure of the system of states and other actors within which diplomacy is practised. Was the classical approach of conducting diplomatic negotiations often in secret ethically objectionable, as Wilson and Lenin both contended in the early twentieth century? Were the different modes of 'open' and 'revolutionary' diplomacy they advocated respectively more effective at achieving the objectives of the negotiators?[12]

It is also important to distinguish the study of diplomacy itself from an important subsidiary component of diplomatic studies: the study of protocol. Diplomatic protocol consists of the visible rituals of diplomatic interaction: everything from how heads of state and government, ministers and ambassadors address one another in person and in writing to seating arrangements at formal dinners, dress codes and etiquette, and the avoidance of inadvertent cultural slights and offences. Most governments take diplomatic protocol very seriously, assigning a senior diplomatic officer to be responsible for all protocol matters. In the United States the post is known as Chief of Protocol and is a presidential appointment. Getting protocol right is important because it facilitates diplomatic communication between representatives. When someone makes a protocol error, it can have a negative material impact upon relations between two countries generally or upon a particular set of negotiations. Hence educational institutions offer training programmes in diplomatic protocol to prepare professionals to specialize in protocol work. The study of the evolution of diplomatic protocol is of great interest to diplomatic historians, but its relationship to the broader study of contemporary diplomacy is that of a technical specialization relative to the broader questions that diplomatic studies seeks to answer.

Ultimately it may be more useful in meeting the objectives of this book to arrive at a working idea of what the study of diplomacy is than to settle on a definition for what diplomacy is and is not. By thinking of the study of diplomacy as the study of the representation and communication between global actors, including (but not limited to) governments, multi-lateral institutions, civil society organizations and large firms, we set our-selves a general roadmap of terrain to be covered without having to tackle in advance all of the difficult cases and resulting questions of whether something counts as diplomacy or not.

Recurring Themes in Contemporary Diplomacy

As we survey the terrain of contemporary diplomacy in the sections and chapters that follow, the core components of representation and commu-nication will surface and resurface as recurring, interacting themes. Although the notions of representation and communication as interlocking central functions of diplomacy do not serve as organizing principles of the book, they will appear in every chapter as they interact with each of the other recurring themes that dominate contemporary diplomacy. We can identify two pairs of recurring themes: the first pair at the level of everyday diplomatic practice, and the second pair at a more philosophical level. At the level of diplomatic practice, the first recurring theme is that of an increasing profusion of diplomatic actors to include not just governments of nation–states, but sub-state governments (Catalonia, Québec), suprana-tional governments (the European Union), multilateral organizations and institutions (the United Nations, NATO), civil society organizations (the International Committee of the Red Cross, Greenpeace) and global firms (Toyota, Microsoft), among others. This broadening of types of actors will be seen to have an impact both on how diplomatic actors represent them-selves (different types of accredited representatives other than 'traditional' diplomats and missions, adoption of corporate techniques of public rela-tions) and on how diplomatic communication is carried out (trade missions composed of government and business representation, public–private part-nerships to promote inward investment, consultation with environmental non-governmental organizations during negotiation of multilateral climate change agreements).[13]

The second theme in this pair is the effect upon diplomacy of the trans-formation in communications technologies. The advent of television, video, global mobile telephony and the internet has changed how govern-ments and other diplomatic actors choose to represent themselves by changing how they are able to be seen and perceived by global publics. It has altered how diplomatic actors communicate both by changing the available channels for communication (secure satellite links, multiple media outlets) and by changing the speed at which communication is possible and at which choices may have to be made ('hotlines', teleconferencing, email). Transformation of communications technologies has also had a deeper impact upon the relationship between diplomatic actors and the constituencies or publics that constitute and legitimate them. When voters can find out most information that may (or may not) interest them about their government through competing media organizations, governments must adjust how they make foreign policy, how they conduct diplomacy, and how they communicate about it to their own constituents so as to build and retain public support and legitimacy for their actions if they hope to remain in office. When stockholders and consumers of global firms can learn about corporate policies and diplomacy in a similar way, managements of firms must adapt their strategies of communication to their stakeholders accordingly. Managers of large civil society organizations face the same challenge in communicating to donors and members.

The second pair of recurring themes reflects more philosophical questions about diplomacy. Of these philosophical issues, the first concerns the significance of change. One of the common debates amongst diplomatic historians (as it is amongst historians in general) concerns to what degree developments in diplomacy are truly new as opposed to being recent instantiations of long-running practices. Is the multi-level diplomacy between European Union member state governments and the EU governmental institutions in Brussels a new phenomenon? Or is it more a contemporary analogue of the diplomatic relationships between the Emperor Charlemagne and the provinces of his empire, which he conducted through appointed emissaries known as *missi*? Is the diplomacy between firms like Citigroup and the governments of the United States and United Kingdom really new, or is it a more current version of the diplomacy that took place between the British and Dutch East India Companies and governments in Europe and Asia in the seventeenth century? This 'meta-historical' debate over what constitutes change not only matters to scholars and students for its intrinsic interest, but is at least as important for practising diplomats. A well-grounded understanding of when circumstances have changed may suggest or even demand a real change in practice in response. If the speed of communications technology increases rapidly and the range of channels proliferates, for example, a ministry of foreign affairs may decide it needs to reorganize its staff to process incoming emails, voicemails, text and video messages 24/7 if it wants to be able to respond to matters now deemed urgent in a timely and efficient manner, much as Britain's Foreign Office decided to hire a night clerk following the invention of the electric telegraph over a century and a half ago.

The second of the more philosophical recurring themes arises from this book's perspective on diplomacy as a useful lens through which to view and understand interactions between actors in the global political economy more broadly. If what diplomats do and how they do it indeed can provide us with a useful picture of interactions between global actors, does this not imply that the norms and practices of diplomacy are in a sense an emergent property of a true global society? The notion of international or global society, with norms and properties of its own, has long been important to the English School tradition within International Relations scholarship, even as it has been contested by scholars who prefer state power-based explanations of change (Neorealists and Neoliberals). This debate matters because, if norms and practices of diplomacy are an emergent property of global society, it suggests that change in diplomatic practice occurs not only when winners of hegemonic wars so will it, but as part of an ongoing process of social construction of international society, in which different types of actors with varying degrees of power all play a part.[14] Just as diplomatic norms and practices changed with the Treaties of Westphalia (1648) and Versailles (1919), the United States has found its foreign policy interests and strategies constrained and even altered by its participation since the 1970s in the Group of Seven / Group of Eight (G7/G8) process of consultation for heads of governments of the industrialized powers.[15]

Organization of the Book

As this book is primarily about contemporary diplomacy, it does not attempt to provide a comprehensive history of diplomatic practice. Many outstanding volumes exist to serve that purpose, of which arguably the most useful and concise is Keith Hamilton and Richard Langhorne's *The Practice of Diplomacy*.[16] This book draws on diplomatic history in a genealogical fashion, as James Der Derian put it so aptly, to use the past to understand the present without imposing the teleology of the present upon the past.[17] The volume is divided into two broad sections: 'Actors and Venues' and 'Processes and Functions'. The concluding chapter addresses the relationship between contemporary diplomatic practice and diplomatic theory and also reflects on the challenges facing contemporary diplomacy going forward. Readers will notice already that making such a broad delineation between actors and processes has a natural correspondence to the core representation and communication functions of diplomacy. This, of course, is not a coincidence. Actors and, increasingly, venues, need to be represented. Processes and functions are primarily the mechanisms through which representatives communicate. At a more theoretical level, political scientists have debated at length the interrelationship between agents and structures in producing change in global politics.[18] The diplomatic dyads of representation and communication, actors and venues, actors/venues and processes/functions are manifestations of the broader need to conceptualize political behaviour and change.

The first section, 'Actors and Venues', begins with a chapter surveying in greater detail the impact of the profusion of different types of diplomatic actor in the contemporary world. Chapters on each of the major types of contemporary diplomatic actor follow: nation–state governments; multilateral, supranational and regional bodies; global firms; and civil society organizations. The second section, 'Processes and Functions', begins with a chapter surveying the multifold impact of change in information, communications and transport technology upon how diplomacy is conducted. Flowing from this survey is a detailed chapter on the most important effects of technological change: the rise of public diplomacy and the rôle of the contemporary media. Chapters that survey how the major functional areas of diplomacy are managed follow: economic, military and security, and cultural diplomacy. The concluding chapter invites the reader to tie together all of the foregoing substantive discussion and analysis of contemporary diplomatic practice by reviewing the state of current debates over diplomatic theory and then proceeds to consider what obstacles a theory-infused diplomatic practice faces in the years ahead. If, as Costas Constantinou has argued persuasively, to practise diplomacy *is* to theorize diplomacy, the consideration of contemporary theoretical debate is most appropriately reserved for the concluding chapter of the book, once the landscape of contemporary diplomatic practice has been documented in some detail.

SECTION ONE

ACTORS AND VENUES

2

The Changing Landscape of Diplomatic Actors and Venues

Introduction: New Stages, Changing Players

* On the 'sidelines' of the World Economic Forum's Annual Meeting in Davos, Switzerland in January 2007, trade ministers of all the world's major trading powers met together, for the first time in many months, to revive the stalled World Trade Organization multilateral trade liberalization negotiations, the 'Doha Development Agenda'. On the last afternoon of the Annual Meeting, at a panel session of leading trade ministers hosted by WTO Secretary-General Pascal Lamy, the Forum announced the trade ministers' accomplishments to the gathered assemblage of global media.

* In 2002, Bono, lead singer of rock supergroup U2 and head of the anti-poverty civil society organization DATA (Debt, AIDS, Trade, Africa), invited Paul O'Neill, US President George W. Bush's first Secretary of the Treasury, to accompany him on a tour of Africa. On their 'Odd Couple Tour of Africa 2002' (as T-shirts produced by Bono dubbed it), widely covered by the global media, Bono and O'Neill met with leaders of governments, local civil society organizations and firms. O'Neill credited Bono with changing his understanding of Africa poverty issues and winning his support for raising the priority of promoting economic development in Africa on the Bush administration's foreign policy agenda.[1]

* In November 2002, Microsoft CEO Bill Gates made an 'official' visit to India. On his visit, Gates's third to India, he was treated, as has been customary, like a visiting head of state. He met with Prime Minister A. B. Vajpayee and the full range of Indian federal and state government leaders, as well as with leaders of top Indian technology firms. On his visit Gates announced that Microsoft would invest $400 million in India over three years.[2] The timing of Gates's visit was significant, as it came only a few months after leaders of Indian and global

World Economic Forum Davos panel meeting

technology firms had brought considerable pressure to bear on Prime Minister Vajpayee and US President Bush over the long-running Kashmir dispute with Pakistan that had spiked in the first half of the year: on Vajpayee to ratchet down military tensions and on Bush to become more active in mediating the dispute. Had this business–government diplomacy not been successful, Gates's subsequent visit to India would have been unlikely.

These vignettes, so familiar to readers and viewers of news on international affairs at that time, help to create an image of the varied landscape of contemporary diplomatic actors that diverges widely from the relatively simpler landscape of nation–state-based diplomacy in the age that followed the 1648 Peace of Westphalia, or even the diplomatic topography of the early twentieth century as international organizations began to emerge in the aftermath of the Great War (First World War). The Peace of Westphalia is regarded by many scholars to have ushered in an international system based upon nation–states. Until the twentieth century, the classical view of diplomacy was that it was linked to representation of nation–state governments to one another and to communication between them. In simplest terms, today we observe a much wider range of actors engaging in the representative and communicative activities of diplomacy: multilateral institutions of various sorts, such as the United Nations and the World Trade Organization; civil society organizations (CSOs), such as the International Committee of the Red Cross, Greenpeace and the World Economic Forum; global firms such as Microsoft, Gazprom and Toyota; even so-called 'eminent person diplomats' such as Bono, Jimmy Carter and Nelson Mandela. But in order to understand to what extent, if at all, this proliferation of types of diplomatic actor is significant, and how, if at all, it has changed the nature of contemporary diplomacy, we must begin by seeking to understand what a diplomatic actor is, and indeed why it is useful to think about diplomacy in terms of stages occupied by 'actors' that play particular types of rôles.

Diplomatic Actors: The Classical View

In the classical, Westphalian notion of diplomacy, who counted as a diplomatic actor was inseparable from the idea of what counted as a nation–state. Both rested on the notion of sovereignty, which itself was evolving. Under the older, more hierarchical structures of political authority that had prevailed in Europe and in Asia, the term 'sovereign' tended to conflate the monarch or ruler with the polity over which he or she ruled. The famous quip *L'Etat, c'est moi* ('I am the State'), attributed to French King Louis XIV, who ruled France from 1643 to 1715 at the dawn of the Westphalian age, perhaps captures this understanding of sovereignty best. Yet Louis XIV was a modernizing monarch who played a key rôle in creating the 'modern' Westphalian nation–state by centralizing state power. Under the Westphalia system, a nation–state was regarded as sovereign if its government exercised effective control over a territory and the people and resources therein. This understanding of sovereignty for purposes of diplomacy was binary: either one had it, or one did not. Hence sovereignty was acknowledged as a form of functional equality between actors. As James Der Derian argues, this sovereignty of nation–states by its nature implies a separation or estrangement between them that required mediation or overcoming through diplomacy.[3] Each government of each sovereign state, large or small, was recognized by the other governments in the system as deserving of the same degree of recognition and level of treatment in matters of diplomatic representation and communication. Thus the recognition of representatives as an act of mediation of the estrangement between sovereign bodies became a defining element both of the international system and of the diplomacy that took place within it.[4] Diplomatic actors, the governments of nation–states, were in effect identified and defined through being recognized by their peers.[5] This was an exercise in social construction of identity in its most transparent form: the international community of sovereign nation–states became a sort of club that collectively set and maintained criteria for membership. Without the club to maintain the criteria for membership, which attributes of sovereign nation–state status were important might not have been readily identifiable at all.

Diplomatic representation itself took on a particular form under the Westphalia system. Governments generally began to exchange representatives with one another on a permanent or ongoing basis. In the centuries preceding the Peace of Westphalia, some sovereigns had already sent permanent representatives to one another. In the late fourteenth century, the stationing of diplomatic representatives by sovereigns of Italian city-states in other such polities on an ongoing basis becomes well documented.[6] Yet the prevailing norm for diplomatic representation in the feudal age was for missions to be undertaken on an ad hoc basis. After the seventeenth century, permanent diplomatic representation came to be identified as one of the standard attributes of sovereign nation–states. Importantly, the rôles of recognition and of permanent representation as identifiers of who counts as a diplomatic actor have persisted into the contemporary period, even as the Westphalian notion of the sovereign nation–state has become less dominant, as we shall explore below. The emergence of permanent representation took on a particular significance for international relations in that it generated for the first time a new cadre of individuals, professional diplomats, who in many respects shared more in common with one another than they did with fellow nationals of their home countries. Professional diplomats tended to be drawn from similar, usually aristocratic, ranks of the domestic societies that they represented. They shared common socializing experiences, and, later, schooling, even before taking up their first diplomatic post. Once assigned to a foreign posting, a diplomat joined a very particular and distinct community of practitioners in a foreign capital or major city that came to be known as the *corps diplomatique*. *Corps diplomatiques* are the communities of professional diplomats posted to the same city from around the world, who share knowledge and relationships to facilitate the conduct of diplomatic business. They serve as monitors of the proper observance of diplomatic practice and procedures by diplomatic representatives and home states alike.[7] Periodically they have occasion to act collectively, as in instances when one of their members is threatened or harmed whilst in post. For example, when the Peruvian terrorist organization Tupac Amaru took several hundred hostages in an armed attack on a diplomatic reception at Japan's embassy in Lima and held some of the hostages for several months, Lima's *corps diplomatique* participated actively in negotiation and mediation to secure the release of their colleagues. Usually 'chaired' informally by the longest-serving ambassador or head of mission, each *corps* has its own customs, norms and hierarchy.

Over the course of the eighteenth and nineteenth centuries, norms of diplomatic practice emerged as an integral part of the Westphalia system of nation–states. Governments exchanged permanent representation. Governments received, recognized and accredited the appointed representatives of other states in similar ways. Governments consulted one another regularly through their diplomats and usually communicated through diplomatic channels before resorting to violence against one another. Diplomatic protocol, the observance of shared customs and manners by diplomats and their interlocutors in government and society, evolved into norms of practice, as, by regularizing expectations of how practitioners of diplomacy would behave, it served to make it easier for them to do their jobs. Diplomatic protocol itself became a form of communication. Seating arrangements at a state dinner, for example, were established means for a host to convey information to guests about their respective ranking or importance in the context of the proximate circumstances surrounding the occasion. Particular forms of language used in official toasts at such occasions performed a similar rôle. Collectively these norms of diplomatic practice could be identified as a distinctive diplomatic culture, which was itself a by-product of the Westphalian nation–states system. Since it came into being, diplomatic culture has continued to evolve in response to technological change, change in the social structure of the states in the system, and other factors. Nonetheless, diplomatic culture has tended to retain its core characteristics despite the emergence of new types of non-nation–state actors, telephonic and internet communications, and the entry of non-aristocratic individuals into their nations' diplomatic services. Hence diplomatic culture can be understood as a distinctive attribute of the Westphalia system of nation–states.[8]

The idea that there is more to an international system of nation–states than the relative size and resources of the states in the system and the distribution of power that results therefrom, which has always been contested, has been advanced by the awareness of a distinct diplomatic culture. Understanding the Westphalia system as consisting of something more than the states within it and the distribution of power between them led

International Relations scholars of what became known as the English School between the two world wars to argue for the existence of 'international society', a distinct entity beyond nation–states and their power relationships that has particular evolving norms and practices of its own. Scholars in the first half of the twentieth century could observe that the Westphalia system of nation–states and the particular rôle for state sovereignty that it encoded was being tested and challenged in new ways resulting from the development of new technologies of production, transport and communication and from the internationalization of flows of goods, services, capital and labour. The Great War of 1914–18, the 'war to end all wars', represented the most taxing of such challenges. They could observe the process, at first slow and halting, through which groups of nation–states began to negotiate new institutional arrangements in which they agreed to pool elements of their traditional sovereignty in order to achieve shared objectives, which ranged from agreed procedures for cross-border communications (the 1865 International Telegraph Union, which became the International Telecommunication Union) to rules for trade (the Brussels Sugar Convention of 1902), to international recognition of property rights (the 1886 Berne Convention on copyright protection), to international security and the prevention of war (the Versailles Treaty of 1919 and the League of Nations Charter). Positing the idea of international society helped to make sense of how and why new international institutions began to emerge from the late nineteenth century as venues within which governments of nation–states could mediate disagreements and facilitate cooperation on issues and projects of mutual interest.[9]

Diplomatic Actors and Venues: A Contemporary View

As the vignettes at the start of this chapter illustrate, there has been a change since the first half of the twentieth century in how and where diplomacy is done, as well as in who is seen to be engaging in diplomacy. This has posed a philosophical challenge for scholars accustomed to thinking about diplomatic actors and functions and about diplomatic culture in terms of the traditional practices of the nineteenth century. The actors that were emerging – multilateral institutions like the United Nations and the International Monetary Fund, global firms like IBM and Infosys, civil society organizations like Médécins Sans Frontières and World Vision – and the venues in which diplomacy was taking place – the World Trade

Organization, the World Economic Forum, the UN Conferences on Women – were more diverse than the classical diplomatic world of meetings between ambassadors of nation–states and occasional multilateral conferences. Did it make sense to think about diplomacy more in terms of a proliferation of diplomatic actors, or instead to acknowledge that diplomacy was now taking place between unlike types of actors? Whilst some scholars of diplomacy have preferred to define interactions with new types of diplomatic actor and some of the newer forms of diplomatic venues as not constituting diplomacy, that choice need not be made. Rather, if the idea of diplomacy is to remain useful, the profusion of types of actor and venue implies that our understanding of what diplomacy is and who does it needs to be broadened accordingly.

The first significant change to note has affected nation–state governments, the most traditional type of diplomatic actor. Although sovereignty has remained important in recent decades, it no longer implies functional equality for nation–states as diplomatic actors in the way that it did in the eighteenth and nineteenth centuries. There has been a dramatic increase in the number of formally sovereign nation–states in the international system since the end of the Second World War, resulting from processes of decolonization and the internal collapse of multi-ethnic or imperial states, and with this increase in number has come an equally dramatic differentiation between the attributes and capacities of the states in the system. As Susan Strange put it so succinctly, size matters.[10] Decolonization of the once vast British Empire has produced nation–states as diverse in population, size and wealth as India, Zambia, Australia and St Lucia. The dissolution of the Soviet Union has spawned oil-rich Kazakhstan, the physically vast and relatively populous Russian Federation, technologically advanced Estonia, and the generally unrecognized Transdniestr Moldovan Republic. Whereas 77 nation–states were founding members of the United Nations in 1945, by 2007 the number of member nation–states had grown to approximately 200. Of the more than 100 newer nation–states in the global community of nations, many are small and poor. As diplomatic actors, whilst formally equal, many of these states are unable to perform many of the core functions of diplomatic representation and communication to anything like the extent of their larger, wealthier and older neighbours. Limited in their ability to train and pay professional diplomats, many newer states send abroad far fewer permanent bilateral diplomatic missions, receive far fewer missions to their own capitals and operate a much smaller ministry of foreign affairs with far more circumscribed capacities.

The impact of this shift away from the functional equality of sovereign states in diplomacy is not as direct as it might seem, however, as it has been mitigated significantly by the rise in the rôle of multilateral organizations as venues for conducting diplomatic business. Governments of smaller, more impoverished nation–states increasingly devote the resources they have available for diplomacy to representation to, and communications with and through, the major multilateral organizations with which they have relationships, such as the United Nations, the International Monetary Fund and World Bank, the World Trade Organization, and regional integration and development finance institutions such as the African Union, the Association of Southeast Asian Nations (ASEAN) and the Inter-American Development Bank. As the chapters that follow discuss, such venues serve not only as fora for much diplomatic business that was once conducted bilaterally, but also as efficient locations for the conduct of necessary bilateral diplomacy with fellow members in the same place for the same purpose.

A further change has affected the nation–state as a diplomatic actor. Not only have nation–state governments as diplomatic actors become more different from one another, but now they are no longer the only type of governmental actor seen to be engaging actively in diplomacy. Sub-national regional governments, such as those of Catalonia and Québec, and supranational actors such as the European Union, Caricom, ASEAN and the African Union, are recognized as diplomatic actors in their own right. Moreover, increasingly, governments of large metropolitan urban areas such as London, Tokyo, Mexico City and New York exchange representatives with other diplomatic actors and engage in diplomatic communications over a range of issue areas extending from crime prevention to attracting international expositions and sporting events.

The case for contemporary diplomacy as consisting of interactions between unlike types of actors is advanced by the convergence between diplomatic actors and venues for diplomacy. This phenomenon is newer and more significant than at first it might seem. From the earliest origins of diplomacy up until the last two centuries, the notion of a venue for diplomacy referred only to the site or location where a diplomatic meeting, negotiation or other sort of communication between sovereigns or their accredited representatives took place. The venue was almost always the court or residence of one of the actors or interlocutors, to which the other actor would have sent an envoy or mission for the purpose of communicating or negotiation. As Costas Constantinou points out in his seminal work on diplomatic theory and practice, *On The Way to Diplomacy*, the word 'embassy' referred to the mission of envoys or representatives sent by one sovereign to another. Only later did it come to connote an actual structure or venue for permanent representation of one sovereign in the capital of another.[11] However, with the emergence of major multilateral conferences or 'Congresses' for conducting diplomatic business in Europe on a regular basis in the nineteenth century, the notion of a venue for diplomacy began to take on a somewhat different aspect. The Concert of Europe multilateral system that maintained the peace in Europe with generally acknowledged success for the best part of a century following the Congress of Vienna in 1815 is the prime exemplar of the change towards venues for multilateral diplomacy. The physical location of such conferences varied, but the standing of the participants was fixed and understood in the context of the particular purpose for which the conference assembled, rather than in the context of an ongoing bilateral diplomatic relationship between host and guest. In fact the failure of the Concert system was attributed by many after the Great War, at least in part, to its lack of a venue of its own. This view contributed to the decision taken at Versailles to give the League of Nations a fixed abode at Geneva.

The next step in the evolution of the venue for diplomacy was the emergence from the late nineteenth century of permanent multilateral organizations in which diplomacy was conducted. Such organizations initially were small and specific to particular issues or needs. The Brussels Sugar Convention of 1902, for example, created a Permanent Sugar Commission, an institution that was tasked with monitoring compliance with the obligations of the convention by signatory countries and non-signatories alike. A sort of proto-World Trade Organization for governing trade in one commodity, sugar, the Permanent Sugar Commission was the first multilateral trade institution empowered to impose sanctions or penalties on states that violated the rules for fair international trade in sugar agreed by signatories to the Brussels Sugar Convention. Although it only lasted little more than a decade, until the outbreak of the Great War, the Permanent Sugar Commission was effective in achieving its objectives, and as such represented a significant development in multilateral commercial diplomacy.[12]

The period after the Great War saw institutional venues for multilateral diplomacy become the norm. The League of Nations was the first great multilateral experiment in entrusting some of the core elements that constituted traditional national sovereignty – protection against attack and the maintenance of peace – to a permanent institution charged with fair administration of mutually agreed rules of state behaviour. Yet not long behind the founding of the League of Nations came the establishment of the International Chamber of Commerce, the first multilateral venue for diplomacy not constituted by governments but by civil society actors: international businesses. The history of the League of Nations and the raft of multilateral institutions that followed it – the United Nations, the North Atlantic Treaty Organization, the Bretton Woods 'triad' of international economic organizations (the World Bank, the International Monetary Fund and the General Agreement on Tariffs and Trade) – was a story of governments and other actors on the global stage becoming at ease with using multilateral venues to pursue different types of diplomatic objectives in different ways. Some venues have been more successful than others. The International Chamber of Commerce's International Court of Arbitration continues to resolve cross-border disputes between firms in the present time, whereas the economic sanctions that the League of Nations was empowered to impose on rule-breaking members were not deemed sufficient for the task by the eve of the Second World War. In any event, however, by mid-century multilateral venues for diplomacy had become part of diplomatic culture and of international society.

These multilateral institutions, as they have evolved, have taken on a diverse range of diplomatic functions, ranging from serving as venues for communication about major global issues such as security and world peace to mediating between nation–states over much narrower economic and technical issues. Some of these functions have made the institutions spearheading them well known to the global public, whilst others by their nature tend not to attract public attention. Organizations involved with security, such as the League and the United Nations and NATO, have tended to have a high public profile, as their decisions and actions, or lack thereof, have received extensive attention in the global media. Other multilateral institutions, such as the Basel Committee on Banking Supervision, which acts to facilitate international cooperation on financial standards for banks, or the International Telecommunication Union, operate largely outside of the public eye.

The emergence of major permanent venues for diplomacy brought with it its own set of operational problems and challenges. A venue for diplomacy by its nature not only connotes the idea of an occasion that is regular or repeated, but also can bear the implication of a physical place or location. Not all multilateral venues for diplomacy acquire permanent physical premises. The G7/G8, for example, are managed on a rotating basis by diplomats of the country serving as that year's chair. But of necessity, when a physical place is created for conducting multilateral diplomacy, it must share that space with whatever nation–states and municipalities already exercise sovereignty over it. For example, the locations of headquarters of institutions such as the United Nations, NATO and the European Union had to be placed within already sovereign states, so both the headquarters facilities and the representatives of members accredited to them had to be accorded the requisite degree of sovereignty by the host state to enable the institutions to perform their duties without fear of prejudice or harm. This has resulted in occasional complications for host states, ranging from issues such as the cost of provision of public services and security to the institution to more challenging problems when host governments have policy disagreements with a multilateral organization located on their territory or find themselves at odds politically with some member states of the organization. Disputes over the cost of providing public services and security have been an ongoing feature of the relationship between the federal government of Belgium and the Bruxelles-Capitale regional government on the one side and NATO and the European Union, which both have headquarters within the Brussels region, on the other. The clash of policies question arose in the relationship between NATO and the government of France, which hosted NATO from its inception in 1947 up until 1967. Following French President de Gaulle's withdrawal of France from NATO's military command structure in 1966, NATO moved its headquarters to Brussels. The third situation has arisen regularly in recent decades when heads of governments deemed hostile to the United States visit the United Nations headquarters and, accorded freedom of movement within 25 miles of UN Headquarters under the UN Charter, use the opportunity to make provocative speeches and public appearances. The visits of Cuban President Fidel Castro have been a prime example, as, more recently, have been those of Presidents Mahmoud Ahmedinajad of Iran and Hugo Chavez of Venezuela. That the interests of a host state and a multilateral institution of which it is a member might differ is not inconsequential. Such differences represent some of the most significant effects upon diplomacy of the emergence of the physical embodiment of institutional venues for the conduct of multilateral diplomatic business.

Over the course of the twentieth century, Switzerland has carved out for itself a particular diplomatic niche: that of a 'venue of venues', as it were. Switzerland has emerged as a natural host location for multilateral organizations, playing host initially to the League of Nations and subsequently to parts of the United Nations infrastructure such as the World Intellectual Property Organization (WIPO), and more latterly hosting a range of institutions extending from the General Agreement on Tariffs and

Trade (GATT) Secretariat and its successor the World Trade Organization, to the International Labour Organization. Switzerland also hosts a group of major civil society organizations, ranging from the World Economic Forum to the International Committee of the Red Cross (ICRC) and UNI, a global umbrella organization for 900 trades unions representing 20 million service workers. Yet at the same time Switzerland has adopted a diplomatic stance of neutrality that it has constructed to take the form of its own government not participating formally in multilateral institutions, declining to join the European Union and not even joining the United Nations itself until 2002. By creating this peculiar sort of offsetting duality through its approach to interacting with the rest of the world, Switzerland perhaps has found a way to avoid at least some of the conflicts that are endemic to nation–states that host venues for multilateral diplomacy.

But going beyond and underlying issues arising from the physical location of venues for multilateral diplomacy is a more fundamental effect that multilateral institutions have had upon contemporary diplomacy. These institutions are far younger than many of the nation–states that created most of them: the UN has been with us for much less time than France and Russia have been, for example. And yet as these young multilateral institutions have emerged and developed as diplomatic venues through the second half of the twentieth century and into the twenty-first, these venues have gradually grown towards becoming diplomatic actors in their own right. Each institution has come to take on aspects of diplomatic 'actorness' to varying degrees, even, in the cases of the League of Nations and United Nations, to the extent of assuming (albeit temporary) authority over the governance of territory in the case of mandates and trust territories in the process of moving towards self-government. Beginning as the creatures of the nation–states or other constituents or actors that created them, these institutions are staffed by officers and, in some cases, employees appointed or elected according to the procedures set by their creators. Yet over time multilateral institutions have evolved their own identities. As they work together, managers and staffs of these institutions shape, and ultimately generate, their own institutional interests and play a greater rôle in setting their own agendas and issue priorities. The institutions then find themselves faced with many of the same diplomatic challenges as nation–state actors themselves. They must represent themselves to and communicate with other diplomatic actors: governments of nation–states and non-state actors, including other multilateral institutions. Nearly all member governments of the United Nations send an ambassador or other permanent representative to New York to represent their interests on an ongoing basis. Many members of the World Trade Organization now have a permanent mission to the WTO headquarters in Geneva. The World Bank and IMF may have permanent or long-term representation in the capitals of the nation–states in which they are funding major projects. The European Union now sends a permanent representative to the United Nations, who functions independently from, albeit cooperatively with, the permanent representatives to the UN of each of the EU's member states. The EU also sends representative missions to other important partners: for example John Bruton, former Prime Minister of Ireland, represented the EU to the USA in the later 2000s.

Actors to Venues

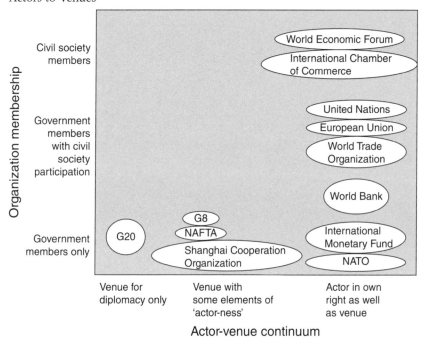

Actor-venue continuum

It is important to recognize that the evolution of diplomatic venues towards becoming actors in their own right contributes to the trend towards differentiation of types of diplomatic actors as well as increasing the number of actors that must interact. Not only does the extent of each institution's 'actor-ness' vary, but the differences between institutions and other types of actors (whether nation–states, firms, CSOs or otherwise) inevitably limit some of the ways in which diplomatic representation and communication between them take place. But the overarching significance for contemporary diplomacy of the evolution of multilateral institutions is that the venues that nation–states created initially in order to facilitate representation and communication between them have now themselves become subjects of diplomatic representation and communication. The efforts of diplomatic actors to respond to change in the contemporary international system, the global economy and technology continue to cause diplomacy to adapt and change. The result of this change and adaptation is that the core diplomatic functions of representation and communication are becoming different rather than becoming easier. A major theme running throughout the remaining chapters of this book is that diplomacy continues to exist and be necessary precisely because diplomatic representation and communication are inherently problematic.

3

Nation–state Governments, Sub-national and Local Governments

Introduction: Evolving Nation–state Sovereignty and Diplomatic Practice

As the Westphalia system of nation–states and the nation–states that comprise it have changed over the past century, the way in which these nation–state actors have conducted diplomacy has needed to change accordingly. The sovereignty of the nation–state and the government that represented it was the cornerstone upon which the Westphalia system was built. Yet even as the inviolability of that sovereignty was enshrined in Article I of the United Nations Charter in 1945, the Westphalia system of nation–states and the idea of sovereignty upon which it rested was already beginning to change.[1] According to James Der Derian, classical diplomacy was founded on the idea of multiple and equal nation–state units, both tied to and at the same time estranged from each other. The nation–states had to be sovereign in the sense of wielding exclusive control over territory, and at the same time independent entities when facing outwards. At the time it represented the complete upending of the hierarchical, universal, mediaeval feudal Christian polity. Yet, functionally, the formal equality of each sovereign nation–state was probably always a necessary fiction.[2] Nation–states and their governments were never functionally equal as diplomatic actors, even if there was a significant tier of nation–state governments that observed the norms of the fiction of equality and generally behaved consistently with it. The great powers that comprised the Concert of Europe in the nineteenth century created new sovereign states, as they did by guaranteeing the sovereignty of the new state of Belgium in the 1831 Treaty of London. But although they granted such states the institutions and symbols of sovereignty, they did not apportion to them an equal measure of the power and influence that was a crucial component of the sort of sovereign authority that they shared with one another. The problem of the existence of the diplomacy of the Holy See after 1870, when it no longer in effect controlled any territory, made the point even more emphatically. Clearly Vatican diplomacy continued to take place, even in the absence of a territorial state for its diplomats to represent. Communist governments in central European countries with large Roman Catholic populations in the 1980s, as they faced the impact of the Holy See's public diplomacy upon their citizenry, might well have found Stalin's contemptuous rhetorical question 'how many divisions does the Pope have?' not to be the relevant question to ask.

Yet even if sovereign equality of Westphalian nation–states was always a myth, the topography of the nation–state system changed significantly enough in the half-century following the Second World War for the changed and changing nature of sovereignty to bring about identifiable changes even in traditional diplomacy between nation–state governments themselves. The configuration of the system itself and the nature of the actors within it shifted dramatically. Decolonization of the old European empires and the break-up of the Soviet Union brought about a roughly fivefold increase in the number of nominally sovereign nation–states in the world in only five decades. In terms of distribution of assets, whether wealth, power or territory, the disparity between nation–state units became vastly greater. The Cold War was the era in which two nation–states (the United States and the Soviet Union) were dubbed 'superpowers' for their ability to organize the rest of the sovereign states in the international system into alliances based on their nuclear power to destroy life on Earth many times over and for their power to preside over the remaking of former European colonies into dysfunctional, corrupt and poor, even if formally sovereign, nation–states. The nation–states system since the Cold War comprises an even greater range of polities, extending from so-called 'hyperpowers' (the most recently applied term for the post-Cold War United States) to great powers (the United Kingdom, France, Germany, Russia, Japan, China, India), microstates (San Marino, Andorra, Monaco, Nauru) and anomalous polities like the Holy See (virtually no territory but a huge diaspora population), Hong Kong (not sovereign but treated by the international community as if it were) and the Republic of China – Taiwan (acknowledged as functionally sovereign by the international community through trade and economic relations, recognized as formally sovereign by a minority of the world's nation–states, even as the majority pretends otherwise in deference to the political power of the government of the People's Republic of China).

This enormous disparity in size and wealth between formally equal sovereign nation–states raises some important practical issues for the conduct of nation–state diplomacy. One of the most important is the sheer cost of the core diplomatic functions of representation and communication. The 2005 annual budget of the Federal Republic of Germany's Auswärtiges Amt (Federal Foreign Ministry) was €1.313 billion, whereas the 2007 annual budget for the Foreign Ministry of the Republic of Georgia was only $40,868,000. Representation costs consist primarily of three very weighty budget lines: the bricks-and-mortar cost of building and maintaining foreign missions (and 'headquarters' base facilities in the home country), human resources costs of training and remunerating professional diplomats and their support staffs, and membership fees in the rising number of international organizations in which most nation–state governments now participate. For example, in the 2007 budget of the Georgian Foreign Ministry, 61.4 per cent of the total budget was spent on diplomatic representation abroad, 22.1 per cent on the home expenditures of the Ministry (over 30 per cent of which went to staff salaries), and 15.1 per cent on membership fees for multilateral institutions. Each of these budget lines has tended to grow rapidly in recent decades. Embassies, consulates and other diplomatic facilities have become more expensive to operate and maintain, not least because of increased security costs, but at even a basic level the explosion in the number of sovereign nation–states has rendered unworkable the traditional European diplomatic commonplace that each sovereign government would wish to maintain an ambassador in each other sovereign capital. The notion that each formally sovereign nation–state would open and maintain a mission in each of the now over 190 other such nation–states has quite unimaginable cost implications. The Georgian Foreign Ministry budget more than doubled between 2004 and 2007; a significant portion of the increase was attributable to opening five new diplomatic missions abroad in 2006 and another five in 2007.[3] Even the wealthiest of nation–states cannot afford to maintain as many foreign missions as their diplomatic services would wish in order to meet the professional standards of diplomacy to which they aspire.

Staffing Levels of Various Ministries of Foreign Affairs

Nation–state	Foreign Ministry staff
United States – Department of State	30,260 (2004)
Germany – *Auswärtiges Amt*	11,650
India – Ministry of External Affairs	3500
European Union – DG *Relations Externels*	5600

Costs of remunerating professional diplomats have risen significantly as well. Foreign ministries, even in wealthy countries, can no longer rely upon the willingness of ambassadors and other senior diplomats from aristocratic, monied families to contribute substantially to their own operating costs whilst in post (living and diplomatic entertaining), as was often the case in the nineteenth and early twentieth centuries amongst the diplomatic corps of older nation–states. The development of information and communications technology since the 1970s with the advent of satellite transmissions, the internet and broadband and wireless voice and data transmission (see chapter 7) has altered significantly how diplomatic communication is done, increasing both the sheer possibilities and the efficiency of diplomatic communication over distance at speed, but again at some considerable cost. Major communications budget lines include building and maintaining communications satellites, installing and maintaining hardware, operating and training staff to operate communications software, and provision of communications security.

The implications of the cost increases in the business of diplomacy for nation–state governments are as evident as they are varied. Diplomatic budgets in wealthy and powerful nation–state governments face increasing competition in appropriations processes from other spending lines that legislators are able to link more directly to specific benefits for constituents. At the other end of the spectrum, very poor nation–states and micro-states cannot afford to create the infrastructure of representation and communication that larger and richer states already have: embassies, consulates, trade development offices and cultural centres. Hence both rich and poor nation–states have moved towards experimenting with different strategies of representation. One strategy is the pooling or sharing of representative offices for specific functions, such as the operation of joint consulates. Some of the smaller, wealthier countries in Europe share consular facilities in a number of third countries. The ambassadors sent by most smaller states to the European Union are also accredited to the Belgian government, and some serve as their sovereign's representative to NATO in addition, as all three bodies are located in greater Brussels. Another strategy is to substitute increased communication for representation. It has become possible increasingly to use advances in technology to carry out from the home country many diplomatic functions that once required on-site personnel in missions abroad (see chapter 7). Meetings, conferences and negotiations (at least at some levels and in some circumstances) can be held using videoconferencing. Much consular business, such as routine visa applications and issuance, can be conducted using the internet.

Another key change in the nation–state system has been the accelerating diffusion of aspects or elements of sovereignty from nation–state governments towards other institutions or structures. As noted in the previous chapter, from early in the twentieth century governments of nation–states and their diplomats have been creating multilateral organizations to serve as permanent venues for mediating estrangement between nation–states. This process has resulted in two significant developments. The first is that a network of multilateral organizations has emerged, stretching from the United Nations and its specialized agencies to the World Bank, the International Monetary Fund, the World Trade Organization, the International Atomic Energy Agency, the Basel Committee on Banking Supervision, and the World Health Organization, to name only some (see chapter 4). These organizations have produced significant regimes of what could be called global governance, albeit over delimited issue areas and competences. In order for this to happen, nation–state governments have had to choose consciously, through domestic legislative and/or executive political processes, to alienate aspects or elements of their sovereignty, their power to govern, to other entities.[4] This legal process of alienation has taken a number of forms: in security, for example, by signing the UN Charter, governments agree to be bound by rules regulating their prerogatives to engage in offensive military action, at least in theory. Perhaps the most common elements of global governance consist in the creation of entities to manage the way that global markets are structured, by setting the parameters within which the actors must make decisions and fixing the matrices of incentives for market actors. These institutional structures and 'rules of the game' frame the decision horizons of the players in the global marketplace. For example, by signing the Treaty of Marrakech in 1994, governments chose to alienate to a new World Trade Organization the power to drive an ongoing process of trade negotiations further to develop a particular sort of neoliberal market structure for global trade in goods and services. They granted to the WTO the power to mediate estrangement between sovereign states over trade: to adjudicate and resolve trade disputes through a supranational dispute settlement body whose decisions are binding upon member state governments.

The second development follows from the first. As noted in the last chapter, the multilateral organizations that were created to serve as venues for diplomacy have become distinct new actors in their own right. The practical implication of this for nation–state governments is that they now must engage in diplomatic representation and communication with the organizations themselves. All members have permanent representation to the United Nations, just as in many cases the UN has representative offices in member countries. All the world's major trading powers, and many smaller ones, maintain permanent missions to the WTO. Most have permanent representation to the IMF and World Bank as well.

A further important shift or evolution in the nation–state system has been the breaking down of the social, political and economic boundaries between the domestic and the international. In the first half of the twentieth century, the political contestation of different domestic economic interests over issues like employment, benefits and government subventions to industry were framed primarily as domestic political debates. Yet since the Second World War and particularly since the 1970s, these one-time domestic debates have come to focus increasingly on international issues like trade, monetary policy and other governments' subventions to industry. Thus foreign ministries and other diplomatic offices that were established initially to mediate between the state – the national government – and other states now increasingly must also engage in mediation directly with civil society within the home state. Businesses with interests to promote, civil society organizations advocating a particular direction in or protesting against the government's foreign policy, and individuals with particular demands and agendas all seek increasingly to advance their objectives by lobbying the government's organs of diplomacy and foreign policy directly. At the same time they continue to use the more traditional channel for bringing political pressure through their elected representatives in the legislature.

The Changing Rôle of Foreign Ministries

How these simultaneous diplomatic mediations are actually done, and how well they are done, depends in large part upon the ministry of foreign affairs and other governmental institutions that are charged with conducting a nation–state's diplomacy. Mediation can be understood as taking place at two levels simultaneously: symbolically, as overcoming estrangement or alienation through representation and communication, and practically, as reconciling differing interests and views. In the classical model for understanding diplomacy, the foreign ministry played the lead rôle in diplomatic mediation at both levels. In many respects this leadership position has persisted, yet the ways in which foreign ministries and other ministries involved in diplomacy work together are evolving in significantly new directions. In order to understand how these changes are affecting both the processes and products of diplomacy, let us begin with a review of the traditional rôle of the foreign ministry itself. The foreign ministry can be seen as exercising a dual mediation function not only in symbolic and practical terms, but also in terms of the international and the domestic. The foreign ministry is best known for mediating between the home state and other states, a representation and communication function that it undertakes using both home-based personnel and various sorts of envoys: embassies, consulates and other missions, some of which are permanent and some ad hoc. But, of equal importance, the foreign ministry must mediate with the rest of the government of the home state and with related private actors, such as policy institutions (think tanks), epistemic communities and lobbyists. This boundary-spanning communication process both disseminates information about diplomacy and gathers information that contributes to shaping it.[5] The foreign ministry informs the foreign policy making apparatus of the state, however it happens to be set up, of the results of the implementation of the state's foreign policy and on how implementation of policy has affected the state's relations with other states.

In performing this communication function the foreign ministry evaluates the effectiveness of policies and uses its expertise to develop policy recommendations for the political leadership that must approve new or amended policy. So in a sense the foreign ministry 'makes' foreign policy, but not on its own. The foreign ministry must accept instruction on policy from the political leadership of the foreign policy making apparatus.[6] The ministry must then implement that policy through its headquarters staff and its envoys abroad. As an example of how this process works, suppose that the US State Department advises the White House that a significant number of potential terrorists are passing into the United States on legitimately issued visas. They recommend better integration of intelligence data into the database used to determine visa eligibility. But instead the National Security Council staff in the White House, whose responsibility it is to make and coordinate foreign policy, decide that the way forward is to require all visa applicants from countries that do not issue passports with electronic data strips to submit fingerprints for identification, which then will have to be re-checked at ports of entry. They inform the State Department, which then must notify all US consulates to begin fingerprinting visa applicants in the relevant countries.

According to the classical diplomatic studies tradition, the other main function of the foreign ministry is what Brian Hocking calls 'the gatekeeper rôle'.[7] The principal function of foreign ministries traditionally has been understood to be that of regulating and coordinating the involvement of other institutions of government in diplomacy. When another ministry – the ministry of finance, agriculture, trade, education, whatever – wants or needs to deal with its foreign counterpart agencies, that interaction would

The Sublime Porte, Istanbul, the gateway where the Ottoman sultan traditionally received foreign ambassadors, and which became the term used to refer to the Ottoman Empire government as a diplomatic actor (*Photo credit: G. A. Pigman*)

need to be approved by and coordinated by the foreign ministry. This gatekeeper rôle historically implied that the foreign ministry took the lead rôle in coordination of the nation's foreign policy. For example, if the Office of the US Trade Representative ('USTR') were keen to negotiate a bilateral trade liberalization pact with Burma in response to lobbying by US garment manufacturers seeking to outsource garment assembly to Burmese facilities, the US Department of State would need to approve direct contacts between USTR and Burmese trade officials. Before approving the trade negotiations, the State Department would be charged with making sure that a potential United States – Burma trade pact was compatible with overall US foreign policy objectives regarding Burma. State Department officials might tell their colleagues at USTR that, whereas in principle a trade agreement would be desirable, negotiations would have to be delayed until the United States could obtain from the generals ruling Burma commitments to liberalize human rights and hold free and fair elections. The State Department's gatekeeper rôle would require them to balance pressure from business to liberalize trade against pressure from civil society to defend human rights, articulated to State by members of

Congress and perhaps by direct lobbying as well. State would need to construct the foreign policy matrix of carrots and sticks to be presented to the Burmese government, naturally all subject to political approval by the White House.

In many countries the foreign ministry's gatekeeper function traditionally extended even to signing off on the diplomatic activities of senior politicians, including legislators as well as administrative officials. This gatekeeper rôle was as much cultural as legislated – it reflected the dominance of the particular diplomatic culture of classical diplomacy. If a British Member of Parliament is invited to visit South Africa, naturally she is going to coordinate her itinerary with the Foreign Office and with the High Commission in Pretoria. The Foreign Office will review the MP's itinerary and notify her if they see any potential problems: places she should avoid because of security concerns, a CEO upon whom she should go out of her way to call because his firm buys a significant quantity of British exports, or a controversial local political official she specifically should not meet because of political sensitivity in bilateral relations.

Yet today we see such diverse practices as finance ministries and central banks meeting regularly to coordinate exchange rate policy and stability of financial markets, justice ministries working closely together to formulate common responses to problems related to migration and terrorism, commerce and trade ministry officials meeting with foreign CEOs on export control issues, and health and agriculture ministers meeting with global civil society organization leaders to coordinate disaster relief efforts, all without nearly the same degree of foreign ministry gatekeeping in evidence. A survey of the practice of diplomacy today might suggest that the increasingly direct rôles of other government ministries in diplomacy have undercut the foreign ministry's ability to perform its gatekeeper function effectively and might even have caused the central position of the foreign ministry in diplomacy to decline. The reality is probably more subtle: in order to maintain their centrality in nation–state diplomacy, foreign ministries have had to adapt their rôle to fit the newer, multi-actor, multi-channel character of contemporary diplomatic interaction.

A Test Case: Emerging Norms of Representation to the European Union

Brian Hocking and David Spence, in *Foreign Ministries in the European Union*, argue that the gatekeeper as a dominant metaphor for the foreign

UNIVERSITY OF WINCHESTER
LIBRARY

ministry's relationship with other government ministries on diplomacy has given way in significant measure to another metaphor, that of the 'boundary spanner'. The boundary spanner rôle is about facilitating communication and cooperation between all of the government ministries involved in diplomacy. The foreign ministry as boundary spanner must ensure that everyone knows what everyone else is doing so that they can achieve policy objectives as efficiently as possible. Hocking and Spence use the diplomacy between member states of the European Union and the EU government in Brussels, a new type of relationship requiring a new approach to diplomacy, as a vehicle to explore how foreign ministries have adapted their rôle. (See chapter 4 for more on the European Union as a supranational diplomatic actor.) Hocking's boundary spanner metaphor addresses the notion of mediating estrangement where boundaries and political jurisdictions are ambiguous, which is an essential characteristic of the relationship between EU member states and the EU itself. He argues that the essence of the boundary spanner idea 'resides in the changing character and significance of boundaries, proceeding from the recognition that these, both in their territorial and policy-related manifestations, are increasingly porous'. In the shifting boundary and jurisdictional environment of the EU, ministries that can act as mediators, as boundary spanners, are particularly important.[8]

The problem of member state – EU diplomacy is an ideal case for exploring the changing rôle of foreign ministries, as well as being revealing in a broader sense, because immediately it problematizes the classical diplomatic notion of states as equal, sovereign and estranged entities and instead focuses on an asymmetric diplomacy between actors possessing different levels of sovereign authority. Member state – EU diplomacy could no longer be just a 'dialogue between states', as Adam Watson would have had it.[9] The creation of the EU required the alienation or pooling by each member state of a partial measure of sovereignty to a shared body. For each member state, creating the EU meant bringing into being a new entity that was neither fully the member state that contributed to it nor fully alien to that state. It raises new questions: is an EU member state's representation to and communication with the EU akin to its relations with another state, that is, with an entirely foreign entity? Or is it more akin to 'intra-state' relations, the interactions that take place between a regional or local government and the central government of a state? For foreign ministries it poses the direct question of what rôle they play in relations with the EU. The EU itself has diplomatic relations with other nation–states, including the United States, Russia and most other states, as well as blocs of developing countries with which it has economic relationships, such as the ACP countries, a grouping comprised primarily of former colonies of EU member states. The EU has a foreign ministry of its own, Directorate General for External Relations ('DG Relex'), within the European Commission, the EU's executive arm, to direct and manage these relations. But DG Relex does not manage EU relations with EU member states, any more than the British Foreign Office manages relations between the national government in Westminster and the regional government of Scotland or Wales.

How have member state foreign ministries dealt with the growth in the various areas of cooperation, and conflict, between the member states and the EU? Most importantly, Hocking and Spence argue, foreign ministries have indeed adapted substantially to the fundamental change in the foreign policy environment for member states that has come with deepening EU cooperation, often showing greater capacity for innovation than other government departments. The emergence of more extensive EU-level cooperation has not meant the end of bilateral diplomatic cooperation between member states. Arguably bilateral relations are more extensive than ever. But some aspects of bilateral diplomatic relations between EU member states have been superseded by institutions and processes of collective, supranational governance in which other EU ministries take leading rôles. For example, most aspects of European competition policy are no longer negotiated bilaterally but are debated and legislated by the European Commission's competition ministry, DG Competition. Policies that are adopted are then implemented by EU-level regulation and supporting member state regulation. Both implementation and enforcement require cooperation from member state governments – by each member state's judiciary, and, in Britain for example, by ministries such as the Department of Trade and Industry and by the Monopolies and Mergers Commission.

Two of the critical boundary spanner functions that member state foreign ministries must now perform, according to Spence, are coordinating the European and international aspects of domestic policies (mediating between the internal and the external), and providing member state input to the EU's own collective foreign policy, or external relations, as it is known. EU external relations is comprised of three policy 'pillars': (I) trade, development, enlargement and technical assistance; (II) foreign and defence policy; and (III) justice and home affairs. In order to conduct these functions, member state foreign ministries maintain embassies in Brussels known as Permanent Representations to the European Union. At each member state's Permanent Representation, lead ministries – the member states' other ministries connected with functional policy areas, such as agriculture, finance, and health and safety – interact directly with one another, and with the relevant European Union DG (ministry) in Brussels on an increasing basis, at least on matters involving the first and third pillars. As boundary spanners the foreign ministries play a coordinating rôle here, for example in preparing meetings of the EU Council of Ministers, which is the EU legislative body consisting of ministers of member state governments. In preparing Council meetings, member state foreign ministries ensure that member state input at Council meetings is coherent, a function that can involve mediating between different home government lead ministries when their interests clash. French foreign ministry representatives, for example, might find themselves mediating between different views held by the French finance ministry and the French justice ministry respectively on an asylum issue to be taken up in the EU Council of Ministers. How this mediation is done varies from state to state. In Belgium and Germany dispute arbitration duties are shared between the foreign and economics ministries, although in Germany the Federal Chancellor's office has a rôle in it as well. But in France and Germany, the Prime Minister's cabinet office tends to perform the arbitration rôle instead. In this sort of context the member state foreign ministry ends up playing more of a monitoring rôle than a supervisory rôle in member state 'domestic' policy making. Other ministries may choose to challenge the foreign ministry's boundary spanner rôle when they perceive the foreign ministry to be acting in their own interest, or even in the interest of other member states, against a domestic ministry's particular interest.

The member states' Permanent Representations are in effect a new hybrid of a traditional foreign ministry's embassy adapted to encompass representation of a broader range of member state government agencies to a new type of polity. As such, the Permanent Representations play both a lobbying and a coordinating rôle for the member states in Brussels. A number of methods of lobbying exist, including influencing the forward thinking of the Commission, receiving early warning of Commission legislative proposals and pre-negotiating thorny issues. The Permanent Representations also communicate with and lobby the EU's legislative organ, the European Parliament, which has the power to amend legislation submitted by the Commission and to vote up or down on 80 per cent of EU legislation (including the all-important budget). The hybrid nature of the Permanent Representation is also evident in that although it is an embassy, organized and operated like a traditional foreign-ministry-run embassy, it is staffed increasingly by representatives from the whole range of member state government ministries that have business in Brussels. Hence other government officials increasingly are called upon to function as diplomats, in the embassy setting. This can have a significant impact upon the management of embassy operations, given that the non-foreign-ministry officials are not likely to be under the direct line management of the ambassador. Thus, for foreign ministries, playing the rôle of the boundary spanner has become pivotal if they wish to minimize a decline in their influence resulting from the diffusion of diplomatic activity into other ministries.

Foreign ministries play substantially more of a coordinating rôle in relation to the second pillar, EU foreign and defence policy, which has resulted in the creation of the EU's Common Foreign and Security Policy (CFSP) in the 1990s and the even more integrated European Security and Defence Policy (ESDP) in the 2000s. The Treaty of Nice in 2000 approved considerable consolidation of foreign policy making power for the EU, including the creation of the European Union High Representative to act as EU foreign policy 'tsar'. It has brought on an increasing shift of policy making activity from the national capitals to Brussels. Yet importantly, much of the work of CFSP remains intergovernmental, so diplomacy between the member state foreign ministries remains key. One of the main aspects of this has been the formation of the Political and Security Committee ('PSC'), which is composed of national representatives at senior ambassador level based in the Permanent Representations, the embassies. The PSC is an intensive working group, meeting twice weekly to oversee CFSP and to work on setting up ESDP. Feeder committees supply the PSC with policy input, on military matters and on civilian aspects of crisis management, for example. So in practice the development of EU foreign and security policy has meant a lot more work for member state foreign ministries, especially ministries from some of the smaller member states that previously had not articulated diplomatically a direct policy interest in many of the European security issues that now arise on a regular basis.

The emergence of the European Union and its massive agenda of issues has required member state foreign ministries to reorganize themselves institutionally to accommodate the shift. Foreign ministries now have separate departments for EU relations and for bilateral relations with member states on non-EU-related matters. The traditional channel for bilateral mediation of estrangement continues, as the need for such functions remains. That said, bilateral embassies, especially those between Britain and Germany, are collaborating increasingly over EU matters on an operational basis, especially to ensure coherence in defending EU policy to the rest of the world.

Ultimately, foreign ministries in Europe, as elsewhere, increasingly have been compelled to adopt the boundary spanner rôle, although that has not stopped them from attempting to play the gatekeeper rôle as well, albeit with less success. Foreign ministries themselves diverge substantially from one another, even within Europe. Within the governmental hierarchies and political cultures of their respective nation–states, some foreign ministries are stronger and more dominant, whilst others are weaker. Denmark is an example of a country with a strong foreign ministry; the Netherlands has a weak one. Ireland had a very weak foreign ministry before the Second World War, whilst in recent times the Irish Foreign Ministry has become second in influence in Irish politics only to its Finance Ministry.[10]

Other Ministries and Governmental Bodies as Diplomatic Actors

Whilst other ministries in the nation–state government have long played a certain part in the making and implementing of foreign policy, in the decades since the Second World War their particular diplomatic rôles have increased greatly. The two ministries outside of the foreign ministry that have played the most important parts in direct representation and communication are those of trade and finance. Given the economic character of so much representation and communication, this is not surprising. Trade and finance ministers and their staffs engage in mediation bilaterally, multilaterally and through multilateral organizations (see chapter 4 and chapter 9). The growing importance of trade on the diplomatic agenda has prompted a number of nation–state governments to re-think their organizational structures for diplomacy in terms of what will serve the national interest best. Most foreign ministries and trade ministries work quite closely together. A number of countries such as Belgium and Australia have amalgamated their foreign ministries and trade ministries into a single government department. Others, like Canada, have taken this step and then subsequently reversed it, more for domestic political reasons than due to lack of success of the organizational reform.

However, the rise of inter-agency cooperation on trade policy should not be taken to suggest that there do not remain institutional differences of interest, and indeed sometimes tensions, over trade policy between different ministries, and that can play itself out in diplomatic interactions.

In the United States, for example, the Commerce Department, the Agriculture Department, and the Office of the US Trade Representative are each responsible for different aspects of trade policy. Sometimes the lines of responsibility are not entirely clear, so occasionally the Secretary of Commerce might be saying one thing to the European Trade Commissioner whilst the US Trade Representative might be saying something rather different in a meeting with leaders of the European Parliament.

Largely for historical reasons, the US State Department still considers itself responsible for the coordinating rôle of ensuring that trade policy supports, or at least does not hinder, more overarching US foreign policy objectives, such as security cooperation. State Department officials do not want a US–EU trade dispute to jeopardize relations between NATO members, for example. Much of the State Department's gatekeeper function on trade was taken away in the 1960s explicitly by legislation that created the US Trade Representative. Yet there is substantial opposition to what residual coordination rôle they do have, as domestic business and labour interests advance their own objectives for US trade policy primarily through Commerce, USTR and Agriculture. Domestic economic interests do not have the same lobbying leverage at State, so they press for their issues to be kept safe from any bargaining or tradeoffs that might result from a coordinating action by State.

Different functional areas of bilateral and multilateral diplomacy between nation–states draw in still other ministries. On finance and banking issues, not only government finance ministries but also central banks, now often independent from government political control, engage directly in diplomatic representation to and communication with their foreign counterparts. Finance ministers and central bankers regularly meet and communicate bilaterally and multilaterally in venues such as the annual meeting of G7 finance ministers and the Basel Committee on Banking Supervision. Emergency summits to deal with international financial crises are now routine, as illustrated by the meetings during the various currency collapses in the 1990s. Communications technology has facilitated the types of close cooperation on a daily and weekly basis between finance ministries and central banks of advanced industrial states that we now see. Going still farther afield, many other government ministries now engage in direct relations with their counterparts abroad on issues such as health and safety, energy, education. The forms and structures that they use to represent themselves and communicate often replicate the original diplomatic culture of representation through foreign ministries. Yet again, technology has made new structures of communication possible, including teleconferencing and working groups that meet on an ad hoc basis online.

Another example of the profusion of channels for diplomacy at the nation–state level appears in the growth in recent times of parliamentary diplomacy, direct communication between legislators across national borders. Parliamentary diplomacy can take place either through bilateral representations and missions or through multilateral inter-parliamentary venues such as the Inter-Parliamentary Union (IPU), NATO's Parliamentary Assembly, and the Council of Europe's Parliamentary Assembly. One of the main drivers of growth of parliamentary diplomacy has been the increased desire of publics to exercise greater scrutiny over the decisions and practices of executive branches of government, which include traditional organs of diplomacy (head of government, foreign ministry, etc.), using their elected legislators. Greater information flows between legislators has resulted in legislatures being better informed about diplomatic questions when they have come to require legislation, such as treaty ratification. Legislatures have been more ready with firmer support for the foreign ministry in dealing with crises that arise. Transfer of best practices, capacities and skills between legislatures has also been facilitated. For example, Dutch parliamentarians have participated in capacity-building projects with their legislative counterparts in Georgia and Kyrgyzstan.[11]

The Diplomacy of Sub-national and Local Governments

The classical approach to studying diplomacy historically has ignored the relationships that in fact have long existed between many levels of sub-national, dependent and local governments on the one hand and external entities – national, sub-national and local governments abroad – on the other. The traditional approach to diplomacy has also disregarded relationships between nation–state governments and some of their own sub-national governments, relationships that can articulate considerable complexities with respect to sovereignty and identity. Yet sub-national diplomatic actors routinely engage in many of the same core diplomatic functions of representation and communication that characterize diplomacy between sovereign states. Likewise, relationships between national governments and sub-national actors exhibit many of the same asymmetric or 'multi-level' relational characteristics as have been observed in the discussion of member state – EU relations above. The engagement of sub-national governments in diplomacy has been observed to be increasing significantly in recent times.[12]

Sub-national governments vary in degree of stature relative to the nation–state of which their region forms a part. Some highly distinct and autonomous regions of member states have long maintained their own virtual foreign ministries, replete with headquarters in the regional capital and missions to those foreign capitals with which they have a particular need for or interest in permanent representation and communication. These missions are no less significant politically, economically and cultur-ally because they are entirely subordinate in a formal and institutional sense to the foreign ministries of their nation state. Their presence and functions are accepted by the nation–state government in return for regional acknowledgement of the nation–state government's ultimate sov-ereignty and authority over the entirety of its foreign policy and diplomacy. Regions known for possessing such institutions include Québec (Canada), Scotland (United Kingdom), Wales (United Kingdom), Catalonia (Spain) and Bavaria (Germany). One level down, many states and provinces send representatives and open offices abroad to focus more expressly upon trade, investment and tourism promotion. In the United States, states ranging from California and Florida to New York and Massachusetts have representation in various foreign capitals, as do Canadian provinces such as British Columbia and Ontario. In the 2000s, Governor Arnold Schwarzenegger of California, a state whose economy would be seventh largest in the world were California a nation–state, increasingly has engaged foreign counterparts directly on issues of energy and environmental policy, visiting and receiving foreign dignitaries and making cooperation agree-ments within permissible bounds under the US Constitution.

A more recent development has seen governments of large cities and urban areas increasingly engage directly in diplomatic activities, opening representative offices in foreign capitals and other major world cities and sending their mayors on ever more frequent 'state' visits to their foreign counterparts. In recent decades, mayors such as Jacques Chirac (Paris), Rudolph Giuliani (New York), Ken Livingstone (London), Yuri Luzhkov (Moscow) and, more recently, Michael Bloomberg (New York) became well known on the global diplomatic stage through their travels. These representations, once largely confined to the promotion of tourism, trade and investment, now focus on sharing approaches to major urban policy problems, ranging from terrorism to transport, provision of social services and environmental issues. They can even take the form of political consult-ing, as when former New York Mayor Giuliani advised former heavyweight boxer Vitaly Klitschko on his bid to become mayor of Ukraine's capital city, Kyiv, in May 2008. The competition to win the award of the quadrennial summer or winter Olympic Games from the International Olympic Committee has become a particular sort of global contest between cities that requires mayors of cities that compete to marshal all of their diplomatic, leadership and marketing skills.

The nature of sub-national governments, particularly those of large, distinct regions, is such that not only do they have a need for diplomatic representation to and communication with other sub-national governments and with more distant foreign powers, but also there is often an estrangement much closer to home that requires mediation. As noted above, relations between sub-national governments and the governments of their own nation–state, whilst not entirely like diplomacy between nation–states in terms of institutions and formalities, nonetheless are often analogous in terms of the core diplomatic functions of representation and communication. Some nation–state governments maintain ministries charged expressly with conducting relations with their own sub-national governments. For example, the British government has a special ministry, the Northern Ireland Office, to manage relations with and administration of Northern Ireland, a component part of the United Kingdom that, owing to its particular history, has had a complex relationship both with the UK and with the adjacent Republic of Ireland. Britain's Northern Ireland Minister acts simultaneously in several rôles: the political spokesperson for the government of the ruling party in Westminster on Northern Ireland policy; the representative of the national government to the people of Northern Ireland; and as representative of the government of the United Kingdom on all-Ireland or 'inter-Irish' matters requiring joint consideration with the government of the Republic of Ireland.

The Westphalia system of ostensibly equal nation–states has evolved into a complex global political environment in which nation–state governments of different sizes and capacities must engage not only with one another but also with an increasing number of sub-state, supranational and multilateral political actors. The diplomatic challenge that governments of each type and every size face is how to deploy their resources for diplomatic representation and communication most effectively towards achieving their policy objectives. If the recent past is any guide, it is likely that the outcomes of diplomatic interaction will continue to redistribute power and influence towards governments that use their diplomatic resources effectively and away from those that do not.

4

Multilateral Institutions, Supranational Polities and Regional Bodies

Introduction: The Evolution of Multilateral Institutions

The twentieth century witnessed a profusion of types of political bodies engaging in diplomacy. Many of these newer entities began initially as venues for diplomacy and gradually took on attributes of diplomatic actors in their own right. In this chapter the diplomatic function of multilateral institutions in all their current guises is considered. These institutions can be organized into a broad topology by structure and function:

- global governance bodies, such as the United Nations, International Monetary Fund, World Bank and World Trade Organization;
- knowledge-generating organizations that serve as institutional venues or settings for diplomacy, such as the Group of Seven / Group of Eight, Organization for Economic Cooperation and Development, World Economic Forum, and International Chamber of Commerce;
- supranational polities, such as the European Union; and
- regional governance bodies and development banks, such as the North American Free Trade Agreement, the Gulf Cooperation Council, the Association of Southeast Asian Nations, the Asia-Pacific Economic Cooperation Council, the South African Development Council, the African Union, the Asian Development Bank and the European Bank for Reconstruction and Development.

At first glance, non-state actors – multilateral institutions like the United Nations and the World Bank, regional governance bodies and development banks – do not look as if they belong in the same category as governments of nation–states. It did not make sense to speak of diplomacy 'between' states and non-state actors, because many of these entities themselves were devised by governments to serve as diplomatic mechanisms through which, or venues in which, governments of nation–states would communicate with each other. However, as these entities have grown and changed in nature, we have had to adapt the way that we understand diplomacy. This is the important 'venue' vs 'actor' question: when does an institution cease to be simply a venue or setting for diplomacy, and when does it become a diplomatic actor in its own right? The classical approach to studying diplomacy would doubt that venues can ever become actors. In order to be able to characterize the interaction between governments and non-state economic entities as diplomacy, we need to identify that a significant number of the diplomatic practices that take place between governments are also taking place between governments and these entities. There need to be mechanisms for diplomatic representation and communication between non-state actors and governments, including professionally staffed organs for that purpose. Diplomats from each side need to be engaging in characteristic diplomatic practices, such as sending and receiving envoys, gathering information, communicating regularly about ongoing issues of mutual interest or concern (both routine and extraordinary), and articulating and advocating their side's respective interests. Each type of actor's diplomats need to engage in negotiations with the other's to achieve a range of objectives, from making agreements that create mutual advantage, to resolving disagreements and conflicts, to managing crises.

Multilateral institutions and other non-state entities have emerged as diplomatic actors over the past century organically, as a result of the technologically driven processes through which more and more of the world's resources, population and economic activity have become interdependent, processes identified today as 'globalization'. However, the emergence of these bodies was often masked by the attempts of governments and their diplomats to maintain their own power and their dominance of the diplomatic discourse. The nineteenth century was by some measures a 'golden age' of nation–state dominance of diplomatic activity, in which bilateral diplomacy predominated and *haute politique* questions of sovereignty, territory and control commanded the largest part of the diplomatic discourse. Yet this first era of economic globalization brought with it proto-structures of global governance. The Concert of Europe was created initially at the Congress of Vienna in 1815 as a mechanism for Europe's 'great powers' to maintain peace and security across the European continent in the wake of the calamitous and global effects of the Napoleonic Wars. Although initially envisaged as a 'Congress' that would meet at regularly scheduled intervals, the system evolved into an understanding or mechanism that, when invoked by one or more of its members, provided for a particularly configured venue for high-level diplomacy intended to avert or resolve security crises. Foreign ministers, other high-level envoys, and on occasion heads of government or of state would converge when required, meet and negotiate, sometimes for an extended period of weeks or months, in search of a solution to the problem at hand. The Congress of London in 1830–1, which resolved a Franco-Prussian territorial dispute by creating Belgium as a nation–state, is a good example of the fruits of their labours.[1] The Concert of Europe is generally credited with contributing substantially to the peace and stability that prevailed in Europe for the greater part of the century extending from 1815 to 1914. That peace and security in turn made a substantial contribution to the stable business climate and political atmosphere favouring trade liberalization, currency convertibility and cross-border financial flows that engendered enormous global economic growth and rapidly increasing economic interdependence. However, the Concert system broke down when Germany refused to attend a meeting of the Concert in 1914, setting off a chain of events that led to the outbreak of the Great War.[2]

Multilateral Institutions as Diplomatic Actors

Notwithstanding its diplomatic successes, the Concert of Europe could in no sense be construed as anything more than a major regional venue for diplomacy. The first actual multilateral institutions with a degree of permanence were established, beginning in the late nineteenth century, to facilitate cooperation in limited areas of mutual economic interest, such as post and telecommunications. For example, the Universal Telecommunications Union was founded in 1874 to standardize protocols for construction and operation of international telegraph and telephone links.[3] As noted in chapter 2, the Brussels Sugar Convention of 1902 established a multilateral body, the Permanent Sugar Commission, to oversee the enforcement of the Convention's ban on subsidized sugar exports. The Permanent Sugar Commission was the first multilateral body given the authority to impose mandatory sanctions on governments – signatories to the convention or not – that were not complying with the Convention's requirements.[4]

Over the course of the twentieth century, governments found themselves having to engage diplomatically with a growing range of multilateral institutions that they themselves, for the most part, summoned (or rather negotiated) into existence. These entities vary considerably in terms of their size, purpose, mechanisms of governance and decision making, and ultimate power relative to the governments that created them. The first group to emerge were institutions established for the purpose of global cooperation on major issue areas. The League of Nations and its successor organization, the United Nations, were founded to promote global security. For managing the global economy, the Bank for International Settlements (BIS) was founded in 1930 and a triad of organizations conceived at an international conference at Bretton Woods, New Hampshire in 1944: the International Monetary Fund (IMF), the World Bank, and the General Agreement on Tariffs and Trade (the GATT), the successor to which was the World Trade Organization (the WTO).[5] For integrating broader concerns of the great powers of the day, there later emerged the consultative mechanism for heads of government that today is known as the G7/G8. Each of these institutions not only established permanent venues at which ongoing diplomacy between member governments could take place, but also provided structures for a measure of global governance that would be conducted by means of that ongoing diplomatic interaction. The United Nations has generated an enormous network of organizations and structures employing approximately 16,000 people in the Secretariat and another 47,000 in all the other UN programmes and related institutions that undertake all the wide range of projects that its member states agree, ranging from peacemaking and peacekeeping to environmental research and protection of workers' rights.[6] The global economic governance institutions took on major projects requiring extensive diplomatic representation and communication between member countries: for example, the International Monetary Fund established and maintained a system of fixed exchange rates that lasted until 1971, and the World Bank established and maintained criteria for financing sound global economic development. In institutional structure, these bodies vary widely. At one extreme, the G7/G8 operates with minimal institutional structure and a Secretariat that rotates amongst its members, whereas the other bodies are highly institutionalized with permanent structures and professional staffs.

Knowledge Institutions, Supranational Polities and Regional Bodies

A second group of non-state actors, bodies such as the Organization for Economic Cooperation and Development, the World Economic Forum and the International Chamber of Commerce, play a more indirect, if more ideational, rôle in global governance. These bodies are characterized by a consultative, knowledge-generating and sharing function. Their principal missions are to disseminate knowledge between their members and to provide members with knowledge and information services. These missions do occasionally take the form of mediating between their members, as in the ICC's International Court of Arbitration for resolving cross-border business disputes. The institutions also undertake joint external projects on members' behalf, as in the World Economic Forum's 'Initiatives' for addressing global problems (see chapter 9), or the OECD's abortive Multilateral Agreement on Investment (MAI) (see below), but these activities do not have the same primary governance function as the activities of the global governance organizations discussed above. The membership or constitution of these organizations also differs importantly from that of the global governance institutions: they are not all constituted by nation–state governments. The membership of the OECD consists of industrialized country governments, whereas the members of the World Economic Forum are large global firms. The ICC's membership is drawn from an even wider spectrum of businesses that operate across national borders. Hence the challenges of diplomacy between knowledge-generating institutions and nation–state governments largely concern gathering the information needed from governments to supply to their members and then actually providing the services. To produce its annual Global Competitiveness Report and other annual league table economic surveys, the World Economic Forum requires the cooperation of both governments and business leaders in each country surveyed to make the data gathered complete and of value. To conduct a survey on the effects of software piracy for its member governments, for example, the Organization for Economic Cooperation and Development would need to obtain data from as many nation–state governments as possible, including some governments that might not be inclined to cooperate in the absence of careful diplomatic negotiation.

Supranational polities are the newest and most unusual category of non-state actor, in part not only because they are both venues for diplomacy and actors in their own right, but also because some would regard them as a form of state as well, even if not in the traditional nation–state sense. The diplomatic structures of supranational polities for representation and communication resemble those of nation–state governments more closely than those of any other non-state actor. The European Union is the only actor in this category at present, although indications suggest that other regional integration bodies (such as the African Union) could evolve in this direction over time. As was discussed at some length in chapter 3, for many reasons the European Union is a *sui generis* sort of entity. However, supranational polities are grouped alongside other categories of non-state diplomatic actors because they share with the other categories the same ambiguity between their status as venue and as actor, and the same newness and uncertainty of identity and standing relative to nation–state governments.

The last category of non-state actor, regional governance bodies and development banks, is comprised of the regional analogues of the global governance institutions discussed above. Like their global counterparts, their membership is comprised of nation–states. They vary across a number of dimensions: focus, age, degree of institutionalization, and ambition, or trajectory of evolution (widening and deepening or stasis), just to name some. The focus of such institutions can range from security cooperation (NATO) to economic integration (Mercosur),[7] economic development (regional development banks), cultural cooperation, or some combination thereof. The Organization of American States traces its institutional origin to a multilateral conference in 1890, making it one of the oldest regional bodies, whilst the Shanghai Cooperation Organization, established in 2001, is amongst the youngest. The North Atlantic Treaty Organization is highly institutionalized (see chapter 10), whereas the Asia-Pacific Economic Cooperation Council is a much more informal venue for regional cooperation initiatives. The North American Free Trade Agreement has maintained a stable remit of activity since its creation in 1993, whereas the African Union, established only in 2002 on the base created by the Organization of African Unity, has a highly ambitious programme for expansion of the range and scope of its integration mission. Importantly, all serve as venues for diplomacy and some have evolved a measure of 'actor-ness' in their own right. Again like its global counterparts, by its ongoing facilitation of diplomacy, each has changed the relationships of its members, one to another. A partial listing of regional governance bodies and development banks appears opposite:

What makes all these types of multilateral institutions diplomatic actors in their own right to any extent, and more than just institutional venues for diplomacy? For each of the institutions as they were created, the ability to carry out their intended functions required the establishment of regularized working relationships with member country governments. Multilateral institutions needed actual diplomats to do the core generic diplomatic functions of representation and communication. Their

African Development Bank
African Union (AU)
Asia-Pacific Economic Cooperation Council (APEC)
Asian Development Bank
Association of Southeast Asian Nations (ASEAN)
Commonwealth of Independent States (CIS)
European Bank for Reconstruction and Development (EBRD)
Gulf Cooperation Council (GCC)
Inter-American Development Bank (IADB)
Mercosur/Mercosul
North American Free Trade Association (NAFTA)
North Atlantic Treaty Organization (NATO)
Organization of American States (OAS)
Shanghai Cooperation Organization (SCO)
Southern African Development Council (SADC)

professional staffs were often drawn from the foreign ministries of member governments or else from defence ministries, finance ministries, trade ministries or the other specialized agencies. But multilateral institutions from the outset took seriously the need to construct their own professional, and hence diplomatic, identities and cultures. They established rigid nationality quota systems for employment and set higher employment standards than member governments in areas such as linguistic ability. By doing so each institution created a cosmopolitan cadre that came to differentiate themselves and their objectives from the staffs of the governments from which many of their members originated. Like other diplomats, UN, World Bank and NATO personnel, for example, are paid tax-exempt salaries and frequently are eligible to drive vehicles with diplomatic number plates. Staffers of the multilateral organizations have tended to find that they come to have more in common with one another than with fellow nationals of their home countries. As the leaderships and support staffs of these bodies have come to work together over time, each group has developed its own perspective on the mission with which it was initially charged, its own set of priorities, its own issue agenda and its own peculiar biases. The sketches that follow are intended to illustrate the similarities, as well as the differences, between these types of institutions as diplomatic actors.

Multilateral, Supranational and Regional Institutions Close Up

The **Bank for International Settlements** (BIS) is the oldest surviving institution, even if the least well known, amongst the global governance bodies. The BIS was established in 1930, initially to address the problems that Germany was facing in meeting its war reparations obligations under the Versailles peace settlement. Its secondary function, to facilitate cooperation between nation–states' central banks, undertake research on monetary and financial stability and act as central banker to the world's central banks, rapidly became its primary function following German abrogation of reparations obligations. In 1974 the BIS created the Basel Committee on Banking Supervision, comprised of central bank governors and bank regulators, from ten industrialized country member states, known as the G10, to promote best practice in global banking supervision. Under the auspices of the Basel Committee the central bankers and regulators negotiated the 1988 Basel Capital Accord, which established a voluntary framework international standard for measuring credit risk, which has been adopted by most countries in the world. It was revised in the summer of 2004 in an agreement known as Basel II to make risk management mechanisms more sophisticated and precise, and to include the risk profiles of new types of financial products that had evolved over the preceding fifteen years.

The largest and best-known of the multilateral organizations is the **United Nations**, which inherited from its predecessors, the League of Nations and the Concert of Europe, the overarching mission of preserving peace among the nations of the world. The UN, whilst its mode of operating and specific decisions are not always politically popular, nonetheless remains the club of which every nation wants to be a member. At the time of writing, 192 of the approximately 200 generally recognized nation–states of the world are members of the United Nations. Since the signing of the UN's founding Treaty of San Francisco in 1945, UN membership has generally been regarded as a key criterion of legitimacy for any nation–state and its government that aspires to be recognized as a sovereign member of the global community of nations. The transfer of the 'China' seat at the UN from the Republic of China government in Taipei to the People's Republic of China government in Beijing in 1971, and with it the permanent seat on the UN Security Council, is a vivid example of the significance of this perception of global legitimacy. Both governments claimed (and still claim) to be the rightful government of China, leaving it to the UN membership (and Security Council politics) to choose upon which to confer that legitimacy.[8]

The two principal organs of the UN, the **Security Council** and the **General Assembly**, can each be viewed as serving not only as venues for diplomacy but as diplomatic actors in their own right. The Security Council is arguably the most powerful of all multilateral institutions, in that it alone is authorized to sanction the use of force to preserve or restore peace between nations. Even the 1949 North Atlantic Treaty, which created the most powerful regional defensive alliance, subordinates its own authority to use force to the UN Charter. The Security Council, which today consists of five permanent member countries (the People's Republic of China, France, the United Kingdom, the Russian Federation and the United States) and eleven members from the rest of the UN membership that rotate on two-year terms, is directed by the UN Charter to take whatever steps are required, on behalf of the overall membership of the UN, to prevent and resolve interstate conflict.[9] The General Assembly, consisting of the entire membership of the UN and in which each member state has one vote, has a much broader remit under the UN Charter in terms of furthering UN objectives as laid out therein. As a venue for negotiation and agreement of multilateral objectives, the General Assembly functions very differently from the Security Council in that the General Assembly's resolutions are non-binding in a legal sense, so its resolutions are only effective to the extent that they serve to motivate governments of UN member states to implement them. Hence much of the diplomacy of the General Assembly is a process of persuasion by advocates of a particular view that members share a common interest not only in agreeing to take action but in implementing what they decide to do. The politics of the two bodies differ substantially as well, in that whereas Security Council politics tends to be dominated by the relationships between the permanent members on any given issue, as each has a potential veto, General Assembly politics on the other hand has been dominated historically by developing countries (although since the end of the Cold War, General Assembly coalitions have been more cross-cutting in nature).[10]

Beyond the Security Council and General Assembly, the United Nations carries out much of the work mandated to it in its charter through functionally specialized economic agencies, such as the UN Council on Trade and Development (UNCTAD), the UN Development Programme (UNDP), the UN Educational, Scientific and Cultural Organization (UNESCO), the UN Food and Agriculture Organization (FAO) and the International Labour Organization (ILO). Some of the specialized agencies, such as the FAO and

ILO, have become the 'go to' multilateral organizations for addressing multilateral issues within their area of expertise, whereas others, such as UNCTAD and UNDP, have had to 'compete' with non-UN agencies (such as the GATT/WTO and the World Bank) that also serve as venues for diplomacy (and in some cases as diplomatic actors) in economic areas such as trade and development.

The principal multilateral institutions that would provide venues for economic diplomacy originated as part of a common, if only partially realized, design. At the Bretton Woods economic conference in 1944, governments of the soon-to-be victorious powers in the Second World War negotiated to create multilateral structures to avert the nationalistic economic conflicts that had emerged in the 1920s and 1930s and contributed to the outbreak of the most destructive world war to date. Diplomats at Bretton Woods envisaged a triad of institutions to facilitate management and administration of the key aspects of the increasingly global economy: monetary relations, economic development and international trade.[11] The so-called 'Bretton Woods twins', the **International Monetary Fund** and the International Bank for Reconstruction and Development (or **World Bank**, as it became known), were constituted in such a way that share capital equated with voting power, which permitted the interests of nation–states that contributed the most to each organization's capital stock to have the greatest influence over the organization's collective policy making process. The World Bank has since morphed into the World Bank Group, which is now a whole family of agencies, including the International Finance Corporation (IFC) to organize private sector development financing, the International Development Association (IDA) to provide very-low-interest loans to the poorest countries, and the Multilateral Investment Guarantee Agency (MIGA) to insure worthy development projects.[12] After the third leg of the triad, the International Trade Organization, was not ratified by the United States Senate in 1948, its trade treaty 'rulebook' and skeletal organization, the **General Agreement on Tariffs and Trade** ('GATT'), took effect nonetheless. GATT rules committed member countries to lower barriers to trade in goods and uphold open trade negotiating principles of non-discrimination and national treatment. The GATT's ad hoc Secretariat functioned until, forty-eight years later, the Uruguay Round of multilateral trade negotiations created the **World Trade Organization** ('WTO') to administer the revised GATT. Initially they took decisions by consensus, which meant in practice the most powerful members sought, and usually received, deference from the others. The WTO redistributed decision making power substantially towards the principle of one nation, one vote, which gave it significant new standing as a diplomatic actor that the GATT with its ad hoc Secretariat had lacked (see below). These three institutions involve the largest number of member governments and serve as venues for the lion's share of economic diplomacy between governments, in addition to functioning as diplomatic actors in their own right.[13]

The **G8**, and the G7 before it, was established initially as a venue for an annual summit meeting of leaders of at least some portion of the world's great powers, at which heads of government and finance ministers could meet in an informal, relaxed setting, develop and cultivate personal relationships and communication, and address major global problems away from the intensive scrutiny of the media. Today its membership includes France, the United Kingdom, the United States, Germany, Canada, Japan and Italy, which meet as the G7 finance ministers, and, with Russia, as the G8 heads of government. Founded in the early 1970s when the international monetary crisis resulting from the collapse of Bretton Woods fixed exchange rates required a new format for multilateral cooperation, the G8 in recent years has become involved actively in addressing a wide range of major global issues from an intergovernmental perspective: bridging the Digital Divide, global climate change, and poverty eradication in Africa, among others. Now more than just a diplomatic venue, the G7/G8 has evolved to a point where it wields substantial influence in its ability to shape the global public policy environment and even in terms of shifting foreign policy agendas and priorities within its major member states.[14]

Amongst the consultative, or knowledge-generating, multilateral bodies, the **Organization for Economic Cooperation and Development** is the most senior and most specialized. Created in 1960 out of the Organization for European Economic Cooperation, the multilateral body set up to distribute American and Canadian Marshall Plan aid to Western Europe, the OECD was tasked with the rôle of monitoring the global economy, conducting research and producing policy recommendations. Its membership consists of governments of industrialized countries, and as such has gradually grown as additional countries have reached a level of development rendering them eligible for membership. Headquartered in Paris with a highly professional staff, the OECD has been effective at providing research and information to its member governments. But in the mid-1990s OECD member governments sought to negotiate a Multilateral Agreement on Investment ('MAI'), which would have created an international regime for cross-border investment flows, using the OECD as their chosen diplomatic venue for the project. The MAI is an interesting case study of diplomacy between multilateral institutions, governments and civil society organizations (CSOs). Whilst the OECD had the knowledge base and expertise to facilitate the negotiations, perhaps it was not ideally suited to manage the diplomacy and the international politics required to bring the agreement to fruition. The OECD became a focus of controversy as a coalition of CSOs and developing-country governments generated enough public opposition to the MAI that ratification by OECD member governments was postponed indefinitely. Opponents criticized the OECD for not making the text of the draft agreement widely available for public scrutiny because the MAI would have redistributed power over investment regulations from more democratically accountable governments towards private 'investors', which tended to be transnational firms.[15]

Another knowledge-generating institution, the **World Economic Forum**, has distinguished itself by creating a venue in which probably the widest range of types of diplomatic actor can meet regularly. The Forum was conceived in 1971 as an annual 'summit' meeting between European business leaders in Davos, Switzerland. Subsequently transforming itself into a membership organization comprised of several hundred of the world's largest firms, the Forum enlarged the range of participants it invited to Davos to include political leaders, the media, academics, cultural figures and other representatives of civil society. At Forum meetings, global problems could be discussed, ideas could be generated and, not coincidentally, deals could be done. Over time the Forum's activities have expanded to include holding regional summits, producing and publishing research on global economic, political and social problems and issues, and undertaking initiatives to facilitate the creation and operation of public–private partnerships to address particular global problems. One such initiative, the Global Education Initiative, is bringing together international development agencies, governments, universities and technology firms to revitalize primary and secondary school education in developing countries, using the latest information technology hardware and software.[16]

The **International Chamber of Commerce** ('ICC') is significant as a multilateral institution in that it serves as a venue for diplomacy entirely amongst non-state actors. Founded in 1919 to be an international association of businesses dedicated to promoting free flows of trade and capital, the ICC has undertaken a series of initiatives over the years to facilitate global business relations. In 1923 the ICC established the International Court of Arbitration to help member businesses resolve commercial disputes across borders. In the 1980s the ICC introduced mechanisms to combat international commercial crime, and in the 1990s produced standards of practice for sustainable development.[17]

The **European Union** differs from the aforementioned non-state actors in that it can be seen as a supranational polity, functioning as a diplomatic actor analogous to that of a nation–state even whilst being constituted as a membership organization of nation–states. The preceding chapter discussed the set of issues and problems that arise as nation–state governments seek to represent themselves to the EU. What is important to note in the context of this chapter, however, is that the EU represents itself (and thus by extension its members) to third countries and multilateral institutions such as the United Nations and the World Trade Organization, just as many governments and institutions represent themselves to the EU. In most cases this representation takes place in parallel with the representations between the EU member states and third countries and institutions. This arrangement can produce diplomatic synergies, as diplomats of EU member states and EU diplomats can cooperate together in a third country capital on common objectives. EU diplomats in Washington, for example, have cooperated with their counterparts at the German, British and other member state missions to press the government of the United States for greater action on mitigating climate change. However, this system of parallel representation can also lead to conflicts of emphases and priorities, if not policies, between the EU and its member states. In the run-up to, and during, the 2003 Anglo-American invasion of Iraq, for example, EU diplomats in Washington and in other capitals were hamstrung to a considerable degree by the wide disparity in the positions of its member governments, with Britain taking a lead rôle, strongly supported by Spain, Italy and Poland, even as the governments of France, Germany and Belgium led international opposition to the conflict.

Issues such as defence and security are complicated for EU diplomatic representation and communication to third countries and institutions. Some EU member states, such as Britain and France, with their permanent seats on the UN Security Council, are already major diplomatic actors on global security issues, even as the EU itself is undergoing a process of developing and evolving its own defence and security identity under the aegis of the European Security and Defence Policy (ESDP). In 1999 the EU created the post of High Representative for the Common Foreign and Security Policy (held at the time of writing by Javier Solana) to represent the Council of the European Union on EU foreign policy issues and conduct negotiations on the Council's behalf.[18] Some have advocated the replacement of the British and French seats on the UN Security Council with a common EU seat. Needless to say, the proposal has met with strong opposition in London and Paris. On certain other issue areas, such as

African and European leaders at the European Union – Africa summit, Lisbon, December 2007

international trade, EU member states have pooled their sovereignty in the European Union formally, so the EU takes on the entire responsibility of representing its member governments to third countries and institutions on issues and conflicts involving international trade, including tariff reduction treaties, free trade agreements and trade disputes. Whilst much of trade diplomacy is conducted at and under the auspices of the World Trade Organization, the EU participates in many bilateral and regional trade arrangements, which must be negotiated and maintained separately. The EU's rôle in trade diplomacy does not preclude diplomats of its member governments from communicating with their counterparts in third countries informally about trade issues, but it does reserve official communication and negotiation for European Union representatives.

Nation–state Governments' Diplomatic Representation to Non-state Diplomatic Actors

Knowing how non-state diplomatic actors and nation–state governments represent themselves to one another and communicate with each other is important for understanding the similarities and differences between the two groups of diplomatic actors. There is a natural asymmetry between the two directions of diplomatic representation and communication that is reflective of the distinctions between governments, multilateral institutions and other non-state actors. The evolving process of multiple channels and levels of diplomatic representation and interaction is all the more important in describing how governments conduct diplomatic relations with non-state actors. This evolution in diplomatic representation has been intensified as the number and type of non-state actors with which they must deal have proliferated. With this proliferation has come a corresponding expansion of channels of government representation, communication, information gathering and negotiation. The most significant non-foreign-ministry diplomatic channels are government departments for international trade, industry and finance, and central banks. Departments for international trade, either in conjunction with or in lieu of foreign ministries, play an increasingly dominant rôle in representing governments to the WTO, OECD and other trade-related institutions such as UNCTAD and regional trade bodies (NAFTA, Mercosur, etc.). In Britain, for example, in the late 1990s the government centralized export promotion activities under a single authority, British Trade International, to facilitate cooperation between the Foreign and Commonwealth Office and the Department for Trade and Industry.[19]

Similarly, finance ministries and central banks take the lead rôle in representing governments to multilateral institutions on issues of monetary policy, global financial management and banking regulation. A government's finance ministry usually directs fiscal and monetary policy formulation and implementation, and, given that matters of global finance are increasingly coming to dominate domestic policy agendas, it is natural to expect that the finance minister will take the lead in implementing policy towards and through the IMF, World Bank, regional development banks and OECD. Gordon Brown, when Britain's Chancellor of the Exchequer, made a punishing tour around Africa to meet other finance ministers and bankers in 2006 prior to attending the World Economic Forum's 2007 Davos Annual Meeting to rally support for a global push to fight poverty in Africa. Finance ministers of developing countries, which are in effect the 'client' countries of the Bretton Woods twins, regularly travel to Washington with their staffs to meet with IMF and World Bank officials. They take the lead in receiving missions from the Bank and Fund to their home countries. Central bankers share in this rôle, in addition to having their own specific tasks. Central bankers are the chief representatives of their governments to the Bank for International Settlements, for example, but when banking supervision is conducted by government agencies other than the central bank, those agencies must be represented at the BIS as well.

When central banks are independent or semi-independent from the political control of their governments, which is increasingly the case, finance ministries and central banks must negotiate domestically over monetary and financial policy involving multilateral economic institutions. They may not necessarily reach total agreement. When central bankers and finance ministers do agree and work effectively in concert, they and their staffs can increase their leverage substantially in economic diplomacy. For example, US Federal Reserve Chairman Alan Greenspan and Treasury Secretary Robert Rubin worked closely together to lead the responses of the IMF, World Bank, regional development banks and consortia of major private international commercial banks to the Latin American financial crisis of 1994 and the Asian and Russian crises of 1997. In the autumn 2008 financial crisis, Federal Reserve Chairman Ben Bernanke and Treasury Secretary Henry Paulson operated similarly, cooperating with their UK counterparts, Chancellor of the Exchequer Alistair Darling and Bank of England Governor Mervyn King, to preserve the stability of US and UK financial institutions.

Other government departments and offices play significant rôles in economic diplomacy with multilateral institutions. Agriculture ministries are particularly important players in farm-related diplomacy. Agriculture departments and their chief ministers are key diplomatic actors in the perennially difficult WTO agricultural negotiations and in negotiations with the UN Food and Agriculture Organization. Heads of government and their staffs will also involve themselves directly in diplomacy with multilateral organizations as needs warrant. Heads of government are often invited to be lead participants in the World Economic Forum's Davos Annual Meeting, as appearances in Davos by US President Bill Clinton, UK Prime Minister Tony Blair, German Chancellor Angela Merkel and successive Israeli and Palestinian leaders attest. Direct involvement by presidents and prime ministers is most common in developing countries, which are visited regularly by delegations from the IMF and World Bank, and where negotiations have to be undertaken that require difficult domestic political decisions on economic policy.

The greatest change in how diplomatic representation is organized institutionally, which parallels the change in diplomatic representation between nation–states, has been brought on by the evolution of communications and transport technology. Governments increasingly require smaller permanent missions to multilateral organizations. Foreign ministries and other ministries involved in diplomacy are able to conduct more diplomatic business from the home country using technology and are able to dispatch teams of representatives of varying size, membership and expertise to different locations at relatively short notice. When the WTO holds its biennial ministerial meeting away from its Geneva headquarters, large countries dispatch huge delegations that are empowered to negotiate and to take many policy decisions on site as required. These delegations have huge technical backup expertise at their disposal. Smaller governments also send teams of diplomatic representatives, but they must operate at the relative disadvantage that smaller numbers and depth of expertise confer.

As most multilateral organizations are operated by professionally staffed permanent Secretariats that conduct the ongoing business of the organization, only relatively limited permanent on-site representation by governments is required. Larger delegations are sent to represent governments at the regular, but occasional, ministerial meetings or plenary sessions that occur. Institutional work programmes involving direct participation by governments may be conducted remotely between governments and the organization's Secretariat or may be convened in locations of the participants' choice. Again the WTO illustrates this evolution well. The WTO is governed on an ongoing basis by a General Council, on which member governments are represented, usually at ambassadorial level. Member governments maintain small delegations or 'embassies' to the WTO's Geneva headquarters. The General Council's authority derives from the biennial WTO Ministerial Conference, which usually convenes at a location other than Geneva (in 2003 it was held at Cancun, in 2005 at Hong Kong). Governments are usually represented at the WTO Ministerial by trade ministers, occasionally by foreign ministers or heads of government. The General Council convenes under different auspices as the WTO Dispute Settlement Body, to receive and adjudicate upon the findings of dispute resolution panels. Member governments involved in a dispute may send a special delegation to Geneva to represent themselves before a dispute resolution panel. WTO work programmes, which include ongoing multilateral trade liberalization rounds and committees to conclude agenda items from previous trade liberalization rounds, are conducted in session in Geneva and other locations convenient to member governments, as well as electronically between capitals.

Multilateral Institutions' Representation to Nation–state Governments

One key factor differentiates how multilateral institutions represent themselves to governments and how governments of nation–states represent themselves one to another. Multilateral institutions must function both in their originally intended rôle as venues to facilitate diplomacy between governments and also in some measure as diplomatic actors in their own right. Each intergovernmental institution came to be as a result of a distinct political process that integrated domestic politics within their founding nation–states with diplomatic interaction between the founding state governments – representation and communication. That process in turn produced a particular organization with an agreed purpose and institutional structure. Initially, each organization's institutional structure, which includes its mechanisms of governance and decision making, as well as its administrative structure (staffing, location of offices, etc.), enshrined the political distribution of power that existed between its founding governments at the time of its creation. For example, the distribution of shares according to initial investment in the capitalization of the World Bank and IMF, with voting rights according to share count, institutionalized a different distribution of power in those organs from the World Trade Organization's one state, one vote principle. However, as noted above, each institution developed an identity of its own as it began to function. As it evolved a sense of its own interests and how to pursue them, beginning to shape its own agenda and advance its own set of policy priorities, each institution thereby became an actor alongside the nation–state governments that constituted it. Multilateral institutions became self-reflexive participants in the ongoing diplomatic processes of monitoring the institution's own achievements and reforming it. For example, the multilateral project to reform the World Bank and IMF that has been going on for several years would be unimaginable without the active participation of the Bank and the Fund themselves. The sorts of questions outside observers ask about this process are themselves an indication of the power of the institutions relative to their member governments: will the Bank and the Fund manage to drive the reform process themselves? Will the shareholder governments be able to impose major institutional reforms, including possible merger or abolition? These sorts of questions presume not only the existence but the power of the Bank and Fund as diplomatic actors in the multilateral debate over their future.[20]

The evolving complexity that has affected diplomacy between nation–states also affects multilateral institutions' representation to governments. It tends to show more in terms of how representation is organized institutionally than of who does the representing. Most of the institutions' small, relatively centralized professional staffs tend to represent themselves as and where needs require. In many organizations, the great majority of the professional staffers function as diplomats, either formally or informally, at least in the information gathering and communications functions. Most are needed to represent their institution to other bodies. Global governance organizations are the most likely to represent themselves to governments through permanent or ongoing missions. Missions to and in client countries – developing countries – are the most similar to permanent diplomatic legations of governments. Annual general meetings of the World Bank, IMF and regional development banks, WTO Ministerial Conferences, World Economic Forum Davos Annual Meetings and the ICC's World Council are analogous to intergovernmental 'summits': member nation–states' interests are represented, disagreements are aired and negotiated over. At these events the host institution also represents its own institutional interests to member governments, therein functioning as actor as well as host.

As governments engage in public diplomacy, multilateral institutions also represent themselves to member governments through publicity: the planned presentation of information to the general public, and thus to the governments that publics elect or are ruled by, about the entity, its objectives and accomplishments. This mechanism has been transformed by technological progress, in particular the advent of the internet. The emergence of communications networks built around internet communications has made it much easier for all sorts of other non-state entities, ranging from global firms to civil society organizations, to interact with multilateral organizations directly, bypassing nation–state mediating institutions that would previously have represented civil society interests before multilateral organizations. The World Trade Organization has taken its public diplomacy one step further by creating a university of sorts that offers training qualifications to students, primarily from developing countries. By doing this, in addition to promoting itself and its interests, the WTO is actively constructing and reconstructing the identities and interests of the people who will be representing their countries to the WTO, the likely future diplomats with which WTO staff will have to communicate and negotiate.

Multilateral institutions are also having to deal more directly with global and more localized social movements based in civil society. Intensive lobbying, publicity campaigns and protest activities have forced global governance organizations (G8, WTO, UN, etc.) to reconsider policies and change actual diplomatic procedures: location and timing of meetings, security, even agenda items. The protests against the WTO at its 1999 Ministerial Conference in Seattle not only forced delays and changes to the proposed multilateral trade round but also brought about changes in the way that the WTO and other multilateral organizations publicize themselves and their activities. Institutions' representation to governments has also changed as particular organizations have been reformed. In the case of the GATT/WTO, diplomacy between nation–states over international trade issues was institutionalized in a particular way by the political process that led to its creation and early development. The ad hoc GATT Secretariat was perceived as weak, relative to nation–state governments. This problem was accentuated by the custom of unanimous decision making that emerged in the GATT Council in its early years. Unanimous decision making enshrined a sort of democratic centralism wherein the most powerful governments, the United States and varying combinations of allies, were often able to silence opposing voices. However, the GATT-led institutional process of trade liberalization triggered structural change in the global economy and change in the perceived identities and interests of GATT member governments, in particular a shift amongst major developing countries towards more pro-trade liberalization positions. This in turn led to a transformation of the institution and its processes through the creation of the WTO with its strengthened Secretariat and its one country, one vote with supermajorities decision making mechanism, which has brought about a redistribution of political power at least somewhat commensurate with the redistribution of power in the global economy in favour of developing countries.[21]

Emerging as venues for diplomacy over the past century and a half, multilateral institutions, supranational polities and regional bodies have subsequently transformed themselves to varying degrees into diplomatic actors in their own right. The emergence and development of this type of diplomatic actor has had perhaps a greater impact upon how contemporary diplomacy takes place than any other development in recent times. The challenge for these bodies going forward lies in how effectively they can fulfil their primary diplomatic function of serving as venues for the mediation of difference between other actors (governments, firms, etc.) who use them as venues to meet, even whilst developing their own institutional interests, agenda and priorities. All of these entities, ranging from ted Nations to the World Trade Organization, the European Union, the World Economic Forum and the regional development banks, have attracted varying degrees of criticism from global civil society arising from their evolution as diplomatic actors in their own right. Even the G8, which has developed perhaps the least degree of 'actor-ness' of the group, is not immune from this. The future success of each of these bodies will be conditioned to a significant degree by their ability to manage and mitigate the negative impact on their public image resulting from their having a diplomatic persona of their own.

5

Global and Transnational Firms

Introduction: Global Firms as Diplomatic Actors

When US Secretary of State Hillary Rodham Clinton made her first official visit to India in July 2009, before reaching New Delhi she travelled to Mumbai (Bombay) to discuss climate change, education and health care with Mukesh Ambani and Ratan Tata. Ambani and Tata were the CEOs of Reliance Industries and Tata Group respectively, two of the largest India-based global firms.[1] The same forces of technological change and globalization that have changed the ways in which nation–state governments conduct diplomacy have also elevated the position of global firms to that of diplomatic actors. Firms differ enormously from one another in terms of size and degree of transnational activity. Whilst many small and medium-sized enterprises do little or even no business across nation–state borders, an increasing number of smaller firms too are transnational in some way. Virtually all large enterprises must operate across borders whether they like it or not. There are a number of ways that a firm can be multinational, transnational or global. A firm can have its headquarters, factories, marketing staffs and stockholders entirely within a single country, and yet still export goods or services all over the world. A firm can spread its corporate offices across several countries, source parts from all over the world, have major assembly operations on three or four continents, trade on several major stock exchanges, and sell in a majority of the world's markets. Unilever, Shell and Ford are examples of the latter. Or, as is the case with many firms, they can fall somewhere in between. But wherever a firm falls on the continuum, it is likely to have a particularly close relationship with one, or in some cases two, 'host' countries. This may be the country that is its biggest consumer market, the country where its corporate registration is filed, the country where its corporate headquarters is located, the location of its largest subsidiary, or the location of
its largest exchange on which its shares trade. It can end up being some
combination of these.

Top 15 Global Firms by Market Capitalization, August 2009

Rank	Company	Market cap (US $ billions)	Registration
1	Trigon Agri A/S	$17,433,014	DENMARK
2	Speymill Deutsche Immobilien Co Plc	$1,319,732	UNITED KINGDOM
3	Nr Nordic Russia Properties Limited	$1,083,960	UNITED KINGDOM
4	New Europe Property Investments Plc	$901,605	UNITED KINGDOM
5	Eurocastle Investments Limited	$394,973	UNITED KINGDOM
6	Exxon Mobil Corporation	$327,803	UNITED STATES
7	Industrial & Commercial Bank Of China Ltd	$233,171	CHINA
8	China Mobile Limited	$229,715	HONG KONG
9	PetroChina Co Ltd	$211,364	CHINA
10	Microsoft Corporation	$211,112	UNITED STATES
11	Wal-Mart Stores, Inc.	$201,806	UNITED STATES
12	HSBC Holdings plc	$186,287	UNITED KINGDOM
13	China Construction Bank Corp	$184,241	CHINA
14	BHP Billiton Limited	$178,410	AUSTRALIA
15	JPMorgan Chase & Co.	$166,938	UNITED STATES

Source: Corporate Information, http://www.corporateinformation.com/Top-100.aspx?topcase=b, accessed 18 August 2009

The relationship between a firm and a host government, and the diplomacy that facilitates it, play a special rôle in firms' ability to do business globally. Even large firms need at least to appear to comply with numerous business, financial, labour and workplace health and safety regulations in countries where they are registered, where their shares trade, and where they produce and sell significant quantities of their product or service. In return for this 'good corporate citizenship', firms can expect services from host governments ranging from favourable tax concessions to export promotion, and protection against 'unfair' import competition, among other things. Hence firms' relationships with their host countries are at least as important as firms' negotiations with governments of other countries where they want to enter a market, trade on an exchange, or source inputs of goods and labour.

It is not always easy to identify a firm's host country. In many cases, the relationship is transparent to the casual observer. Toshiba has that relationship with the government of Japan. Shell has host country relationships with both the Netherlands and Britain. Until selling off its Chrysler unit in 2007, DaimlerChrysler had relationships of this sort with Germany and the United States. Microsoft has this relationship with the United States and now also has a strong secondary relationship with Britain, and thus, by extension, the European Union. In other cases, detecting a global firm's host country can be more problematic: a firm can appear to have several host countries or none. News Corporation, for example, is closely linked to the United States, the United Kingdom, Israel and Australia. On its investor relations website, News describes its business geographically as follows: 'The activities of News Corporation are conducted principally in the United States, Continental Europe, the United Kingdom, Australia, Asia and the Pacific Basin.'[2] In 2004, News Corporation, originally incorporated in Australia, re-incorporated itself in the United States with the approval of its shareholders worldwide, to facilitate raising capital on US capital markets.

In addition to firm–state diplomacy, global firms increasingly need to engage with multilateral institutions and civil society organizations. Firms may have interests related to international trade that they seek to articulate at the World Trade Organization multilateral rounds, for example, even if the WTO's structure requires their partnering with governments to do so. When CSOs have objections to the labour or environmental policies of global firms, both organizations are likely to have structures in place to facilitate communication and, when necessary, negotiation. Hence the contemporary global firm's diplomats interact with the full range of other diplomatic actors.

How State–Firm Diplomacy Has Changed

Technological change, especially change in information and communications technology, is making the behaviour and the governance of states and firms more similar. This process has been underway for many decades, as Susan Strange observed, but arguably it continues to accelerate with no end in sight.[3] Increasingly, how well each conducts diplomacy with the other determines how successful each is at achieving objectives within resource constraints. Firms and governments increasingly are having to respond to their respective constituencies using converging approaches. There has been a democratization of communication driven by communications technology. As technology has made it possible to disseminate information more rapidly and through more different channels, the global public have come to expect and demand more and more information from governments and firms alike. The private and public sectors have come to share notions of best practice, or at least common practice, in both style and content. Hence public relations, public diplomacy and propaganda content increasingly are designed, articulated and disseminated by govern-
    ~~~ and firms in similar styles. A firm's investor relations publicity ma-
    w resembles the literature that local governments send to voters

to inform them of how their local taxes are being spent. The convergence of information provision styles and content in turn has contributed to reshaping the subjectivities of the members of the public receiving the information. As the streams of information reaching individuals became richer, they came to understand who they are differently. Thus the ways in which individuals relate to firms and governments, what can be thought of as corporate and state membership behaviour – the rôles of citizen, investor, stockholder, consumer, client – are also converging. Individuals, whether wearing their voter or their stockholder hat at any given time, increasingly demand greater accountability from leadership: elected officials, bureaucrats and managements of firms. The voter demands that her tax money not be wasted in much the same way that the shareholder expects management to maximize shareholder value, even if the metrics for assessing value in each case may differ.

A related factor affecting this transformation was the end of the Cold War, which proceeded from the fall of the Berlin Wall in 1989. The bipolar superpower rivalry between the Soviet Union and the United States, containing within it the threat of mutual assured destruction in the event of an exchange of nuclear weapons, in many ways defined and constructed the relationship of citizens to governments. By ensuring the priority of a discourse of security over other discourses in which citizens engaged, the Cold War produced a degree of ultimate deference from citizens towards their governments that was neither originary nor permanent. The security discourse gave governments of nation–states a stronger structural position from which to compete for the loyalties of individuals. The end of the Cold War removed the absolute prioritization of the security discourse.[4] But the relationship between the end of the Cold War and the convergence of information flows is complex rather than monodirectional. We can understand the end of the Cold War as both a cause and effect of this information democratization, because the information technology revolution had begun well before the fall of the Berlin Wall. The proliferation of the videocassette recorder (VCR), which predated the internet and the DVD player, facilitated the dissemination of Western information flows in the Soviet bloc in the 1980s. Yet clearly the end of the bipolar security regime accelerated this process once it happened.

The objectives of governments and firms in this technology-enhanced, communication-rich, post-Cold War global environment have also now increasingly come to resemble one another. Whilst the responsibility of governments to protect their citizenry against external or internal violence has remained central, the importance of providing for the economic well-being of their citizens as a primary objective has risen dramatically. In their desire to promote the creation and retention of high value-added jobs, attract inward investment, maintain stable consumer prices and currency exchange rates, and promote exports of goods and services, a government of a nation–state resembles nothing so much as the management of a large firm seeking to compete in the global economy. Likewise, although pleasing stockholders to the extent that a firm's stock price rises or stays high remains a publicly traded firm's core objective, firms find themselves needing to spend increasing amounts of time and effort winning and retaining public support for their endeavours. This applies whether the firm is selling into a particular market, building a factory or a facility where services are provided, sourcing inputs to production processes, or engaging in corporate social responsibility projects. Hence the behaviour of governments and firms has converged in objectives, in field of action and in approach as well.

As state and firm behaviour becomes more similar, state–firm diplomacy becomes both more necessary and more likely. Governments, in order to create and retain high value-added jobs and attract inward investment to their territories, must communicate with firms directly. Governments increasingly are finding that domestic economic policy and politics is becoming global economic policy. Therefore, policy making requires the cooperation of many actors: not just other governments and other non-state entities, but also large firms, which have the capacity to create or remove jobs, which can contribute to the tax base or not, and which can join in public–private partnerships to achieve social objectives or not, depending upon how they are engaged. For the managements of firms, especially global firms, the same pattern emerges. Corporate strategy, which was the analogue of domestic policy and politics, has become global policy, which needs the cooperation of governments. If a firm wants to build a plant in another country, if it wants to list its shares on another country's exchange, if it wants to start exporting goods and services into a country's market, the firm is likely to need to communicate and negotiate with a government. Sometimes it will need to communicate only with a local government, but often it will involve some organ of a regional or national government.

In order to make this type of communication regular and productive, governments and firms alike must establish structures and procedures for representation of themselves and their interests. Some of these diplomatic representations and communications may involve other types of non-state actors, such as regional development banks and civil society organizations.

Microsoft co-founder and former CEO Bill Gates with former US President Bill Clinton at the Clinton Global Initiative annual meeting, New York, September 2008

Although diplomacy, by encompassing more types of actors, becomes more complex, some generalizations about outcomes are still possible. Governments and firms increasingly may share particular interests, such as facilitating a particular investment or acquisition, or building a factory that will create a significant number of highly paid jobs. Hence, in a broad sense, state–firm cooperation is becoming more likely. Yet at the same time the outcomes of state–firm diplomacy in individual instances are not necessarily becoming more predictable. The European Union's antitrust charges against Microsoft of the mid-2000s, and the ensuing legal battles that have persisted for many years after the US government's case against Microsoft was resolved, would seem to go against the expectation for greater cooperation between entities that we might assume would have naturally overlapping interests.

As there are more different types of estrangements to be overcome, so more diplomatic mediations are required. The actual structure of representation between states and firms varies considerably, much more so than the more standard missions of governments to one another: embassies, consulates and trade offices. The representation of firms to governments is not greatly unlike that of governments to one another. Large transnational firms tend to have sizable government relations offices in one or more of their headquarters locations, which function analogously to the foreign ministry of a nation–state government. ExxonMobil is a good example of a firm with a large 'political department'.[5] In similar fashion to governments, firms maintain permanent representative offices in capitals and other distant cities where they have regular diplomatic business. But within a government, who is empowered to communicate to the firm's representatives and act on the government's behalf varies according to the breadth and depth of the relationship between the government and firm. A diplomatic mediation between a government and a firm is always going to be asymmetric in several respects. Most importantly, in most cases a government does not send a permanent representation *to* a firm in a physical, geographical sense, whereas firms will often have representative offices in important national capitals devoted exclusively to diplomacy with that country's government. A firm has a different sense of 'place' from a country or a government, so a government's representation to a firm is not territorially located in the same way as a firm's representation to a government or a government's representation to another government. Yet governments do have offices and personnel specifically for conducting representation and communication functions with large global firms. They may be found in trade ministries, finance ministries, tax services or all of the above.

When firms plan significant investments in a country, negotiations with the government are likely to become regular necessities. In 2004 Kia Motors, a subsidiary of Korean industrial conglomerate Hyundai, decided to invest in a vehicle manufacturing facility in Slovakia to produce 200,000 automobiles and other vehicles annually for sale in the European Union market. Hyundai sought and received concessions, including favourable tax treatment, free land and infrastructure commitments from the Slovak national government to build their plant in the north of Slovakia. The Slovak government competed against other governments, that of Poland in particular, to convince Hyundai to locate the plant in Slovakia. The agreement was considered a success by both sides.[6] But the agreement was only the beginning of the relationship. It would take two years for the plant to become operational, during which period numerous issues were likely to arise. Hyundai and Kia officials could expect to have to return to the Slovakian capital, Bratislava, several times in each year, to negotiate the renewal or extension of tax and other concessions granted by the government. Once the plant was built and operating, the balance of power would shift to some degree towards the government, as the firm would have a large quantity of assets invested in the physical plant, with a lot riding on its ongoing profitability. Hence, in order to be successful in retaining the most favourable business conditions possible, the managers would need to convince the Slovak officials that the plant was creating enough jobs and growing the local economy sufficiently to warrant continued favourable tax treatment. So a firm like Hyundai needs to develop an ongoing diplomatic relationship with the Slovak government, consisting of representation and communication through regular channels. Were the relationship extensive enough, it would convince Hyundai of the importance of opening an office in Bratislava specifically for dealing with the government as the need arises. These types of representative offices may perform a mixture of government relations, public relations, and lobbying functions as required, but an office of this kind is in effect an embassy from the firm to the government.

Diplomacy Between Firms and Host Governments

As noted above, one particular configuration of state–firm relationship, one particular diplomatic mediation, has special importance: that between the firm and its host government or governments. Diplomacy between a firm and its host government traditionally was considered domestic political bargaining or interest group politics. This is still true for the vast majority of small and mid-sized firms in the world, and for firms that for historical reasons are concentrated entirely or mostly within one single state. But size matters: when a firm is large and global enough, the relationship with the host state, and negotiations when required, start to look more like economic diplomacy between two governments. Even the largest firms need a host government to provide a home base with legal structures for their incorporation and market parameters where their stocks and bonds can trade. Many firms need stable access to resources on which they depend, whether intellectual capital, labour, land or raw materials. Even the largest firms cannot do altogether without amenities that governments provide, leaving no alternative to establishing a mediation, at least with a host government.[7]

However, the largest global firms have a degree and type of leverage over their host government that smaller and less global firms do not, which is what places the firm as interlocutor more in a position of functional equality and less in the rôle of client or supplicant relative to a government. In some cases large transnational firms possess an ultimate sanction that they can deploy in negotiating with a government: the threat of exit. A firm can leave a state altogether, taking its capital and jobs elsewhere. Many negotiations between firms and states do not lead to mutually agreeable conclusions. As in the case of negotiations between governments, each side seeks to use the most effective mix of carrots and sticks to achieve their negotiating objectives. As noted above in the Hyundai example, withdrawal may be a more credible threat for a firm to make to a government prior to its actually locating physical assets in a state's territory. But under the right circumstances it may make sense for a firm to use the threat of exit in a negotiation with the host government, or even simply to take the rational decision to relocate operations to a more propitious setting.

Numerous recent examples of exit or threat of exit exist. The Hongkong and Shanghai Banking Corporation (HSBC) was long headquartered in British Hong Kong, but by the 1990s it was already a global financial services firm with operations in many countries. Among its portfolio of assets were the British Bank of the Middle East and a mid-sized New York-based bank called Marine Midland. In the early 1990s HSBC bought one of the 'Big Four' High Street commercial banks in Britain, Midland Bank. As the scheduled handover of British sovereignty over Hong Kong to the People's Republic of China in 1997 approached, HSBC's management, after negotiating with the British and Chinese governments, took the decision to move the bank's corporate headquarters from Hong Kong to London. HSBC's top managers decided that the legal structures, business climate and political transparency of Britain were more favourable to the firm and its shareholders than the somewhat less certain environment of Hong Kong under Chinese sovereignty. They did not pull their business interests and operations out of Hong Kong, but they established a relationship with a different host government. Although the Chinese government in Beijing would have liked to retain HSBC's headquarters in Hong Kong, prior to their assuming sovereignty over Hong Kong they did not have sufficient leverage over HSBC to dissuade the bank from relocating. For similar reasons, several large South Africa-based firms, including the mining and precious metals firm Anglo-American and the financial services firm Old Colony, decided to shift their corporate headquarters from South Africa to

Britain before the transition to majority rule in South Africa in the early 1990s. These firms did not abandon their business operations in South Africa, but they preferred the greater stability and transparency of business climate that British politics and the British legal system provide over an indeterminate period of political and economic uncertainty that they anticipated for South Africa.

Another example of exit illustrates that the distribution of power between host governments and firms can remain in a government's favour. In the late 1990s, a number of US-based insurance companies and other firms moved their headquarters to Bermuda. Bermuda remains a British crown colony, with a government of its own. With the encouragement of the Bermudian authorities, some managements of US-based insurance firms and other businesses realized that they could achieve substantial alleviation of their tax liabilities if they moved their corporate headquarters to Bermuda, a nearby location with a comparable legal and political system. However, legislators in the US states that stood to lose the most in terms of tax revenues and jobs as well from these corporate migrations used public diplomacy (see chapter 7) effectively to head off, and in a few cases reverse, this trend. They rallied opposition amongst the American public to the firms that were planning or undertaking the move, thus threatening these firms' income streams from US consumers. Negative publicity for the firms changed the decision making calculus that their boards of directors used when voting to move or stay.[8] Jade Miller argues that US Congressional hearings on internet freedom in 2005 and 2006 played a similar rôle in exerting soft power (through mobilizing public opinion) to discourage US-based information technology firms Google, Yahoo!, Microsoft and Cisco Systems from being too cooperative with China's government in Chinese efforts to conduct internet censorship. According to Miller, in this instance hearings and proposed legislation did not go as far as pressing the technology firms to exit the Chinese market, but still put them on notice that the US public expected them to observe US business and political values in their diplomacy with other governments.[9]

These examples illustrate how the leverage of the state in state–firm diplomacy can vary, both over time and in terms of the distribution of power between particular states and particular firms. In order to succeed at diplomacy with large global firms, governments of nation–states have had to adapt their rôle and objectives from that of the intervention state, which focuses on regulation, to that of the transformative or promoter state, which facilitates business agreements that benefit the public and private sectors alike.[10] In this type of 'catalytic' diplomacy described by

Brian Hocking, the promoter state seeks to use policy and the techniques of diplomatic negotiation in relationships with firms in such a way as to benefit its citizens and its finances to the greatest extent possible.[11] In the three cases above, neither China nor South Africa as intervention states was in a position to raise the cost of exit to HSBC or Anglo-American high enough to prevent moves by significant transnational firms, nor could they provide enough enticements as promoter states to convince the firms to stay. The United States, by contrast, was in a position to raise the cost of exit for its firms to a level greater than the enticements of the Bermudian government. Importantly, this suggests that relative size matters considerably to negotiating outcomes and in state–firm diplomatic relationships generally.

Size Still Matters: The US Government and US-based Firms as Diplomatic Actors

Susan Strange observed that size remains of great importance in assessing the power of nation–states in a world of ever more non-state actors. In keeping with Strange's observation, there was a widely held view in the 1990s that the US government and US-based firms were disproportionately important in this transformed world of state–firm diplomacy.[12] In the 1990s, the argument ran, the US economy was the greatest engine of world economic growth, driven by technological advances and trade expansion. President Bill Clinton's Big Emerging Markets programme promoted large developing countries with booming middle classes as new US export markets.[13] US-based firms globalized rapidly, moving production to many sites, raising capital in different markets, listing their shares on many exchanges around the world. To keep up with these trends, the US government's efforts to regulate business practices appeared to spread way beyond US borders. For example, US regulators pressed other countries to adopt Generally Accepted Accounting Principles (GAAP), the US regime of accounting standards. US government regulatory agencies, such as the Securities and Exchange Commission, the Federal Reserve, and the Food and Drug Administration, all sought to work with their foreign counterparts to coordinate and standardize business regulation. Major bond rating agencies such as Standard & Poor's, Fitch and Morningstar, which perform the all-important function of pricing corporate and sovereign debt, were for the most part US-based, and, in the boom of the late 1990s, the US dollar seemed to become a de facto world currency in many areas.

By this sort of structural argument suggesting a historical moment of global US dominance, the mediation between the US government and global firms had become unusually important: in effect, just as important as state–state relations. To make successful economic policy, Washington needed to build a winning coalition of governments, multilateral organizations and civil society organizations. To craft a winning business strategy, US-based firms needed to do much the same thing. To what extent did the US government and US-based firms rise to meet this challenge? In terms of acting as a promoter state, the Clinton administration was effective. Their economic policy team cooperated with Federal Reserve chairman Alan Greenspan in supporting a policy of low interest rates to stimulate economic growth. They promoted trade liberalization agreements such as the North American Free Trade Agreement ('NAFTA'), APEC, and the 1994 Treaty of Marrakech, which created the World Trade Organization. They promoted US exports to new markets through the Big Emerging Markets countries and with high-level trade missions to other markets, such as Russia. They sought to reinforce the conversion of former communist states to market economy systems through projects such as the Gore–Chernomyrdin Commission, a bilateral commission that met twice a year to facilitate US–Russia trade in energy and high-technology goods and services (including commercial satellite launch services).[14] The Clinton team succeeded in getting the US Congress to approve granting most favoured nation (MFN) trade status to China, which expanded export opportunities for US-based firms significantly. Likewise, the administration and Congress cooperated with US-based firms on important issues that once would have been seen as domestic economic policy in order to benefit US economic interests globally. The 1996 Farm Bill facilitated liberalization of the traditionally heavily regulated global agricultural trade, and for the most part in ways that did not hurt US family farmers. Another example is the 1999 financial services reform legislation (see below). But Clinton was unable to win Congressional support for key initiatives involving traditional state–state economic diplomacy, such as renewal of 'fast track' negotiating authority for trade agreements, and for his goal of negotiating a pan-American free trade accord, the Free Trade of the Americas initiative. The administration also failed in state–state diplomacy in important areas that would have helped US firms, such as launching a new WTO trade liberalization round or bringing to a successful conclusion the Multilateral Agreement on Investment.

How effectively did US-based global firms use firm–state diplomacy in the 1990s to achieve their business objectives? On one hand, US firms achieved an impressive record of economic growth, whether measured by market capitalization or by brand presence and visibility, without needing to negotiate extensively with governments. As the so-called 'new' high-technology economy emerged, firms leapt from obscurity to prominence in the global marketplace: internet firms like AOL and Yahoo!, business software producers like Oracle and Computer Associates (CA), networking hardware firms like Cisco Systems and Juniper Networks, and semiconductor equipment companies like Applied Materials. On the other hand, US-based firms missed a lot of opportunities for growth that could have been pursued through closer cooperation with a 'promoter state' US government. US companies could have worked more closely with the Clinton administration to establish a more significant presence in many big emerging markets, such as Russia. US financial firms in particular did not do enough to reduce risks by attempting to prevent, rather than just reacting to, global crises that ended up costing them a substantial amount of business, such as the Mexican peso crisis in 1994 and the Asian and Russian financial crises of 1997–8. Neither the US government nor US-based firms have used diplomacy well enough to leverage resources to achieve policy objectives where their interests may be at odds. For example, US firms that would have benefited from ending the US government embargo on trade with Cuba following the end of the Cold War did not bring sufficient pressure to achieve that objective in the 1990s. Likewise, the Federal Aviation Act of 1958 restricts the carriage of air passengers between US cities to US-registered air carriers and restricts foreign ownership of US air carriers to 24 per cent. US airlines and non-US air carriers alike over many years have failed to make the case to the US government that repeal of the relevant legislative provisions would preserve US jobs in the airline industry by permitting mergers between US-based and non-US airlines, which would create stronger end-to-end international route networks. Several US-based airlines have downsized or gone bankrupt, and large numbers of airline jobs were lost in recent decades, because non-US-based carriers are still prohibited from purchasing the US carriers.

If the 1990s were arguably some sort of global moment for state–firm diplomacy that benefited public and private interests in the United States particularly, the decade following has seen a number of structural shifts. The rise in importance of the European Union as an actor in business regulation, and the strengthening of EU diplomacy, have meant global firms have to devote more time to diplomacy with the European Union. The collapse of the 'dot.com' technology boom in the early 2000s meant that a number of major US-based firms lost some of the lustre that they held in the 1990s and thus found themselves in a less strong position when negotiating with governments. Several ambitious corporate mergers designed to create ever larger global competitors, such as those of AOL and Time Warner Communications and of Citicorp and Travelers (see below), have not proven to be the competitive successes that their pro-tagonists envisaged. A series of financial scandals on both sides of the Atlantic, which began with Enron, WorldCom, Health South and Parmalat, continued through the subprime mortgage and credit crisis of 2007–8, which began in the United States and subsequently spread into a global recession. This triggered a general crisis of legitimacy for the model of global market regulation that had been promoted by US governments and firms alike. US proposals to harmonize global business regulation along US lines have largely stalled. For example, perceived inconsistencies between conventions for accounting in different countries have long been regarded as a financial risk to investors seeking transparency of accounts as they make investment decisions. The European Commission has called on US regulators to adopt International Accounting Standards (IAS), the European accounting standard, after the European Commission in 2005 required firms in member countries to observe IAS-based International Financial Reporting Standards rather than Generally Accepted Accounting Principles (GAAP), as American regulators would have preferred.[15] Following the global financial turbulence of 2008, interest in regulatory harmonization revived on both sides of the Atlantic. Only time would tell if that revival of interest was sufficient to close deals and get implementing legislation passed.

Case Study: the Citicorp–Travelers Merger and US Financial Services Reform

One of the more interesting recent case studies of diplomacy between a firm, Citigroup, and its host state, the United States, illustrates how each actor used its respective strengths to achieve an outcome that up to then had not been achievable. In the late 1990s, two US firms – a bank, Citicorp, and an insurance company, Travelers – wanted to merge in order to create a financial services company that their managers believed would be large enough to compete successfully in the global financial services marketplace with major overseas rivals. But up until 1999 such a merger was not possible because of longstanding US restrictions on aggregation of financial firms. Since 1933 the Glass–Steagall Act had separated commercial banking from securities underwriting, other investment banking activities and the insurance business. Glass–Steagall had been enacted as a response to the 1929 stock market crash and resulting public perceptions that financial services firms in the 1920s were too powerful and did not serve the public interest. For many decades, banking and finance in the United States and in other industrialized countries was a staid business that grew at a moderate rate and did not change rapidly. However, globalization and the progress of technology that enabled capital to flow across borders more easily generated pressure for change. Financial services reform began in the 1970s with deregulation of the limits on interest rates that banks could pay on savings accounts. In the 1980s, the 'Big Bang' financial reforms on Wall Street and in the City of London (the UK financial sector) heralded more far-reaching deregulation of securities trading, and barriers to interstate banking gradually were lifted. Nonetheless, in the United States the general consensus remained that financial services liberalization should be slow and incremental. Some large financial firms had been lobbying for total repeal of Glass–Steagall since the 1970s, but these efforts had failed repeatedly in Congress. A major challenge for prospective financial services reform was how to reorganize financial regulation amongst the several regulatory bodies to make the system more effective and provide an adequate level of supervision in a liberalized environment. Opinion was sharply divided over who should have regulatory authority in a reformed structure within each financial services subsector: commercial banking, investment banking, and insurance. Opinion was similarly fractured within the relevant government regulatory bodies: the Federal Reserve, the Treasury Department's Office of the Comptroller of the Currency, the Federal Deposit Insurance Corporation and the state-level insurance regulatory agencies.

By the mid-1990s, the Clinton administration, the leaders of the House of Representatives and Senate financial committees, and the managements of major large financial firms recognized the impact of financial globalization and the financial reforms of the 1980s and the resultant need to modernize US financial regulation to preserve and enhance US competitiveness in global financial markets. But a winning political coalition to pass a financial reform bill in Congress still had not emerged. In 1998 Congress tried and failed to pass a financial reform bill. Then, in a single year, internet revenues stampeded the financial services industry. Suddenly, firms were showing very different results depending on how well and how fast they adopted e-business strategies. In the borderless world of the internet, global competitiveness for US financial services firms became paramount in policy terms as never before. In November 1999 Congress passed the Gramm–Leach–Bliley Act, which in effect repealed the Glass–Steagall Act and the 1956 Bank Holding Company Act. Under the new law, commercial banks, investment banks, insurance companies and mutual funds were permitted to merge and compete in each other's markets. Congress drew a new line on permissible financial mergers by deciding to keep big retailers like Wal-Mart and Dillards out of banking.[16]

What finally tipped the scales for Congress over just one year? Citicorp and Travelers announced their merger in April 1998. The $140 billion transaction at a stroke created the largest US financial institution by far, with 100 million customers and operations in 100 countries.[17] Under existing law Citicorp and Travelers would be allowed to form a bank holding company that could hold all existing businesses for up to five years, but they would then have to divest significant chunks if the law were not changed in the meantime. The merger announcement was a daring and hugely significant diplomatic *démarche* by Citicorp CEO Sandy Weill, following on from public and private negotiations with members of Congress and Clinton administration officials. Weill in effect challenged the government to enact financial services reform within the required time window. By the public act of announcing the merger Weill staked his company's reputation on his commitment to the need for the merger to enable Citicorp to compete globally, and in effect dared Congress not to pass financial reform legislation. Citigroup negotiated, and they calculated correctly the leverage of their combined assets. This deal, too big to fail by virtue of its sheer size and importance to US competitiveness, tipped the political balance in favour of passing reform. The Citigroup merger, and the Gramm–Leach–Bliley Act that enabled it, changed the global financial landscape. For the first time it allowed US firms to compete on a level playing field with big European financial firms like Deutsche Bank, which had bought US financial firms Bankers Trust and Alex. Brown Securities. The merger facilitated a wave of cross-border financial mergers that reshaped the industry worldwide. HSBC, which was already in the US market, subsequently expanded further by buying additional US banks. The Royal Bank of Scotland acquired a fast-growing group of US banking and other financial services assets. Citigroup rapidly went on to buy the UK brokerage house Schroders. Ultimately this begs the question of whether Citigroup management, by later in the first decade of the twenty-first century, still regarded the merger as the best business strategy for maximizing the value of their businesses. The point remains, however, that, in the environment of the late 1990s, senior management judged it the best way forward, and they used their skills effectively to communicate their resolve to the US government.[18]

The Citicorp–Travelers case study illustrates this chapter's main point that transnational firms that organize resources effectively in a diplomatic strategy to achieve business objectives can make major gains. Successful firm–state diplomacy includes establishing an ongoing relationship with a government – a mediation – and planning how to utilize the leverage they have in negotiating with government officials. Citigroup reshaped the US financial services regime to its own advantage and in the process generated broader benefits for US interests in the global economy after decades of Congressional inaction. Firms that neglect diplomacy can face adverse conditions despite their size, wealth and global reach, not only in terms of unfavourable policy and regulatory decisions by governments, but also in relation to their competition with other firms. Another firm may do a better job at negotiating with the host government in a strategy to capture economic rents. Firms such as Netscape, Sun Microsystems and Oracle effectively brought pressure on the US government to bring an antitrust case against Microsoft in the late 1990s, in large part because Microsoft had paid so little attention to diplomacy with Washington up until that point.[19] But, of equal importance, governments need to maintain good diplomatic relations with global firms headquartered in their territory to achieve global economic policy objectives. As promoter states, governments need to maximize opportunities for cooperation. Large firms have a degree of sovereignty against host governments (depending on the mobility of their assets) in that they can move away, a threat that could be very costly to execute but possible nonetheless, and hence a potentially potent negotiating tool.

Large private firms that operate across national borders in the contemporary global economy, whilst different in structure and function from governments of nation–states, increasingly engage in diplomacy with governments and with one another. Neither political leaders and their diplomats nor senior managers of global firms can afford to ignore the opportunities for public and private benefit that can result from this type of diplomatic engagement. The challenge for the managements of transnational firms is to develop the diplomatic structures and skills required to represent themselves and to communicate and negotiate effectively with their counterparts in governments, multilateral organizations and civil society organizations. Firms that have acquired this diplomatic expertise have already more than demonstrated its value through faster growth and greater profit, but also through broader social gains created by effective private–public cooperation. Firms such as Microsoft and Citigroup, by showing the way through their own learning curve, have made it likely that more and more firms will come to operate effectively as diplomatic actors.

6

Civil Society Organizations and Eminent Person Diplomats

Introduction: Civil Society and Diplomacy

The idea of civil society traditionally has been understood to refer to social organization outside of that undertaken by governmental, military and judicial bodies. As such, civil society includes business as well as organizations and movements with political interest-based, social and charitable objectives. One of the results of the broadening of access to and participation in diplomacy discussed in previous chapters has been the creation of space for civil society actors to engage in diplomatic representation and communication with other actors directly, rather than being required to have their interests represented by the diplomats of nation–state governments. This chapter focuses on two other major types of civil society actor: civil society organizations and eminent person diplomats. In the twentieth century, civil society organizations (CSOs), also known with somewhat less precision as non-governmental organizations (NGOs), emerged as another major category of non-state diplomatic actor. In the latter half of the century, these organizations and their activities became highly visible to the global public. The campaign by Greenpeace to convince governments and global public to oppose nuclear testing in the 1980s received media coverage worldwide. In 1985 Greenpeace's efforts culminated in one of the century's more notorious failures of diplomacy, in which French government security forces sank the Greenpeace ship *Rainbow Warrior* whilst it was anchored at Auckland, New Zealand, in order to prevent the ship from interfering with planned nuclear tests in the South Pacific. In the way in which CSOs carry out the core diplomatic functions of representation and communication, CSOs are analogous in a number of key respects to the types of organizations engaging in diplomacy considered in previous chapters, such as governments, multilateral organizations and large global firms.

Another group of civil society diplomatic actors, so-called 'eminent person diplomats', increasingly have made their presence felt on the global

Sunken Greenpeace ship *Rainbow Warrior* in Auckland harbour, Auckland, New Zealand, August 1985

stage in recent decades. For example, in the late 1970s Elliot Richardson, former US Attorney General and Ambassador to the Court of St James, acting in a purely private capacity, negotiated a resolution to the Beagle Channel boundary dispute between the governments of Chile and Argentina, heading off a conflict over a navigable waterway between the Atlantic and Pacific Oceans near the southern tip of South America that threatened to erupt into war. Yet as the discussion that follows illuminates, eminent person diplomats are very different from any of the organizational types of actors discussed thus far. An eminent person diplomat does not have the same sort of relationship with whomever she or he is representing as the relationship between an ambassador of a nation–state and her government or a vice president for government relations of a global firm and his CEO and board of directors.[1]

Yet another group of organizations can be considered to be 'civil society' organizations and to engage, to limited and varying degrees, in diplomacy: the group that includes transnational criminal organizations (TCOs) and organizations employing extreme tactics (warlords and terrorist organizations). Organizations such as these can be understood as forming the limit or boundary of contemporary diplomacy. Whilst most such groups undertake limited measures of diplomatic representation and communication, as when al-Qa'eda engages in public diplomacy by sending video cassette messages to al-Jazeera to generate support amongst the global Muslim public, nonetheless for the most part these organizations can be characterized by their unwillingness to engage in the sort of diplomacy that each of the other types of actors hitherto discussed pursues.

Civil Society Organizations as Diplomatic Actors

The term 'civil society organizations' covers a wider range of entities than initially appears to be the case. Like firms, they vary in size from very small and localized to enormous transnational organizations. When most people think of CSOs, they think of large, transnational bodies established to undertake charitable missions such as protecting the environment, treating the ill and fighting poverty: organizations such as Greenpeace, the International Committee of the Red Cross (ICRC), Médécins Sans Frontières (MSF), and World Vision. Yet what differentiates CSOs from multilateral institutions is that their constituencies are not composed of governments. In addition to charitable organizations, CSOs include transnational interest groups, such as the Socialist International and the World Council of Churches; transnational religious organizations, such as the Soka Gakkai International Buddhist society and the Church of Jesus Christ of Latter-Day Saints; and business organizations. Many of the largest transnational CSOs that increasingly are recognized as diplomatic actors fall into five broad categories: anti-poverty organizations, such as Oxfam, World Vision and Save the Children; health and medical organizations, such as MSF and the ICRC; human rights organizations, such as Amnesty International; environmental organizations, such as Greenpeace and Friends of the Earth; and business or political interest representation organizations, such as the International Federation of Trades Unions and the Socialist International. Yet CSOs do not need to be large to be transnational: DATA, for example, has had a significant global impact despite its relatively small size due to the high visibility of its head, Bono, and its ability to form partnerships with other organizations.

Although in this book the International Chamber of Commerce and the World Economic Forum are treated as multilateral organizations owing to their each having some sort of rôle in global governance (see chapter 4), they too qualify as civil society organizations, as neither is constituted by or of governments. On its own website the World Economic Forum identifies itself as a CSO. One of the distinguishing features of CSOs is that each is constituted for the purpose of pursuing a mission or objective. Friends of the Earth, for example, is dedicated to protecting the global environment. CSOs appeal to other organizations and individuals to join with them and support them in achieving their mission. Their legitimacy is generally judged by the global public in terms of how effective they are at doing what they set out to achieve.

Civil society organizations are different from both governments and firms in that they do not have a dedicated source of revenue, such as taxes or sales, and thus usually require external funding to do what they do. They may be funded by governments, by firms, by other private contributions, or a combination thereof. For example, of the ICRC's annual budget for 2007, which was between $600 million and $650 million, 85 per cent was supplied by industrialized country governments.[2] How well funded a CSO is can be viewed as a proxy for its legitimacy on the global diplomatic stage. But sources of CSO funding shape the degree of their independence as diplomatic actors, in that if CSOs depend on government funding they can be dependent upon government officials and policies. Even if a CSO is quite large, this dependence can constrain or limit its independence and freedom of manoeuvre. Yet government funding of CSOs is not intrinsically compromising, and it has become ever more common in recent decades as governments have increased their cooperation with non-governmental bodies that perform or assist in performing public services. As Cooper and Hocking point out, CSOs often work with, for, or in lieu of governments to deliver the sorts of services that traditionally only governments delivered to populations: services ranging from disaster relief to feeding the poor, delivering social services like education or rural health care, and conflict resolution. In this process, the structure of the relationship between a CSO and a government can vary considerably. The CSO can function as a subcontractor, a facilitator, or a joint manager, among other possibilities.[3] In order to succeed at a particular project, each relationship between a government and a CSO must be negotiated carefully in the first instance and then tended through regular communication over the duration of the project. A more wide-ranging relationship extending over multiple projects must be institutionalized to a greater degree, with clear structures of representation and channels of communication.[4] As they do with governments and multilateral organizations, CSOs have relationships with global firms that are involved in projects of mutual interest. For example, the Bill and Melinda Gates Foundation and Microsoft are cooperating to distribute technology to upgrade education in developing countries, and big pharmaceutical firms such as Merck are working with health-care CSOs to deliver HIV medications at affordable prices in Africa.

What this means is that, as is the case with global firms and governments, CSOs and governments have found that they need to establish ongoing relationships with one another – mediations – that consist of diplomatic representation and communication. And so too a similar situation arises between CSOs and global firms in cases in which there is a need for an ongoing relationship. For CSOs this need for diplomacy can be a bit more problematic than it appears at first. Some CSOs have made their name and reputation, and earned their perception of legitimacy, through engaging in critical, even violent, acts, rather than by conducting diplomacy with other actors through the customary practices of representation and communication. Der Derian has characterized as 'anti-diplomacy' a utopian approach to diplomacy sometimes taken by revolutionary movements, such as the French and Russian revolutionaries, who viewed traditional class-based diplomatic culture as part of the problem of how nation–states interacted with one another. For anti-diplomats, mediating the universal alienation of humankind from itself was more important than mediating the particular alienations between nation–states.[5] Long after its days of confrontation with the French government over nuclear testing, Greenpeace, for example, pursued the Japanese whaling ship *Nisshin Maru* through the Antarctic waters of the Southern Ocean in January 2008 in an effort to monitor, publicize and ultimately disrupt what it viewed as illegal whaling by Japan. Greenpeace's tactics could be seen as a good example of Der Derian's notion of anti-diplomacy. But as they chart their way forward, organizations like Greenpeace have faced the same dilemma that revolutionary anti-diplomats must face: once you have acquired a measure of power and influence, what is the most effective way to deal with other actors to achieve your goals? Is confrontation as a strategy to attract global condemnation of an adversary more effective than negotiation?

This more confrontational approach by civil society organizations to relations with governments, multilateral organizations and firms reached a peak in the early 2000s immediately following the highly successful disruption of the World Trade Organization's ministerial meeting in Seattle in November 1999 by a group of CSOs. CSOs such as the Confédération Paysanne Française, a French ruralist organization, and the Association pour la Taxation des Transactions pour l'Aide aux Citoyens (Association for the Taxation of Financial Transactions for the Aid of Citizens), an anti-neoliberal economic reform group known by its acronym ATTAC, continued this new model of aggressive protest at the 2001 G8 Summit in Genoa, Italy, and at the Davos Annual Meetings of the World Economic Forum in 2000 and 2001. The Genoa protests resulted in violent confrontation with Italian police that left one 23-year-old activist, Carlo Giuliani, dead, and in the process generated much of the negative global media attention on the G8 leaders that CSOs had hoped to achieve. By protesting at the Davos meetings, CSOs again sought to attract media attention to the World Economic Forum's activities and, by doing so, to convince the Forum to broaden its issue agenda and its range of invited participants to include more CSOs. The Forum leadership and members were very willing to oblige, provided that the CSOs were willing to abide by accepted rules and procedures for participating at Davos. In the ensuing years many CSOs have become active participants in the Davos Annual Meeting.

In January 2001 a new institution, the World Social Forum, was launched at Porto Allegre, Brazil, with the objective of bringing together civil society organizations from around the world for the same sort of brainstorming about global problems that was already taking place at Davos under the aegis of the World Economic Forum, but with a different agenda set by the CSOs. At the time of the first World Social Forum, its aspirational link to anti-diplomacy was reinforced when Jose Bové, the leader of the Confédération Paysanne Française, participated in a raid on a farm near Porto Allegre owned by global agribusiness firm Monsanto, in which the raiders uprooted experimental genetically modified crops. Yet as it evolved, the World Social Forum in many ways reproduced the form of the venue upon which it was modelled, the Davos Annual Meeting of the World Economic Forum, and thus cannot be seen as a form of anti-diplomacy in itself. The 2005 World Social Forum annual meeting in Porto Allegre drew more than 100,000 participants from over 2,000 organizations and from at least 119 countries. By 2006 the perceived successes of the World Social Forum in broadening public debate over how the global economy should be organized and in getting many of their agenda items included in the discussions at Davos had raised significant questions for World Social Forum organizers about their organization's future. A debate has ensued over whether the World Social Forum had achieved its principal objectives by succeeding in getting their agenda addressed at Davos, or whether there remains a need for the World Social Forum to raise public consciousness of their agenda from outside of the structure of the World Economic Forum.

The World Social Forum debate serves to highlight the extent of success achieved by CSOs in having their identities and issues recognized by other actors on the diplomatic stage. The more obvious CSO successes in participating in diplomatic initiatives to further their objectives, such as the 2005 G8 Gleneagles summit on poverty reduction (see case study below), are underpinned by much broader institutional links between CSOs and major global multilateral institutions, such as the United Nations and the WTO. The UN, for example, has established a series of partnerships with CSOs to address specific issues linked to the UN's Millennium Development Goals. In recognition of the need for institutional change, UN Secretary-General Kofi Annan in 2003 appointed an eminent persons' panel, chaired by former Brazilian President Henrique Cardoso, to examine the rôle of CSOs in UN operations and make recommendations for how CSO participation could be increased and how the UN's engagement with CSOs could be improved. The panel's 2004 report to the General Assembly recognized the importance of CSOs to the UN's objectives and recommended a series of reforms. These included increasing CSO participation in UN intergovernmental bodies, such as the General Assembly, funding increased participation by developing-country CSOs, improving the CSO accreditation process, and enlarging the CSO partnerships programme. As the panel report noted, '[m]ore effective engagement with NGOs also increases the likelihood that United Nations decisions will be better understood and supported by a broad and diverse public'.[6]

In order to achieve their enormously varied objectives, civil society organizations depend upon recognition, support and financial backing from individuals: the public of which civil society is constituted. As noted above, for each organization the number of individual and corporate backers combined with their aggregate level of financial backing can be viewed as a metric for the legitimacy or claim of the CSO to be able to speak on behalf of the cause or mission to which it is dedicated. Greenpeace, for example, claimed to have had 2.8 million subscribing members within the past eighteen months as of January 2007, and it reported its net annual income for calendar year 2006 at €128 million.[7] Hence, in order to be successful, CSOs need to make extensive use of public diplomacy: techniques to influence publics to press their governments, through their domestic political systems, for policy changes (see chapter 8). CSOs generally can increase their diplomatic leverage as they go global, develop brand identity and attract more independent funding that can free them from dependence on powerful donor governments. Large transnational CSOs such as MSF, Greenpeace, Friends of the Earth, the ICRC, Oxfam, Amnesty International and Save the Children have benefited in their fundraising and in their core mission work from recognition that their brand identity carries.

Many of the activities of large transnational CSOs consist of direct delivery of services to the constituencies that they are chartered to serve, as when the ICRC distributes medications to villagers to prevent cholera following a typhoon. However, an increasing portion of CSO activities require engagement in the representative and communicative functions of diplomacy in order to be successful. Organizations such as Oxfam and MSF, in order to operate a refugee camp near Darfur or establish a feeding station in Somalia, may need to negotiate and then communicate on an ongoing basis not only with one or more governments, but also with warlords and terrorist organizations if they are willing (see below), and also with private firms that have agreed to provide logistical support, such as transport for facilities and staff or security for the camp or station. The mission of some CSOs is more expressly diplomatic in nature. The ICRC is granted specific rights and duties under public international law to aid and protect combatants and civilians in conflict situations. Since 1990 the ICRC has held observer status at the UN General Assembly.[8] Amnesty International, after receiving reports of torture of prisoners by a government, have a variety of tactics available to them. They may seek to negotiate directly with the offending government in order to convince them to cease torturing the prisoners. They may lobby the governments of powerful nations, such as France, Britain, Japan and the United States, to bring pressure upon the torturing government to desist. Or they may seek to engage the global (or a regional) public through a campaign to publicize the alleged atrocities so as to motivate citizens of powerful states to press their legislators to bring pressure upon the accused government to end the torture. Still other CSOs may engage in a different form of public diplomacy involving more directly confrontational tactics. When a Greenpeace ship shadowed the Japanese whaling ship *Nisshin Maru* in the Antarctic in 2008, a BBC reporter was 'embedded' aboard the Greenpeace vessel to provide information that would catalyse global public opposition to Japan's whaling programme, which the Japanese government maintains is undertaken only for purposes of scientific research.

Eminent Person Diplomats

From ancient times, history is replete with examples of private individuals, usually of high standing, occasionally being drafted to serve as go-betweens in sensitive or difficult diplomatic negotiations between estranged sovereigns. Such mediation can be needed when the good offices of such an individual are required to open or maintain a line of communication that would otherwise be closed. However, in recent decades there has been a rise in the visibility of high-profile private individuals acting in the diplomatic milieu in a more widely recognized, institutionalized way. These individuals serve as representatives of the interests of others to diplomats of governments, multilateral organizations and other actors and by communicating with these counterparts on an ongoing basis. Often, but not always, such individuals have distinguished themselves and made themselves well known to the public through endeavours in their own careers. Careers of eminent person diplomats are diverse, extending from political and religious leadership to entertainment and sport. In his defining work *Celebrity Diplomacy*, Andrew F. Cooper has chronicled much of the recent activity of these diplomats and explored the important questions that arise from their undertakings. At one extreme amongst famous examples of eminent person diplomacy is the visit of the Revd Jesse Jackson to Syrian President Hafez Assad to seek the release of a US Navy pilot shot down whilst on a mission to bomb Syrian positions in Lebanon in 1983. At another are the anti-poverty campaigns undertaken by Bono since the 1990s, the most visible of which have been in his 2002 'Odd Couple Tour of Africa' with US Treasury Secretary Paul O'Neill and his rôle at the 2005 G8 Gleneagles summit. Bono's objective in 2002 was to raise O'Neill's consciousness about the problems facing Africa, ranging from HIV to lack of clean water, and O'Neill, formerly CEO of US aluminium firm Alcoa and then a relative neophyte regarding development issues, expressed a willingness to learn.[9] It is worthwhile to note that Bono has acted not only as a celebrity diplomat, but has gone on to build around himself a civil society organization, DATA (Debt, AIDS, Trade, Africa), to raise funding for his anti-poverty projects.

It becomes immediately obvious that eminent person diplomats are not analogous to a government, a multilateral organization, a transnational firm or even a civil society organization itself, in that they are not representing and communicating on behalf of an entity. They are representing and communicating ideas or positions to which they themselves are committed.[10] They may also be hired, or volunteer, to represent the interests of another entity, but without being a part of that entity, hence taking on the rôle of mediator of an estrangement one step farther by being truly in the 'middle', in between and independent of the estranged parties. It makes sense to consider the activities of these individuals as diplomacy because, importantly – at least when they are successful – they and the messages that they bear are received by the interlocutor with which they wish to communicate. They are accredited as having standing and legitimacy by the counterparts to whom they seek to make an argument or with whom they seek to negotiate. They are engaging in the core diplomatic functions of representation and communication in the same way that their counterparts in governments, multilateral and civil society organizations and global firms do, and by doing so they play a key rôle in mediating estrangement between other actors.

The first major distinction that needs to be drawn when considering the rôle of eminent person diplomats is that between independent persons who agree to act as representatives of another actor in the spirit of public service, often for no formal compensation, and persons who decide to act as diplomats on behalf of a cause or objective to which they are already committed personally. In the former category can be located figures such as retired heads of government and similar politicians of stature, and United Nations Goodwill Ambassadors. Retired heads of government and senior politicians are often called upon by either their own or other current heads of government to act as mediators and to serve as observers of the proper conduct of elections. Former US Presidents Jimmy Carter and Bill Clinton, former South African President Nelson Mandela, former Irish President Mary Robinson and retired Archbishop Desmond Tutu have played these rôles many times. The UN Goodwill Ambassador function originated in the 1950s, with actors such as Danny Kaye, Audrey Hepburn and Sir Peter Ustinov being appointed as UN 'Ambassadors-at-Large'.[11] More recently, the actress Angelina Jolie has served as a Goodwill Ambassador for the UN High Commissioner for Refugees (UNHCR). By volunteering to make visits to war-torn countries in Africa and Asia and by writing about her experiences, Jolie helps to draw the attention of the global media to the plight of refugees and raises the profile of the UN's mission in aiding them. Tennis star Roger Federer serves in a similar rôle for the UN International Children's Emergency Fund (UNICEF). As UNICEF explains on its website, 'Celebrities . . . can make direct representations to those with the power to effect change. They can use their talents and fame to fundraise and advocate for children and support UNICEF's mission.'[12]

The latter category of eminent person diplomats consists of individuals who decide to act on the diplomatic stage to further a particular cause or interest to which they are committed. Religious figures such as the Revd Jesse Jackson in the United States have sought to take on a mediation rôle, often in international conflicts involving the United States, in part to make a point that US foreign policy and the diplomacy required to implement it were not being carried out in the most effective way possible by US offi-cials. Entertainment celebrities such as musicians Bono and Sir Bob Geldof each became committed to the cause of alleviating poverty, particularly in Africa. They realized that they could use their personal celebrity to gain access to leaders both in developing countries and in donor countries in order to promote the development and improvement of structures for delivering aid. Bono and Geldof found that they could be effective at mobi-lizing the public to press for policy change, as well as in outright fundraising for the cause. As their projects grew, they subsequently found it advanta-geous to build up civil society organizations around them to further their objectives.[13]

To ask what determines whether eminent person diplomats are effective is really to ask whether someone can be counted as an eminent person diplomat or not. An eminent person diplomat is successful to the extent that an ambassador, head of government, cabinet minister, CEO of a global firm or other diplomatist is willing to receive and communicate with him or her. When effective communication to the global public is all that is required, such as to publicize a refugee crisis, for example, the eminent person may succeed in his or her mission merely by being him- or herself in the necessary high-visibility situation so that the media can capture the moment and transmit it widely. However, if negotiation is required, a different and much more extensive set of skills, both reputational and instrumental, is needed. To act in a high-profile mediation rôle, an indi-vidual must be regarded as of high ethical standing, having both political credibility and the capacity to be impartial and thus meet differing notions of what counts as 'fair'. Two or more sides that are far apart in a disagree-ment have to be willing to accept the same individual and give to that person their trust. Often religious figures, such as Archbishop Tutu, are sought for these reasons. Former political leaders of outstanding ethical and moral standing, such as Presidents Carter, Robinson and Mandela, are seen in the same light. Strong negotiating skills can be found in the same individuals, but there is not always a perfect match of the same capacities. Former US Senator George Mitchell, who presided successfully over the implementation of the Good Friday Agreement between the factions in the long-running Northern Ireland conflict in the 1990s and 2000s, is a good example of an eminent person generally regarded both as trustworthy and as a highly skilled negotiator. Mitchell was appointed by US President Barack Obama to serve as special envoy to the Middle East in a bid by Obama to meet this most intractable of diplomatic challenges for the United States.

One indication of the evolution of the rôle of the eminent person diplomat in international society and in diplomatic culture can be observed in the foundation in 2001 of the Elders, a grouping of distinguished former heads of state and government and other senior world leaders who have come together to share resources and make themselves available to consult on and negotiate solutions to problems and conflicts between nation–states and between states and other actors. The idea for the Elders emerged from a 1999 conversation between two Britons, musician Peter Gabriel and business leader and philanthropist Sir Richard Branson. Gabriel and Branson then convinced former South African President Nelson Mandela, Mandela's wife and former Mozambican First Lady Graça Machel, and former Archbishop Desmond Tutu to convene the body that exists today. They signed up an A-list roster of highly respected global leaders, including Grameen Bank founder Muhammad Yunus, former US President Jimmy Carter, former Norwegian Prime Minister Gro Harlem Brundtland, former Irish President Mary Robinson, Burmese democracy leader Aung San Suu Kyi, Indian Self-Employed Women's Association founder Ela R. Bhatt, former Brazilian President Fernando Cardoso and UN diplomat Lakhdar Brahimi. The Elders' first mission was to Sudan in October 2007 to heighten global awareness both of the Darfur crisis and of potential paths to its peaceful resolution. Subsequently they participated in negotiating a resolution of the Kenya election crisis in December 2007 and spoke out in defence of democracy in Burma and Zimbabwe.[14] The Elders' methods combine using the diplomatic talents of their members to negotiate solutions to conflicts and their members' public profiles and high visibility to raise public consciousness and focus public opinion on situations where public pressure on their own elected officials may make a difference in shaping policies. Funded thus far by private support, the Elders is developing an organizational structure of its own, and by doing so may become a hybrid that joins eminent person diplomats under the umbrella of a CSO to facilitate and amplify the impact of their activities.

A Darker Side to Civil Society Diplomatic Actors

Organizations that engage in extreme or terrorist tactics and transnational criminal organizations (TCOs) are civil society organizations in that they are organized entities that exercise a measure of power and command a measure of support from a constituency or population, but without the same kind of legitimacy that formal sovereignty or legal business registration confers. At one end of the spectrum of such entities, transnational criminal organizationss such as the Cali and Medellin drug cartels, the Mafia and Camorra, Russian-based crime syndicates, and the East Asian triads and yakuza are akin to global firms in a number of ways. They conduct business across borders with a variety of other entities, including businesses and in some cases even governments. Other organizations may control territories and populations within states but without the consent of their governments, such as the Revolutionary Armed Forces of Colombia, known by their Spanish-language acronym FARC, which controls a portion of Colombian territory; the Taliban, which at the time of writing controls small areas of territory and populations within Afghanistan and Pakistan; and the 'warlords' or tribal leaders that have exercised control of portions of Burma, Somalia and Afghanistan in recent times. Both of these types of organizations are happy to send and receive representatives and to communicate as much as needed to further their objectives. Their ability to engage in diplomatic representation and communication is constrained primarily by the unwillingness of sovereign governments, multilateral institutions, global firms and CSOs to recognize them and accredit them as legitimate diplomatic actors.

Yet other organizations, such as al-Qa'eda, are non-territorially based entities that engage in terrorist tactics to achieve an agenda of political objectives and appeal for support from segments of the global public. These groups, whose tactics Der Derian has characterized as 'anti-diplomacy', tend to be opposed ideologically to the forms and rituals of diplomatic representation and communication. They do not want to communicate and negotiate; they wish to achieve their objective through different, often more violent, means. The difference between these types of CSOs and those heretofore discussed is that these types of organizations engage in relatively little of the substance, let alone the ritual, of diplomatic representation and communication, in which other CSOs engage, and which makes other CSOs analogous to other types of diplomatic actors. Hence they must be identified as lying at the outer boundary of what can be studied under the rubric of diplomacy. Nonetheless there are occasions when even these bodies have need to communicate, to represent themselves to others, and to acknowledge representation from and communications by other actors.

On these albeit infrequent occasions, the norms and practices of diplomacy emerge on an as-needed basis. Two examples illustrate this phenomenon. Following the Mumbai terrorist attacks of November 2008, which were attributed to Pakistan-based terrorist organization Lashkar-i-Taiba,

Maulvi Faqir Mohammad, deputy leader of Taliban forces fighting the Pakistani and Afghan governments from border regions, publicly offered support to Pakistan's government in the event of an outbreak of war between Pakistan and India.[15] Earlier the same month, when Barack Obama was elected President of the United States, al-Qa'eda second-in-command Ayman al-Zawahiri chose to comment publicly on its significance for relations between al-Qa'eda, or at least those populations for whom al-Qa'eda purports to speak, and the United States. Al-Zawahiri claimed that the Obama election represented a victory for al-Qa'eda in that it was a rejection of Bush administration Middle East policies, in particular the invasion of Iraq.[16] In both examples, the respective organizations are using public diplomacy (see chapter 8) to increase their own popularity and legitimacy with Muslim populations from whom they seek support. In the Taliban example, the Taliban were also using a public channel to send a classic diplomatic message to the Pakistani government, indirectly, that the Taliban were willing to set aside hostilities to form a common Muslim front against majority Hindu India. Neither case can be construed as a conventional example of diplomatic representation and communication, but in both situations the organization involved needed to represent itself to outsiders and to communicate to constituents using recognizable diplomatic processes.

Case Study: CSOs, Eminent Person Diplomacy and Africa Poverty Reduction[17]

The campaign to reduce poverty in Africa in the mid-2000s, generally regarded as having achieved some measure of success, documents the interaction between a broad array of types of diplomatic actors – CSOs, eminent person diplomats, multilateral organizations and governments – that culminated in the G8 summit at Gleneagles in Scotland in July 2005. The process began in 2001, when Bono, who for several years already had been using his celebrity status to champion the cause of reducing poverty in Africa, met Condoleezza Rice, at the time US National Security Adviser, at the Genoa G8 summit. Bono, according to Andrew Cooper, is the most skilled of celebrity diplomats owing to his capacity to gain access to the highest level of diplomatic interlocutors in governments and non-governmental actors alike.[18] Bono discovered that Rice was a fan of U2, and the beginnings of a Habermasian *Lebenswelt* began to be created between two rather unlikely diplomatic interlocutors. Bono started lobbying Rice for Africa poverty reduction at that time. After getting Rice's input at Genoa, Bono's civil society organization, DATA, began to develop proposals that would link Africa poverty reduction assistance to the good governance agenda favoured by Bush administration policy makers.[19] Using what Cooper calls his 'diplomacy of voice' with consummate skill, Bono played a key rôle in convincing US President Bush in 2003 to double US official development assistance (ODA) through the Millennium Challenge Account programme and to launch a new initiative to combat AIDS.[20]

During the 2005 UK presidency of the G8, for a constellation of domestic and exogenously driven political reasons, Her Majesty's Government chose to focus their G8 presidency on eradicating poverty in Africa. Prime Minister Tony Blair and Chancellor Gordon Brown tried to outdo each other in fighting poverty in Africa in the run-up to the May 2005 UK elections. Yet poverty reduction in Africa remained less of a foreign policy priority in Washington, even after the 2002 Bono – Paul O'Neill 'Odd Couple Tour'. President Bush and Secretary of State Rice remained much more focused on more traditional 'hard' security issues such as democratizing the Middle East, fighting the 'Global War on Terror' and controlling nuclear weapons development in North Korea and Iran. Yet ending poverty in Africa and global climate change were the main agenda items selected by the British government for the Gleneagles summit in July 2005. Another eminent person diplomat committed to the Africa cause, former Boomtown Rats lead singer Sir Bob Geldof, convinced Prime Minister Tony Blair to establish a special Commission for Africa in 2004, creating a sort of policy 'bandwagon' on which it became politically important for Chancellor Gordon Brown to travel as well. The Commission report, entitled *Our Common Interest: An Argument*, was released to the public in March 2005, four months before the summit, to huge public fanfare. The report created public expectations for action at the summit by calling for a long list of concrete steps by all the major global players, public and private. Specifically, the report called for the developed countries to increase support for Africa by $50 billion a year.[21] The civil society organization established by Geldof, Make Poverty History, produced a short, pamphlet-style book published in the UK called *Make Poverty History: How You Can Help Defeat World Poverty in Seven Easy Steps*, to communicate directly to the general public about how they could participate personally in achieving the poverty reduction goals proposed for the G8 summit.[22]

Entertainment industry celebrities, in addition to producing a certain number of eminent person diplomats such as Bono and Geldof, increasingly function collectively as a global civil society network that can affect worldwide public opinion about issues with which they choose to engage. In the United States, effective public diplomacy by Hollywood celebrities on behalf of the Africa poverty reduction cause contributed to constructing public expectations for G8 action at Gleneagles. Film star Brad Pitt used an hour-long interview on a major US TV network evening chat show, *Primetime Live*, to focus attention upon the issue immediately prior to the Gleneagles summit.[23] It became clear that it would be increasingly difficult for Bush, Blair and the other G8 leaders to escape public scrutiny on the issue. In spring 2005 Geldof argued that it was still about getting President Bush on board. Geldof credited Bush for trebling aid to Africa already, albeit from a very low level, and even if he attributed the reason for the administration's concern to fears that China was competing ever more aggressively for influence in Africa. But in Geldof's view, this was not nearly enough: 'So Bush can come to it, and he can come to it because this particular prime minister [Blair] is probably the only person in the world who can talk to him at this level this well . . . I think he can ask Bush, "Do this one for me, George".'[24]

The British governmental hosts focused on transparency before and during the summit, holding close deliberations with other CSOs, who were given access to Gleneagles and the press centre.[25] Civil society groups were consulted directly on the Africa aid and debt relief plan. Sir Bob Geldof's 'Make Poverty History' campaign played a major rôle in heightening the global public's awareness of the Africa issue, as millions worldwide purchased and wore white rubber wristbands embossed with the words 'Make Poverty History'. Over 200,000 people marched in Edinburgh on 2 July 2005, just before the summit began. CSOs set up a huge encampment outside the Gleneagles security perimeter, easily accessible for full media coverage. Bono led a full court press in calling on the G8 leaders publicly to meet their aid commitments to Africa.

Notwithstanding the terrorist bombings that occurred in London on 7 July 2005, the first day that the G8 leaders were scheduled to meet at Gleneagles, the summit agenda stayed centred on its two main themes: poverty eradication in Africa and climate change. Reflecting the immediacy of the London attacks, the summit accomplishments were constructed in the G8 communiqué written by the British government in the language of an 'alternative to hatred'. There clearly were significant accomplishments. The final communiqué included the following specific goals:

- Double development aid to $48 billion by 2010;
- Write off debt initially for eighteen African countries;

- Provide 'as close as possible' to universal access to treatment for HIV/AIDS; tackle malaria, TB and polio; education; and train a further 20,000 peacekeeping troops;
- Open dialogue between the G8 and developing countries on climate change, with the first meeting in London in November 2005, but no targets for cutting carbon emissions;
- Provide $3 billion a year for the next three years for the Palestinian Authority to help build up institutions;
- Establish a credible end date for a trade agreement to eliminate export subsidies.[26]

Some aspects of the summit were considered successful by both the media and CSOs. Geldof, for example, publicly gave the aid plan for Africa a '10 out of 10' and the debt relief plan '8 out of 10'.[27] However, some other CSOs gave a less rosy assessment, and Geldof himself was accused of 'selling out' by giving the G8 leaders an overly sympathetic assessment of their accomplishments.[28] The media generally lauded the direction of the Africa package, whilst noting that time was already running out on reaching the much celebrated objectives of the Millennium Development Goals. However, the other major item on the agenda, climate change, did not receive the same positive coverage, and most of the blame for that was heaped on the Bush administration. Some claimed that the climate change portion of the communiqué was 'watered down' in order to achieve American approval.[29] Tony Blair responded to that allegation, saying, 'my fear is that if we do not bring the US into the consensus on tackling climate change, we will never ensure the huge emerging economies, particularly China and India, are part of a dialogue.'[30]

The G8 Gleneagles case illuminates a number of aspects of the emergence of CSOs and eminent persons as diplomatic actors and the changing nature of diplomatic relationships between CSOs and governments. To achieve key objectives, governments increasingly need CSOs, whilst to a large degree CSOs remain dependent upon governments. If mediation of estrangement through CSO–government diplomacy is successful, both types of actors can benefit. Governments can profit from using CSOs to help to build support for important foreign policy initiatives. CSOs need governments to obtain access for their staff and their agenda items to many multilateral organizations that still do not accredit fully the diplomats of CSOs, such as the World Trade Organization and the United Nations. A further emergence of an estrangement requiring mediation has ensued since the 1980s. Many governments have chosen to privatize some of their functions into quasi-non-governmental organizations, best known by their Commonwealth acronym 'quangos'. A quango performs functions formerly carried out by governments, but with powers devolved into autonomous management structures. Whilst many quangos are regulatory in nature, others provide public services, such as transport. Some quangos, such as the still publicly owned German passenger railway Deutsche Bahn, are sufficiently large as to operate extensively across national borders, raising the question of how these new hybrid diplomatic actors that blur the boundaries between governments, CSOs and firms must conduct diplomacy with those other types of actors, of which quangos themselves are a hybrid.

Civil society organizations, eminent person diplomats and even transnational criminal organizations are playing an increasingly significant rôle in the complex new networks of diplomatic relationships between governments and non-governmental actors. CSOs (and TCOs) in recent decades have come to play a pivotal rôle in representing interests of individuals and groups on the global stage in ways that governments are unable, or do not choose, to do. Eminent persons, if skilled and if accorded access and credibility, can facilitate communication between governments, multilateral organizations, firms and CSOs, which in turn can help to meet global policy challenges more effectively. As with firms, the challenge for CSOs is to develop the structures and skills needed to represent themselves publicly and to communicate and negotiate effectively with their counterparts in governments, multilateral organizations and global firms. The diplomatic successes of CSOs like the ICRC and MSF have demonstrated the gains to be achieved through more effective diplomacy. Yet some CSOs, and the members or constituents whose interests they represent, remain at least somewhat ambivalent about whether diplomatic engagement as a strategy is compatible with all of their other values and interests. Hence the prospects for CSOs as effective diplomatic actors are likely to be less uniformly promising than those of global firms, and the resulting social gains more uneven.

SECTION TWO

PROCESSES AND FUNCTIONS

7

Technological Change and Diplomatic Process

Introduction: Diplomatic Processes and Functions

In this second section of the book, the focus shifts from diplomatic actors and venues for diplomacy to a more in-depth examination of the diplomatic processes and functions in which the actors engage. As such, the chapters that follow will focus extensively on the core diplomatic activities of representation and communication. Towards what objectives are representation and communication directed? This section highlights how these core functions are directed towards the effective management of diplomatic relationships. As diplomacy is by its nature a relational concept, effective diplomacy at its heart is about strong relationship management. Diplomatic relationships can exist between any two or more actors. Such relationships also exist between a government or firm and a public constituency, as public diplomacy reveals (see chapter 8). Diplomatic processes and functions that manage a relationship successfully minimize the likelihood that crises will occur. Negotiating and signing of agreements and treaties, for example, is only the first step towards resolving a dispute or preventing a dispute from becoming a crisis. Creating effective diplomatic mechanisms for enforcement and monitoring of compliance with agreements is crucial to ensuring their successful implementation.

This chapter frames the broad discussion by highlighting the ways in which technological change over recent decades has affected how diplomatic processes and functions are carried out. The following chapter addresses the most significant effect of technological change upon diplomatic processes: the flowering of public diplomacy. The chapter examines in detail how public diplomacy has been changed by the revolution in information and communications technologies (ICTs) and how that revolution has changed the rôle of media in diplomatic communication. Three subsequent chapters address the management of substantive issue areas in which diplomacy takes place every day: economic, military and security, and cultural diplomacy. These chapters examine contemporary issues and problems across each of these issue areas and evaluate how the techniques of diplomacy used to deal with them have evolved. The concluding chapter reflects upon trends in diplomacy in light of the findings of the book and considers prospects for diplomacy going forward, exploring different theoretical approaches that have been applied to understanding diplomacy.

Assessing the Impact of Technology Upon Diplomacy

Technology has the broadest and most far-reaching effects upon how diplomacy is done and even what it is, extending from the structural and abstract level right down to the practical level of everyday diplomatic practice. As noted previously, technology determines how communication can take place and, critically, at what speed. At a broad level communications and transport technology has driven globalization, which in turn has permitted new types of actors to become diplomats in an arena that once was dominated by nation–states: multilateral institutions, global firms and CSOs, in particular. Technology has accelerated the speed at which diplomatic processes and functions can be carried out. In two centuries, technology has developed from an age in which communication between governments could only take place at the speed at which a horse or camel could travel between the two capitals to a time of instantaneous telephonic and internet communication, of every diplomat holding a handheld mobile communication device. The oft-employed Cold War metaphor for this acceleration was the twenty-minute distance between the Soviet and American ICBM launchers and their respective targets. Following the 1961 Cuban Missile Crisis, US President John F. Kennedy and Soviet Communist Party General Secretary Nikita Khruschchev agreed to install the infamous 'hot line' between the White House and the Kremlin to provide for instant communication to be used in emergencies as a means of avoiding the sort of nuclear Armageddon that could result from a misunderstanding or a miscommunication. At the most superficial level, as technology speeds up communications, the assumption is that diplomats become obliged to respond ever more rapidly. Shortening the amount of time available to formulate considered and measured responses to communications should increase the risk of ill-chosen or immoderate responses. Diplomatic decisions could, paradoxically, end up being taken based on less information rather than more, as less time becomes available to do background research. As Iver Neumann found in his research on the Norwegian foreign ministry, procedures govern the writing and approval of official foreign ministry communications to the outside world expressly to prevent decisions from being taken and policies being articulated too rapidly and without the full backing of foreign ministry personnel.[1]

Another fundamental question that the ubiquity of transport and communications technology raises for diplomacy concerns the extent of the ongoing need for diplomatic representation at all. Transport and communications technology makes it practical today for much diplomatic work of communication and negotiation that is done by delegated representatives to be conducted directly between the principals involved in each relevant issue. The agriculture ministers of Norway and Canada, for example, could agree terms of a bilateral agreement by telephone, by video-conference or at a face-to-face meeting after a flight by one of them lasting at most a dozen hours. To a certain extent these practices have become more common. Why then retain resident ambassadors and foreign missions at all? Some argue that more direct, less delegated diplomacy is more efficient and effective, because it reduces the scope for mis-understandings to emerge as leaders and ministers communicate to their diplomatic representatives, who in turn communicate to their counter-parts, who then communicate to their own leaders in a variant of the traditional children's game of 'telephone'. In recent times, diplomatic 'summit' meetings between heads of government or between government heads and leaders of non-state actors have become more common. Summits at which substantive negotiation takes place have displaced more tradi-tional 'state visits' – ceremonial meetings between heads of state – to some degree.[2]

Yet direct communication and negotiation between principals such as occur at summit meetings, in the absence of the detailed preparation and pre-negotiations done by their respective representatives, can be fraught with peril and uncertainty. Such meetings can lead to embarrassment for one or both parties and an overall negative outcome. The best example of such a situation narrowly averted was the 1986 Reykjavik summit between US President Ronald Reagan and Soviet President Mikhail Gorbachev, in which, as the two presidents discussed nuclear arms reduction, Gorbachev dramatically proposed to Reagan that the two countries agree to eliminate their entire nuclear arsenals. Reagan, struck by the idea, was tempted to agree in the magic of the moment, at least until his advisers reminded him that to do so would leave the Soviet Union with a major advantage over the NATO allies in conventional forces and weaponry in Europe. Often those diplomats who are best positioned to add value to key preparatory work and pre-negotiations are precisely those who are (or have been in the past) stationed in a foreign mission. Technology notwithstanding, these officials are likely to have a greater knowledge of the politics and culture of both the home country and the country in which they are stationed. They may also have had the opportunity to develop personal networks of official and unofficial communication that can prove vital on occasions when sensitive and difficult issues need to be negotiated.

As the next chapter discusses in greater depth, this development and spread of communications technology has increased the importance of public diplomacy. Radio, television, the internet and rapid, inexpensive travel have permitted progressively greater disintermediation of the relationships between individuals who belong to different estranged nation–states or other diplomatic actors. In earlier centuries, the principal way that individuals in one country learned about another country or place, its government and its inhabitants was through reading books or print media (newspapers and magazines) or by meeting migrants. Today individuals can and do learn about and follow developments in other countries in real time through electronic media. They travel to other countries for purposes of business and tourism and interact with visitors from abroad in their home countries in numbers never before imagined. This increase in the quantity and contemporaneity of interactions between peoples across borders has had the paradoxical effect of making others both more familiar and at the same time more strange. For example, if the publics in the United Kingdom and the United States become aware through the media that there is an ongoing debate in Turkey over whether the Turkish government should permit women to wear traditional Islamic *hejabs* (headscarves) in public places or not, it may increase British and American understanding of contemporary Turkish social, economic and political issues, whilst simultaneously making Turkey and its people seem more different from Britain and the United States than might have been the case previously. This heightening of estrangement occasioned by greater familiarity between peoples can make diplomacy between governments, and between governments and peoples, more challenging and more complex.

The evolution of telecommunications technology has increased the power and reach of media organizations. As multimedia information providers like the BBC and CNN have used this expanded power and reach to democratize and legitimate mediations, the views of the public on relationships and issues requiring mediation have become much more important. Governments, multilateral organizations, global firms and CSOs all have to conduct more public diplomacy than ever, and the way that each type of diplomatic actor does it is becoming more and more similar, as is explored further in chapter 8. But, equally importantly, despite the increase in the importance of public diplomacy, the rôle of traditional non-public channels of diplomatic communication has not diminished. Most diplomatic communication, both between governments and within governments, is conducted privately, and, when necessary, using 'secure' communications channels (see below). If anything, these non-public lines of communication are more important than ever, as leaders more frequently now need to communicate with one another to correct (and, if necessary, resolve) misunderstandings created by statements made in the public domain and disseminated widely through the media. The difficulty today lies in the fact that non-public diplomacy, however routine, increasingly tends to attract public criticism. Whilst many people understand that non-public diplomatic communication is necessary, the public is generally less tolerant of it than before, to a considerable degree because they know more about it. People increasingly tend to associate routine and necessary non-public diplomatic communication with secret diplomacy, which they in turn tend to think of in the context of dictators and bad consequences. The 1940 Molotov–Ribbentrop Pact, for example, was one of the most notorious outcomes of secret diplomacy between Hitler's and Stalin's governments, as it facilitated Hitler's invasion of Poland and the division of Polish territory between Nazi Germany and Soviet Russia. Hence, in democratic nations in the current era one of the standard critiques of the foreign policy of incumbent governments made by challengers is that the government is doing a poor job at diplomacy. This refrain is often coupled with a criticism of diplomatic negotiation conducted in secret and a call for greater transparency, which fuels public expectations of greater conduct of diplomacy in public, which may be entirely at cross purposes with the same public's demand for more effective diplomacy.

At a more routine level, technology has changed how and where the ordinary day-to-day business of diplomacy is done. Diplomatic personnel ranking from the foreign minister right down to junior clerks and security guards are linked in real time by email, instant messaging, mobile telephony and handheld data communication devices. Files and databases that once were confined to physical offices, either in foreign ministry headquarters or in particular overseas missions, are now accessible electronically by diplomatic staff around the globe. Foreign ministry staffs are also now linked electronically to personnel of other ministries and agencies engaging in diplomacy, such as trade, agriculture and commerce ministries, central banks and ministries of defence. This electronic linking up of the staffs of foreign ministries and other government ministries engaged in diplomacy and the merging of their files and databases in cyberspace means that the practices of diplomatic representation and communication can now be done in different ways and in different places from the traditional foreign ministry–embassy configuration. At a practical level, it means that meetings can be conducted by conference call or video link with participants in several locations, often on several continents. When these meetings take the place of meetings that would otherwise have needed to take place in person, they reduce the time and cost of travel needed to get business done. In some cases these remote encounters sacrifice the opportunity for all the different levels and interfaces that face-to-face communications entail. Yet teleconferencing permits meetings to take place that previously might not have taken place at all, which can improve channels of communication and mediation of differences.

Another effect is more organizational and bureaucratic in nature. As Kurbalija argues, the advent of instant communications technology means that the work of diplomacy no longer needs to be organized geographically in the way that it once did, which has paved the way for functional organization of diplomatic work to emerge alongside geographical organization.[3] Teams dedicated to particular functions, such as cooperation in combating international organized crime or containing the spread of infectious diseases, can be organized within the foreign ministry and between the foreign ministry and other agencies without needing to be based in the capital city or another single location. Staff no longer need to have a line manager in the same location where they work. This phenomenon does not presage the disappearance of geographically organized functions, in particular many country-specific tasks, but it allows for greater efficiency and effectiveness by permitting work that naturally lends itself to functional organization to be done thus. It further facilitates opportunities for staff to work both geographically and functionally at the same time. An economic counsellor at a foreign mission can work closely with fellow economic counsellors in other missions electronically on broad policy implementation issues whilst at the same time working with political and consular staff in the same mission on issues specific to the country to which they are assigned. This sort of re-drawing of organizational charts of diplomatic personnel across geographical and agency boundaries also heightens the importance of the foreign ministry's ability to perform the boundary spanner rôle of coordinating diplomatic work in given locations without needing to act in the gatekeeper rôle of controlling the diplomatic work of other agencies (see chapter 3).

Technology, Diplomatic Communication and Security

The transformation of information technology has also transformed the rôle and importance of information security for diplomacy and for diplomats. Foreign ministries and other government agencies have long had communications security protocols in effect to ensure that communications between foreign ministries and missions abroad are not intercepted or monitored by other governments or private listeners. These protocols began with the diplomatic 'pouch', a regular (in the case of large missions, daily) mailbag hand-carried between the foreign ministry and the mission, and in the twentieth century extended to the operation of secure, or encrypted, communications links between national capitals and overseas missions: telegraph and telex lines initially, followed by telephonic connectivity. However, the development of mobile telephony, the internet and broadband communications hardware, videoconferencing, and placing of files and databases online have raised the challenge of providing security against unwanted listeners to an entirely new level. Foreign ministries and other agencies engaged in diplomacy increasingly rely upon government communications satellites to transmit the huge quantity of bytes of text, voice, video and other data that now travel between locations around the world every minute of every day. The satellites in turn depend upon a network of transmission and reception facilities ranging from large base stations in the home country to smaller 'dishes' and other receiving equipment often placed on rooftops of embassies, consulates and other structures in overseas missions. This creates the challenge of protecting both the hardware and the software needed to keep the communications infrastructure functional.

Threats to the privacy of electronic diplomatic communication occur primarily at two levels. The first level is that of hacking. Some individuals and groups attempt to crack the encryption codes that protect diplomatic communications, sometimes in an effort to learn what is being said for very personal, individual reasons, in other cases as part of political agendas that can involve political opposition to the targeted state. Other individuals hack simply because they relish the challenge of cracking the code and gaining access to information from which others have sought to keep them. Others yet hack to inflict damage on secure communications systems because they resent the power of technology to create a barrier of privacy from the public domain. Whatever its motivation, hacking holds the potential to cause anything from mild disruption of routine diplomatic business to a more catastrophic breach of security during a period of sensitive negotiations.

The second and more serious level of threat to privacy of electronic diplomatic communication is electronic espionage or surveillance, which is most often conducted by the very governments from which another government wishes to keep its communications private. Global firms are also major parties to espionage. Some firms seek to learn commercial secrets of their rivals. In other cases, governments seek to learn confidential business plans of firms that can affect job creation and tax revenues. This type of spying, which has gone on ever since electronic communication was invented early in the twentieth century, is conducted often using the most sophisticated hardware available. The technological 'arms race' between encryption and shielding technologies and electronic surveillance technologies is not likely to abate in the foreseeable future. Electronic surveillance of diplomats that relies upon much simpler technologies, such as 'bugs' or listening devices placed in the homes, offices and cars of diplomats, is still often effective, as so many James Bond films dramatized vividly in both their Cold War and post-Cold War instantiations. Physical location continues to play an important part in government-conducted surveillance, as line-of-sight access to surveillance targets, such as foreign ministry buildings, continues to confer substantial advantage. It is no wonder that the Soviet government were so keen to acquire the site of the former Veterans Administration hospital on Mount Saint Alban in Washington, DC. The Soviet embassy that was constructed on the site, now the embassy of the Russian Federation, has line-of-sight access to most of the significant government buildings in the city of Washington, as well as the Pentagon and other sites across the Potomac in neighbouring northern Virginia.[4]

At yet another level, the increased dependence of diplomats and foreign ministries upon high-technology communications infrastructure has created a level of vulnerability that makes government communications infrastructure a potential target in the event of war, revolution, insurrection or other armed conflict. During the Cold War, this danger first became known to the general public in the form of the possibility that an electromagnetic pulse (EMP) resulting from the detonation of weapons in a nuclear exchange could disrupt or destroy military and civilian electronic communications networks. However, it does not require nuclear weapons to disable the ability of one's enemy to communicate, whether those communications be military or diplomatic. Nor does it require sophisticated technology. One of the primary tools of information warfare, as it has become known, is the very low-technology so-called 'denial of service attack' on the internet, in which the internet is flooded with data of sufficient quantity at the same time that other necessary communications cannot get through. The US missile strike destroying one of its own disabled espionage satellites in decaying orbit in early 2008 by means of an inert ('dumb') projectile that caused it to explode illustrated that a similarly low-technology approach could be effective against an opponent's communications satellites during wartime. If diplomacy remains one of the prime means to avoid war between states, safeguarding the communications infrastructure for diplomacy of necessity has become a primary objective, not only for foreign ministries but for governments as a whole in the contemporary period. Practically speaking, this has required a steadily increasing cooperation between foreign ministries and defence ministries, as defence ministries and military establishments face essentially the same security threats to their communications as those faced by diplomats and foreign ministries. Different means of protecting defence and diplomatic communications infrastructure exist, of which providing redundancy of hardware and software is amongst the most important, so that if one satellite or network is knocked out, another can take its place.

Technology, Language and Translation

The advance of technology has had significant cross-cutting effects upon the problem of how diplomats overcome the specific problem of how to communicate and understand one another across different languages. Historically the difficulty was avoided by having an official language for diplomacy, a language that the educated, trained aristocracy from which diplomats generally were selected could understand and use to communicate, irrespective of what tongue they spoke at home. For many centuries during and following the decline of the Roman Empire, in Western societies this language was Latin. The use of Latin for 'universal' communication has persisted to this day within the global community of the Roman Catholic Church. By the time that the Westphalia system of nation–states had emerged in the seventeenth century and generated the norms of classical nation–state diplomacy, the diplomatic *lingua franca* (and the language of most European court society, from which diplomats were chosen) had become French. In the twentieth century, from the League of Nations onwards, French had to share its linguistic hegemony in diplomacy with English, as it became the norm for official texts of multilateral treaties and other diplomatic documents to be rendered in both French and English, with equal authority ascribed to each. The United Nations designated six official languages, creating the obligation for translation of official texts into each. But the twentieth century witnessed not only an expansion of official languages for multilateral diplomacy, but also a significant increase in the use of translation of bilateral treaties and other diplomatic texts into the languages of the nation–states that were parties to them.

Since the Second World War, technology has facilitated the expansion of the norm of translation beyond texts into meetings of multilateral organizations such as the United Nations. Interpretation, or simultaneous translation, performed by a staff of trained experts, enabled representatives to bodies such as the UN and NATO to participate in plenary sessions, negotiations and other diplomatic processes whether or not they understood the speaker's language or even one of the official languages of the organization. This had the effect of broadening the range of potential participants from each country well beyond the old educated elites from which classical diplomats traditionally had been selected.

Technological advances in translation and interpretation between languages for diplomats have, on the one hand, facilitated communications that used to be much more cumbersome and problematic, but in turn they have opened the way for a democratization of linguistic communications that brings both new advantages and problems. We see in the European Union the most detailed and extreme example of this phenomenon. With twenty-three official languages now in the EU and more likely to come, interpretation and meaning has become problematic as never before. The EU provides simultaneous translation of oral communication in meetings of the European Commission, European Parliament and European Council, and all major texts have to be translated into all of the official languages. This requirement has created particular challenges that did not exist when the EU was comprised of a small group of countries that spoke major European languages. Today there is a shortage of professionals who can translate and interpret directly between all of the less commonly spoken tongues of the European Union. Some less common language pairings, e.g. Maltese to Latvian, now routinely have to be translated via one of the major languages, like English, French or German. Hence the possibility for slippage in meaning is magnified. Likewise, when diplomats from 'small language' countries have to use their second or third languages to carry on routine communication, they can be disadvantaged in power terms relative to their colleagues who can do most of their communicating in their native tongue. English in a sense can be seen to have become the 'court language' of contemporary diplomacy and of techno-diplomacy, using Der Derian's terminology, just as Latin was the language of proto-diplomacy and French the language of classical diplomacy and neo-diplomacy. But it is important to recognize that it gives native English speakers extra power advantages in diplomatic interaction.

Ultimately language is a tool that permits two diplomatic interlocutors to come to know one another, to communicate and, ideally, to mediate a difference or reach agreement on an issue or problem. In many cases, but by no means always, they find that communication is easier when they share a language (even imperfectly) and do not require interpreters. Some senior officials choose to use interpreters even when they understand the language spoken by their diplomatic counterpart, so as to afford them additional time to reflect on the meaning and intent of what their counterpart says during a meeting or negotiation. Language by its nature contains ambiguity, even when all the speakers are using the same tongue. Experienced diplomats, in order to be effective, must develop a political sense of when a negotiated agreement should preserve ambiguity of interpretation, allowing different signatories to understand its meaning differently, and when the objective of an agreement is precisely to eliminate such ambiguity. For over 150 years, for example, there has been political and scholarly debate over the differences between the English and Maori translations of the 1838 Treaty of Waitangi between the United Kingdom and the Maori Confederation. However, the dynamic of that very debate has served as a foundation for a social and political dialogue between *pākehā* (European settlers) and Maori in recent decades, geared towards constructing a bicultural identity for contemporary New Zealand.[5] Advances in communications and translation technology have the capacity to facilitate translation when it is required, but ultimately they can have little impact upon the essentially political challenges for diplomats of understanding and making oneself understood, and of managing the ambiguity and precision of meanings.

Technology, understood in its broadest sense, is probably the single greatest factor conditioning the evolution of the core diplomatic functions and processes of representation and communication. Technologies of travel and communication have affected how diplomatic representation is undertaken and how communication takes place. Technology has accelerated the speed of diplomatic communication dramatically, for better and for worse, and has complicated the security of diplomatic communication. New technologies, whilst facilitating translation between unfamiliar languages in diplomatic communication, are not able to address the deeper

UNIVERSITY OF WINCHESTER
LIBRARY

difficulty that diplomats face in communicating in such a way as to make themselves understood. The challenge for diplomats in undertaking representation and in communicating is to manage technological change and utilize technology effectively without allowing technology to dictate the form, substance and results of diplomatic interactions. Whether to communicate, who is to do it, to whom to speak, through what channel or means, how often, and whether and how fast to respond remain basic questions that a diplomatic actor must decide based on what is likely to yield the best result. In the era of email, videoconferencing and electronic surveillance, the gap between diplomatic actors who can subordinate technology whilst employing it skilfully and those who cannot is likely to grow, and their respective diplomatic accomplishments to diverge accordingly.

8

Public Diplomacy

Introduction: The Rise of a Not So New Tool of Diplomatic Communication[1]

One of the most significant effects of the transformation in information technologies that has taken place in the decades since the Second World War has been an increase in the need for public diplomacy. At its broadest, public diplomacy refers to communication that governments and other diplomatic actors make to the general public. Public diplomacy has been employed to generate support for a government's foreign policies, the objectives and operations of a multilateral organization, and even the policies of global firms. Contrary to some contemporary popular perceptions, public diplomacy itself is not a new development in diplomatic practice. According to 1930s historian C. K. Webster, late nineteenth-century German Chancellor Otto von Bismarck responded to the rise in the importance of public opinion, which resulted in an increased focus by the print media on foreign affairs, by manipulating German and foreign media organizations 'to disseminate hopes and fears among the people of Europe'. Webster specifically describes as public diplomacy US President Woodrow Wilson's efforts to 'sell' his plans for a post-World War I international settlement to the US domestic public on his stump speeches.[2] The characterization of public diplomacy as we tend to think of it today is generally credited to professional diplomat and later Dean of Tufts University's Fletcher School of Law and Diplomacy Edmund Gullion, who described public diplomacy in 1965 as dealing with the influence of public attitudes on the formation and execution of foreign policies. Gullion regarded cultivation by governments of public opinion in other countries as increasingly important, as communication between diplomats and journalists became necessary due to the growing link between the reporting of foreign affairs in the media and the resulting impact on the making of foreign policy.[3] Another professional diplomat-turned-scholar, Kishan Rana, argues in *The 21st Century Ambassador* that public diplomacy has become a 'lobbying' and 'networking' practice.⁴ Joseph Nye has described foreign policy behaviour of governments that is intended to 'win hearts and minds' as 'soft power'.⁵ Jan Melissen describes soft power as 'the post-modern variant of power over opinion'. Political communication in general, and public diplomacy in particular, are key instruments of soft power.⁶ Governments today are cognizant of the need to reckon con-sciously with the necessity of engaging in public diplomacy, and to be seen to be doing so by their own citizenry and the global public.

But if, for Bismarck in the nineteenth century, public diplomacy was an instrument for manipulating the media to communicate to publics in a mono-directional way about Germany's foreign policy, successful public diplomacy today increasingly is viewed more broadly as a bi-directional process of inter-cultural communication. As media channels have prolifer-ated and become progressively more disintermediated, governments and other diplomatic actors have come to perceive the importance of com-municating to and listening to foreign publics as they form, implement and adjust their foreign policies. Today's media have not only given govern-ments, firms and civil society organizations an unprecedented multiplicity of channels through which to communicate to global publics. Contemporary media have also given global publics the ability to talk back: to respond directly or indirectly to diplomatic actors about the policies with which they may agree or not. The recent growth of public diplomacy is a testa-ment to the tightening of this feedback loop, through which governments can take account of how their policies are being received by targeted audi-ences and make adjustments accordingly.⁷

Public Diplomacy or Propaganda?

Public diplomacy, when viewed as a mono-directional communication of information, has been linked in the minds of some observers with propa-ganda. In the twentieth century propaganda was associated with the dis-tribution of false information by governments about their states and societies. The word 'propaganda' stems from the Latin word *propagare*⁸ ('to propagate'), meaning to foster growing knowledge of, familiarity with, or acceptance of (as in an idea or belief).⁹ Pope Gregory XV coined the word propaganda in 1622 in response to Catholic fears about the spread of Protestantism, establishing the Office for the Propagation of the Faith (Congregatio de propaganda fide) to supervise the Church's missionary efforts in the New World.[10] First World War allies Great Britain and the United States gave the term a more pejorative cast by defining the communications and persuasion tactics of their enemies as propaganda. In the meantime they themselves were producing propaganda of their own in order to conjure up public support for the war efforts against the 'barbarian' Hun.[11] Gradually, as the evidence of Allied propaganda was exposed to the American and British publics, they became outraged by the half-truths, exaggerations and outright lies that were told to them by their own governments.[12]

Today, public opinion tends to regard propaganda as a deceitful and dangerous practice, even though a more descriptive definition of propaganda might be more neutral.[13] Propaganda analysis pioneer Jacques Ellul defines propaganda as 'communication employed by an organized group that wants to bring about the active or passive participation in its actions of a mass of individuals, psychologically unified through psychological manipulation and incorporated in an organization'.[14] Randal Marlin calls propaganda 'the organized attempt through communication to affect belief or action or inculcate attitudes in a large audience in ways that circumvent or surpass an individual's adequately informed, rational, reflective judgment'.[15] Karen Johnson-Cartee and Gary Copeland contend that effective propaganda requires taking into account the predispositions of the audience: 'Propaganda is not brainwashing – or the introduction of new ideas, attitudes, and beliefs – contrary to the individuals' cognitive structure. Rather, propaganda is a resonance strategy, the discovery of culturally shared beliefs and the deliberate reinforcement and ultimately aggrandizement of those beliefs.'[16] Ultimately, public diplomacy and propaganda have many of the same goals, the most important of which is to 'influence public attitudes' or to 'influence people's opinions'. Traditional scholars of diplomacy have tried to demarcate propaganda normatively and thereby discourage its use in the practice of public diplomacy. But although propaganda may have a negative connotation, its use may prove to be effective in reaching specific goals under particular limited conditions. In analysing and measuring the effectiveness of contemporary public diplomacy, the feedback loop emerges as crucial. Hence a key factor in distinguishing effective public diplomacy campaigns from those that are not is trust. Those governments that are perceived by publics, domestic or foreign, as regularly engaging in deceptive public diplomacy, whether labelled as propaganda or not, come to find that they are not trusted. This in turn limits their ability to engage in effective public diplomacy in future.

Techniques of Public Diplomacy

One of the most common, and most successful, approaches intended to project a positive image of a country abroad is the sharing of its culture through cultural diplomacy: arts, educational and sporting exchanges, as discussed below (see chapter 11). Beyond what can broadly be considered as cultural diplomacy, many of the specific techniques that can prove effective in conducting public diplomacy are the same techniques that are favoured by public relations practitioners. Making the best use of the media – print, audiovisual and electronic – is at the core of most public diplomacy strategies. Advertising and sponsorship of media programming and events have the advantage of being able to be targeted specifically to the desired audience, whilst running a greater likelihood of viewers perceiving the promotional objective directly. This approach can be effective, provided that the state that is advertising or sponsoring does not have a significantly negative impression in the minds of viewers at the start of the campaign. Publicity is a strategy of making use of media to cover events that feature the country in a positive light. Publicity has the advantage of appearing more spontaneous and less scripted, allowing the viewer to make his or her own positive associations between the story told and the country concerned, but the audience reached may not be able to be targeted as effectively as through advertising and sponsorship.

Whereas advertising, sponsorship and publicity tend to be largely mono-directional communicative strategies, a media relations strategy moves more towards bi-directional communication. Media relations involves meeting and communicating with journalists, editors, producers, radio and television chat show hosts, bloggers and other personalities. Diplomats provide background information on the country and related issues on an as-needed basis to help journalists to produce accurate stories and to assist them as they plan stories, features and coverage in a broad sense. Diplomats may suggest ideas for media coverage that might end up producing advantageous results. For example, one of the first things that former advertising executive Charlotte Beers did after being appointed US Undersecretary of State for Public Diplomacy and Public Affairs in autumn 2001 was to engage Christopher Ross, a former US ambassador and fluent Arabic speaker, to be available to Arabic-language television network al-Jazeera to rebut anti-US broadcasts by al-Qa'eda.[17]

The media relations component of public diplomacy is challenging for a number of reasons. For example, when working with media it is not enough simply to have a well-written pitch. Diplomats must know the publication to which they are reaching out, be aware of the types of stories that the publication covers, understand the topics that interest the editor or journalist and be able to explain why the information or messages the diplomat wants included are valuable to the readership.[18] Particularly important, however, is to be media-savvy enough to grab the editor or journalist's attention and capture their interest. What may facilitate this ability more than anything is the capacity to listen to, take on board and respond sensitively to what the media figures are saying. Often media in target countries will understand their own countries and what people on the ground are thinking better than anyone else, even if they do have their own interests. Hence media relationships can prove crucial in feedback loops for implementing, testing and validating foreign policy. If media figures, like other interlocutors, are able to perceive that their input forms part of an effective policy feedback loop, their ongoing willingness to engage in a productive relationship is likely to be much higher.

Other strategies are likely to succeed or fail similarly to the extent to which they are conducted in a dialogic manner. Hosting and participating in public events in target countries is a vital way both to communicate and to listen. Conferences, symposia, panel discussions, roundtables and academic seminars are all venues not just for disseminating, but for exchanging and developing, ideas. Events with a wide range of participants, including political, business and other civil society figures, will often produce the greatest effects.[19] The sending abroad of 'goodwill ambassadors' selected from amongst prominent achievers in sport and the arts can also be an effective tool for communicating and listening. Nation–state governments and multilateral organizations alike make use of this strategy. The US State Department appointed figure skating champion Michelle Kwan in 2006 and baseball star Cal Ripken, Jr, in 2007 to serve as 'Public Diplomacy Envoys' and promote better relations and perceptions of the United States through sporting cooperation. Kwan toured China and Russia, meeting with youth in both countries, and Ripken was engaged in a baseball training exchange with China in 2007 in which he trained Chinese coaches at his Aberdeen, Maryland training academy and later went to China to participate in training young players directly. At the August 2007 announcement of Ripken's appointment, Secretary of State Condoleezza Rice said,

> Public diplomacy cannot be an American monologue; it must
> be a dialog [*sic*] with people from around the world. That dialog
> [*sic*] must be sought out and conducted, not only by people like

us in government, but by committed Americans from all walks
of life, Americans like Cal Ripken, Jr. He truly exemplifies
America at its best, our aspirations to be a better nation and to
help build a better world.[20]

Multilateral organizations have also found this public diplomacy technique
effective. UNICEF appointed tennis champion Roger Federer to be a goodwill ambassador after he had mobilized the sport to raise funds for the relief
of children harmed by the Boxing Day 2004 Indian Ocean tsunami.
Similarly, the Council of Europe appointed former model and actress
Bianca Jagger to be their goodwill ambassador for their campaign against
the death penalty in 2003.

Public Diplomacy and Public Relations: Convergence of Public and Private

Within the governments of the United States and the United Kingdom, the
challenge of prosecuting the war in Iraq over several years without broad
public support led many policy makers to draw the conclusion that older
approaches to public diplomacy were not working. This of course begged
the question of whether the problems were the result of how governments
were attempting to do public diplomacy, the content of the policies they
were attempting to 'sell' to global publics, or both. Governments' perceptions that their public diplomacy strategies were not succeeding have
resulted in their turning increasingly to the private sector for support and
assistance. This in turn has resulted in a convergence between the practices
of public relations and public diplomacy. Traditionally, public relations and
public affairs are said to differ from public diplomacy in that public affairs
involves governments communicating with their own domestic publics
and public relations involves communications between private actors
(firms, civil society organizations, etc.) and their audiences and constituencies. In practice, today these boundaries are considered increasingly blurry,
as often the same individuals may be communicating to more than one
audience using the same techniques, skills and messages. Kathy Fitzpatrick
argues that effective public diplomacy, as in public relations, must have at
its core the building and managing of relationships. This again ties back to
the idea of public diplomacy as a bi-directional communication.[21] In public
relations campaigns and public diplomacy campaigns today, there is little
difference in process. Both require research on the prospective message,
organization of the strategies and tactics that will best achieve expected

goals, and the creation of a measurement structure to analyse the success of a campaign's strategies and tactics. As Pierre Pahlavi observes, one of the greatest challenges faced by diplomats engaging in public diplomacy is how to develop reliable and consistent mechanisms for evaluating the effectiveness of public diplomacy strategies.[22]

The increasing competitiveness and density of the global media environment and the correspondingly greater access of global publics to streams of information serves as another reason why governments perceive it as progressively more difficult to undertake public diplomacy successfully on their own, using only their own diplomatic personnel.[23] In 1999 the United States folded its US Information Agency (USIA) – since 1953 a freestanding agency for public diplomacy – into the Department of State, ostensibly on grounds of improving operational efficiency and coordination of message, but in practice as a result of a political negotiation between Secretary of State Madeleine Albright and Senate Foreign Relations Committee Chairman Jesse Helms (Republican – North Carolina).[24] The shift was generally viewed by outsiders as driven by a need to cut budgets and a perception that at least some of USIA's work might be achieved more effectively by non-government personnel. Governments of small and poor states already often face a lack of budget, personnel and skills to undertake successful public diplomacy campaigns in-house within their foreign ministries. But governments of large and wealthy states may suffer from the very weight that their exercise of power has upon the credibility of the stories that they seek to tell the world about themselves. The media-saturated cynicism of populations of industrialized countries accentuates the problem of trust. As Nye observes, 'postmodern publics are generally skeptical of authority, and governments are often mistrusted. Thus it often behoves governments to keep in the background and to work with private actors.'[25] Peter Van Ham argues that 'marketing experience teaches that it is more important to *show*, than to *tell*' (italics original).[26] Government practitioners of public diplomacy have come to see benefit not only in the methods and techniques of public relations but also in the process of working directly with external public relations and political communications professionals in the client–consultant relationship. One of the key elements in that relationship is the ability of the consultant to view the client's problem, or objective, with 'fresh eyes' and 'fresh brains', and, in working with the client to develop a project proposal agreeable to the client, to help the client to see their own problems differently and modify their objectives accordingly. Private firms are also experienced at developing and employing much-needed metrics for evaluation of the success of their work, which they need to present to clients as they attempt to seek follow-on business.

Hence private actors have taken on an increasingly significant rôle in public diplomacy in recent times, both by providing human resources to foreign ministries and by doing the actual public relations work that governments are no longer choosing to do 'in-house'. Not only are private individuals and firms increasingly engaging in public diplomacy on behalf of governments on a contract basis, but public–private partnerships engaging in national brand-building are becoming more common as well. Government contracting of private firms to provide public diplomacy takes a variety of forms. Training or capacity building of government diplomats is probably the most common type of contracting. For example, one week before 11 September 2001, US Undersecretary of State for Public Diplomacy Charlotte Beers brought in a former Madison Avenue colleague of hers, Ogilvy & Mather branding expert Steve Hayden, to lecture to State Department staff on how firms and countries can escape their reputations for dominance. Telling his audience of diplomats that consumers prefer leadership to dominance, Hayden advised the diplomats to adopt a public relations strategy similar to that followed by Nike in the early 1990s, after public perceptions of Nike's market dominance and unfair labour practices in developing countries caused them to lose market share. Hayden advised the State Department to undertake an emotional campaign, enlisting the support of intellectuals, writers and thought leaders to make the US case to the global public – in effect, to enlist others to make a case for the United States that the US government would be less effective at doing itself.[27] In 2002, Washington, DC public relations firm Qorvis received $14.6 million from the Embassy of Saudi Arabia to engage in public diplomacy for a six-month period intended to increase perceptions amongst the US public that Saudi Arabia was committed to supporting the 'War on Terror' and Middle East peace in general. According to the *New York Sun*, the $14.6 million payment was the largest ever received by a US firm to represent a foreign government in a given reporting period.[28] Qorvis, according to the *Washington Post*, lobbied Congressional staffers, Bush administration officials and US journalists on general Middle East issues and specifically on a political communication strategy for the Saudi Crown Prince's meeting with President Bush.[29]

Another strategy for conducting public diplomacy that has proven increasingly effective is the public–private partnership. Governments are forming partnerships with business and other civil society actors to promote themselves and their exports of goods and services as national 'brands' and, through developing a positive marketing identity, to promote inward investment and tourism.[30] National chambers of commerce, which are associations representing business interests within a country, for many decades have served as information portals for foreign firms wishing to do business with domestic firms. According to branding and marketing specialist Wally Olins, governments too have long been in the business of projecting to the outside world a national image that is distinct and readily identifiable. Olins cites the repeated undertakings of successive French regimes to reinvent France for outsiders with new symbols and images representing revolutions, empires, restoration and republics. Similarly, founder of the Turkish Republic Mustafa Kemal Atatürk undertook an aggressive project to reinvent Turkey's image, following the fall of the Ottoman Empire as Western, secular and technologically advanced.[31] Lebanese-based transnational political organization Hezbollah, which has aspired to control the Lebanese government, paid to line Lebanese motorways with billboards selling their controversial summer 2006 attack on Israel to the Lebanese public as a national triumph for Lebanon. With bold slogans proclaiming 'la Victoire Divine' ('divine victory'), Hezbollah sought not only to claim credit for the victory, but to cast enemies of Hezbollah, both domestic and foreign, as enemies of God himself.[32]

Recent evidence suggests that governments and business associations (such as chambers of commerce) have come to see significant synergies in strategies for achieving their respective objectives of public diplomacy, namely to promote a positive image of the state abroad and positive brand awareness of the nation amongst potential external investors, importers and tourists respectively. A best-of-breed model for how public–private collaboration in building a national brand and undertaking public diplomacy together is the India Brand Equity Foundation (IBEF), a collaborative venture between India's Ministry of Commerce and the Confederation of Indian Industry (CII), which is one of India's leading business associations. IBEF serves as a forum for brand vision development, coordinates strategic marketing initiatives, and operates a resource centre for firms that wish to trade with and invest in India. IBEF uses aggressive marketing language to pitch India and itself at the same time: 'Achievements. Successes. Growing consuming class driving demand. Vibrant democracy. People who dare to dream. Indians and India have a story to tell. IBEF collects, collates and disseminates accurate, comprehensive and current information on India.'[33]

Among its numerous publications, IBEF publishes *India Now – A Perspective*, a glossy bimonthly magazine featuring business success stories and opportunities in India, and thick pamphlets such as 'UK Companies in India: Success Stories', which illustrates how British firms have profited from investing in India. IBEF has played a leading rôle in the discursive construction of India as an emerging great power in the eyes of the global public since India's economic liberalization took off in the early 1990s, prominently featuring slogans such as 'India: fastest growing free market democracy'. At the World Economic Forum 2006 Annual Meeting in Davos, IBEF launched what they characterized as India's most ambitious brand-building campaign yet, entitled 'India Everywhere'. IBEF's work has contributed substantially to the global public perception of India as a great power and the concomitant boom in trade with, investment in and tourism in India since the late 1990s.

The move towards public–private partnerships has even extended to a need felt by business actors in some circumstances to undertake public diplomacy on behalf of their nation without participation of the government itself. Building on research on negative global perceptions of the United States that he began after the 9/11 attacks, Keith Reinhard, Chairman Emeritus of leading advertising agency DDB Worldwide, founded Business for Diplomatic Action (BDA) in 2004. BDA characterizes itself as a private sector task force whose mission is 'to enlist the US business community in actions to improve the standing of America in the world with the goal of, once again, seeing America admired as a global leader and respected as a courier of progress and prosperity for all people'.[34] The impetus for BDA arose from growing business perceptions that the US government, for many years, was failing to conduct successful public diplomacy on its own. Weber Shandwick Worldwide CEO Harris Diamond observed: 'As a person who makes his living from building reputations, I would argue that neither the Clinton nor Bush administrations have had a comprehensive public diplomacy or brand-building strategy in place, or an experienced, capable team to implement one.'[35] BDA seeks to address the problem of rising anti-Americanism around the world, which its member firms have identified as a threat to US interests, both public and private. With a membership of major US firms with global presence across a range of industries and an academic advisory council packed with heavyweight names, BDA seeks to generate and disseminate ideas for improving the global image of the United States, utilizing all Americans who travel, particularly business-people and students, as 'ambassadors'. On their website BDA frame the problem thus:

> This effort is not about ads or selling – it's about sensitizing Americans to the extent of anti-Americanism today and its implications, transforming American attitudes and behaviors as necessary, building on the many positive perceptions of America that still exist, and building new bridges of cooperation, respect, and mutual understanding across cultures and borders through business-led initiatives.[36]

BDA have assembled a formidable archive and database of research on public diplomacy, available for downloading by the public. BDA's 'World Citizens' Guides' for business travellers and students, in which they impart common-sense advice on how to behave abroad to reinforce positive images of the United States, were prepared in response to research documenting a link between behaviours by Americans abroad and negative foreign perceptions of the United States. Other principal causes of negative perceptions identified by the research include US foreign policy, negative effects of globalization, and the pervasiveness of US popular culture.[37] BDA's pedagogical efforts accord with Paul Sharp's conception of citizen diplomacy. Sharp argues that all members of the public who interact with foreign nationals and entities, whether at home or abroad, act as diplomatic representatives of their own state to other actors.[38] Hence, it serves their own interests for them to behave accordingly.

Case Study: US Public Diplomacy as a Hard Sell

The public diplomacy of the US administration of George Bush the Younger serves as a prime example of how difficult it is to use public diplomacy to 'sell' a foreign policy that is broadly unpopular abroad, even when a serious effort is made to improve public diplomacy techniques. The administration faced a major challenge after the terror attacks of 9/11 in how to communicate to the global public in such a way as to win popular support for their 'Global War on Terror'. The Bush administration's first major attempt to improve US public diplomacy was to appoint private sector public relations expert Charlotte Beers in September 2001 to serve as Undersecretary of State for Public Diplomacy and Public Affairs. Beers, who had headed such advertising giants as Ogilvy & Mather and J. Walter Thompson, was tapped to bring the public relations expertise of Madison Avenue 'in house' and to develop a strategy to 'sell' the Global War on Terror and later the project of invading and democratizing Iraq to the person in the Arab street and to the global public more generally.[39] Beers directed a public diplomacy initiative known as 'Shared Values', which was intended to communicate to Muslims around the globe that the United States embraced Muslims and their religion and culture alongside all of the other religions and cultures in the US melting pot. Videos showing happy Muslim American families were produced and shown to target audiences in countries such as Indonesia. Yet feedback from target audiences was negative, because their concerns about the United States were not about the conditions for Muslims living in the United States, but rather focused on US foreign policies towards Muslim areas of the world such as Palestine and Iraq. Within a fairly short space of time, Beers's 'Shared Values' project was perceived as not gaining any traction, and by March 2003 she had left the administration.[40]

Critics of the Bush administration blamed the failure of Beers's approach on the general incommensurability of strategies and methods for selling consumer products with those for selling the United States, its values and objectives.[41] However, many public relations professionals explained at the time that the problem was not her introduction of strategies and tactics used by private public relations and advertising firms, but the way in which she decided to implement them. As communications expert Nancy Snow argued, Washington has to 'tap into the voluntary organizations and the thousands and thousands of US citizens (Fulbright scholars, academics, business people) in constant contact with the world who can effectively communicate outside the bounds of government'. Snow was identifying the importance of using third parties to communicate about a government's policy in a way that would be perceived as credible by audiences. Jack Leslie, Chairman of public relations firm Weber Shandwick Worldwide, stressed that 'the lesson you learn when you're communicating on behalf of a government is that you have to use a holistic approach. You can't divorce the issues from the message.'[42]

The Bush administration's first foray into remaking US public diplomacy illustrates vividly how closely public diplomacy is related to its professional cousins public relations, public affairs and propaganda. Each of these functions involves using language skilfully to communicate to public audiences, using media channels, and the management of publicity and 'brand image'. The subsequent chapter in the Bush administration's public diplomacy strategy reinforces how they continued to view public diplomacy and public relations as a sort of seamless professional space. Beers's brief tenure in the public diplomacy and public affairs post at the State Department was followed by a similarly brief tour of duty by Margaret Tutwiler, a former press secretary to Secretary of State James Baker under President George Bush the Elder. President Bush then appointed longtime insider and con-

US Under Secretary of State for Public Diplomacy and Public Affairs Karen Hughes meeting with Vice President Richard Cheney and President George W. Bush, August 2006

fidante Karen Hughes to the job in 2005. Hughes had come from a background in television journalism and politics. Like Beers, Hughes was a skilled political communication professional.[43] Backing up Secretary of State Condoleezza Rice's view that American values would win over global hearts and minds if only they could be communicated successfully, Hughes proposed mobilizing regional 'rapid response' teams to rebut anti-American content in foreign media.[44] Yet coming from their commercial backgrounds, neither Beers nor Hughes may have been able to recognize the complexities of inter-cultural communication that they faced. The appointments of Beers and Hughes were emblematic of the global migration of methods and techniques from the private sector world of public relations, marketing and advertising into the very public realm of public diplomacy, which had once been the preserve of the diplomatic corps with their very different professional background of training and experience.

Since the eighteenth century many professional diplomats had been conditioned historically to disdain business and particularly the ensemble of practices actually connected with selling.[45] Thus it has required a considerable accommodation for the denizens of traditional diplomatic culture to harness the expertise of professionals from other fields. As governments have come to need the methods and techniques of public relations to communicate to publics in an increasingly competitive and media-intensive global environment, increasingly they have hired public relations experts and political communication professionals to teach their skills to diplomats and other government officials seeking to communicate better and to 'win hearts and minds' to their foreign policy objectives. One approach that the State Department has undertaken in recent times has been to hire private sector professionals to join the government at fairly senior rank, bringing their ideas and talents to an area of diplomatic practice still in its early days and yet nonetheless having to respond to rapidly changing media and global public opinion.[46]

At the end of the day, however, many analysts considered that no matter how effectively the Bush administration conducted its public diplomacy, it would never be enough. The problem for the State Department during the Global War on Terror at root was that the policy was unsellable to foreign publics, irrespective of the skill level of their approach to public diplomacy.[47] To the extent that this is true, it makes the case that the best metric for evaluating public diplomacy is how effectively the actor uses it dialogically as part of the foreign policy making process. Regarding the Global War on Terror as a failed foreign policy brand, the incoming administration of Barack Obama abolished use of the tag and vowed to engage in bi-directional communication about US foreign policy with allies and adversaries alike. Only time would tell whether this shift in approach would bear fruit.

Public Diplomacy in Multilateral Venues

With increasing frequency, meetings of multilateral institutions and other international gatherings are serving as effective venues for the full range of diplomatic actors to conduct public diplomacy. Some occasions, such as large international gatherings that draw attendees from the ranks of politics, business and civil society and attract the attention of the global media, can serve as useful stages or venues for the practice of public diplomacy. Meetings of the United Nations General Assembly and its functional agencies, World Trade Organization ministerial meetings and similar gatherings of multilateral institutions can be used effectively in this manner, because they bring major diplomatic actors and their audiences together (through the media) in one place and time. In a recent example, Venezuelan

President Hugo Chavez maximized global media attention and public perception of his government's global political stance when he attended the UN General Assembly meeting in New York in September 2006. A day after calling US President George W. Bush 'the devil' in his speech to the General Assembly, Chavez announced at a speech in traditionally poor Harlem that he was doubling the amount of discount price oil that Venezuela ships to poor citizens of the United States. Media around the world engaged in a 'feeding frenzy' of coverage of both speeches over two days. Whilst the Bush administration was predictably antagonized, Chavez won plaudits not only from poor Americans but from the populations of poor and weak states elsewhere in the world.

Increasingly in recent times, privately hosted venues have also proven to be effective platforms for public diplomacy. The World Economic Forum's regional 'summits', as well as the Davos, Switzerland, annual meetings, at which global business leaders, political leaders, academics, journalists and leaders from civil society gather to discuss and seek solutions for global problems, are a good example of events that attract global media attention and, in many respects, are ideal venues for a government or a firm to promote its brand and focus public attention on its image, especially if it is seeking to change its image significantly. At a Forum regional meeting, and even more so at the Davos Annual Meeting, governments, firms and CSOs have what is in effect a captive audience of regional and global opinion leaders, with the added advantages of extensive media coverage and the inevitability that the assembled opinion leaders will interact with one another as they receive new information. In the early and mid-2000s, Pakistan's government used Forum events particularly effectively to shift the focus of public attention from political instability in its tribal regions and to refocus global business leaders, academics and the media on the story of Pakistan's accelerating economic growth and increasing attractiveness as a destination for inward investment. Pakistani Prime Minister Shaukat Aziz used a media interview at Davos in January 2005 to announce that the following week he would propose to India's Prime Minister Manmohan Singh a new set of bilateral confidence-building measures without prejudicing the resolution of their dispute over Kashmir.[48] Aziz also took advantage of the attention from global business leaders at Davos to market the Pakistani government's economic reform programme.[49] At an invited breakfast for Davos attendees in January 2007, Prime Minister Aziz promoted the positive impact of Pakistan's enactment of gender reform liberalization upon the investment climate in Pakistan. Following the formal presentation, female Pakistani attendees of the breakfast reinforced the Prime Minister's message, in informal conversations with non-Pakistani attendees, that the gender reforms are substantive and not just window dressing. At the 2007 Davos meeting, Cisco Systems and Computer Associates ('CA') were able to showcase the use of their proprietary technologies in improving education in developing countries. Cisco and CA were the lead private sector participants in a World Economic Forum-sponsored initiative intended to modernize teaching and learning in Jordan and other countries. Media coverage at the Davos panel presentations brought strong positive visibility for Cisco's and CA's global corporate social responsibility undertakings.

Another important category of privately hosted venue for public diplomacy is international sporting events. Governments and global firms based in a particular country use the quadrennial summer and winter Olympic Games and the FIFA World Cup (football/soccer) in particular, but also other events ranging from the America's Cup in sailing to the cricket World Cup, to communicate to global publics about their culture and about their desirability as destinations for investment, tourism and trade. These events differ from events such as the Forum's Davos Annual Meeting, in that significant numbers of the general public attend the event, meet with local people directly, and form their own opinions about the place, its government, its firms and its culture. An even vaster global television and internet media audience view the events and the media coverage of the location from afar. Governments making plans from a public diplomacy perspective can influence but not control altogether the perceptions that global visitors and media consumers form. Creating the best possible impression requires careful coordination of event planning, communications strategy and message design between national and local governments, international and domestic sporting authorities, and sponsor firms. The government of the People's Republic of China faced a major challenge before and during the Beijing Olympics of August 2008 to present China and Beijing to the world as a modern and welcoming place, whilst deflecting criticism of their human rights policies in regions such as Tibet. Most outside observers gave China generally high marks for achieving their objectives. A similar challenge faced South Africa in hosting the 2010 FIFA World Cup to present the nation as a safe, modern country with sound infrastructure and efficient transport.

Public diplomacy has become a much more important part of diplomatic process for governments and other diplomatic actors alike, owing to the transformation in communications technologies. Although its effectiveness is difficult to quantify directly, public diplomacy's effects are felt ever more

powerfully in the support for and receptivity to policy initiatives undertaken by governments, multilateral organizations, global firms and CSOs.
The challenge for governments and other diplomatic actors is not only to
marshal the most effective ensemble of practitioners and skills to conduct
public diplomacy effectively, but also to conceive of public diplomacy in
terms of relationships to be built and managed. The extent to which diplomats are able to construct a reliable feedback loop through which they
are able to listen to the views and ideas of the public, abroad and at home,
and use that information as part of their own process of shaping policy, is
likely to have a major impact on the effectiveness of their overall diplomacy going forward.

9

Managing Economic Diplomacy

Introduction: Contemporary Functional Areas of Diplomatic Practice

The next three chapters examine broad functional areas of diplomatic practice: economic, military and security, and cultural diplomacy. The three often overlapping categories are used as an organizing principle, and as such should be understood as referring to the dominant functional area of the particular issues in diplomatic practice being discussed. The objective of each chapter is to understand how the business of diplomacy is done in each functional area, by whom, and through which mechanisms, instruments and approaches. The key functional areas of diplomatic practice are addressed through the lens of relationship management: the process by which diplomats representing one actor manage the necessary relationships with diplomats representing other actors with respect to a particular functional area. Hence each section begins with a discussion of needs, asking which aspects of diplomatic relationships need to be managed in each functional area. A discussion of approaches to managing relationships with respect to economic, security and cultural issues, respectively, follows thereafter.

Diplomatic practice that deals with both economic and security issues can be broken down into two broad categories. The first consists of the processes of negotiating and agreeing upon how regimes or arrangements for managing particular functional relationships, such as international trade or arms control, should function, and how such regimes or arrangements should be amended or modified when required. These processes are overtly political, often highly partisan and contested, and hence often require the highest level of representative and communicative skills if estrangements are to be mediated and new forms for managing relationships on an ongoing basis are to be created. The second and no less important category consists of the processes of implementing and enforcing or ensuring compliance with agreed economic and security regimes and arrangements, such as the WTO Dispute Settlement Mechanism or the Conventional Armed Forces in Europe (CFE) Treaty verification inspections. Whilst the issues in contention may be less partisan and more juridical in character, they are often no less political than the first category of processes, and as such they require a similar set of diplomatic skills and expertise. Beyond these two broad categories, the management of economic and security crises can be thought of as areas for diplomatic management in and of themselves, over and above the management of other aspects of relationships with respect to economic and security issues. The principal areas on which diplomatic management of economic relationships is focused are international trade, foreign investment, monetary stability, financial markets, economic development, and migration. The management of environmental issues (such as energy, water, pollution and climate issues and conflicts), which can be understood as falling within the economic and security functional areas equally, will be addressed in the following chapter under managing military and security diplomacy.

Economic Diplomacy: International Trade

What in many respects is the oldest functional area of economic diplomacy remains one of the most important and one of the largest and most time-consuming: the management of trade relations. In ancient times, the earliest trade missions and diplomatic missions were often one and the same. Since the beginning of human civilization foreign trade has been an act of bridging difference, a mediation of estrangement, as the goods sent and received from abroad themselves served as embassies, as representatives of the sender to the recipient. Trade in ancient and mediaeval times consisted almost entirely of the exchange of unlike products, whereas today, trade in like products is common: Japan and Germany each ship automobiles to the other, for example. Engaging in trade and gaining access to different and unfamiliar goods produced abroad made participants in both countries more familiar with the differences between each trading partner. To engage in foreign trade successfully required negotiating an agreement with foreign authorities that was as much political and military as economic in nature.[1] When the Venetian Republic ('La Serenissima') sent missions in search of spices and other exotic products to the Orient in the fifteenth century, agreement had to be reached not only on the price of goods to be acquired but on a guarantee or understanding of safe passage home for the mission with their acquired goods, lest they otherwise be subjected to piracy, pillage and plunder. The nineteenth century is viewed by many as a sort of 'golden age' for the liberalization of movement of goods around the globe, as naval protection of maritime shipping lanes by governments (particularly by Britain's Royal Navy) effectively enabled trade agreements to be negotiated between governments without a significant military component. Diplomats were able to concentrate upon the 'rules of the game', such as the lowering of tariffs and other barriers to trade and the implementation of 'fair' trading practices across nations, enabling trade itself to be privatized to a large extent.[2] The first multilateral trade agreements, signed in the late nineteenth century, permitted the free movement across borders of commercial samples, which enabled more effective marketing of goods to potential foreign buyers.

Today, international trade diplomacy is even more regularized than it was a century ago, although it is vastly more complex. By the mid twentieth century the nations of the world had come to accept the idea of an international regime for trade that consisted of a general body of rules and of accepted practices and processes for encouraging general observation of the rules. By the early twenty-first century, these rules have become vastly more extensive and complex. Trade rules today consist not only of permitted levels of tariffs, quotas, and other barriers to trade, but also of allowed levels of subsidies and other government subventions to industries that engage in trade, health and safety standards for traded goods, and a common global system of classification of traded merchandise, the Harmonized System of Tariff Classification (HSTC). Trade rules apply not only to trade in goods, as they did in the nineteenth century, but also to trade in services, to foreign investment regulations affecting trade, to intellectual property protection and, increasingly, to environmental and labour regulations affecting trade. Trade rules impose limitations and prohibitions on various 'unfair' trade practices, including the selling of goods abroad below the price at which they are sold in the home country (known as 'dumping'), trade in counterfeit or 'grey market' goods, trade in products made by child or prisoner labour, and goods manufactured under unsafe working conditions.

The primary rulebook for international trade, the General Agreement on Tariffs and Trade (GATT), was signed by twenty-three nations in 1947 and was amended most recently (as of the time of writing) by the Uruguay Round of multilateral trade negotiations in the 1990s. The GATT has been administered by the World Trade Organization (WTO) since the WTO was created in 1995 by the Treaty of Marrakech, which concluded the Uruguay Round. Most multilateral trade rules today are proposed, negotiated and agreed under the auspices of the WTO. If they are not, they at least need to be constructed through direct bilateral or multilateral negotiations in such a way as to be 'GATT legal'. However, it falls to member governments to enforce WTO rules and judicial rulings through their individual national legislation and regulations. This has the effect of separating trade diplomacy from trade law enforcement functions within member governments. Diplomats who work on trade issues must do the negotiating of agreements and revisions to agreements, and they must take the lead in making representations before judicial organs such as the WTO's Dispute Settlement Body (DSB) (see below), but they are not tasked with enforcing the rules that they bring about.[3]

The management of trade diplomacy consists primarily of constant monitoring of one's trading partners' compliance with trade agreements and multilateral trade rules. This requires diplomats to make representations to protect national interests when perceived violations occur or when disagreements or questions of interpretation of agreed rules arise. In addition, there is a huge surge of activity researching, mediating between competing domestic interests, and negotiating with foreign counterparts during the period when GATT/WTO multilateral trade negotiation rounds are underway. In many nations, responsibilities for trade diplomacy are often spread between staff at numerous different government agencies. In the United States, the Office of the United States Trade Representative (USTR), located administratively within the Executive Office of the President, is the principal executive agency tasked with making trade policy and negotiating trade agreements, whereas the Department of Commerce has the principal responsibility to promulgate and enforce regulations implementing US trade policy and obligations under the GATT and other trade agreements. The Commerce Department also plays a rôle in making trade policy, primarily through engaging in trade promotion and otherwise articulating the interests of domestic industries affected by trade conditions. The US Department of Agriculture takes the lead in making US agricultural trade policy, sending staff to all trade negotiations involving agriculture. Other US executive agencies, such as the Departments of Energy and Environmental Protection, are involved in making trade policy as well.[4] In the European Union, responsibility for trade diplomacy is more concentrated, falling predominantly under Directorate-General (DG) Trade. Other DGs, such as DG Agriculture, do play rôles as well.

Whilst the majority of trade diplomats are based in the headquarters of the different executive agencies for which they work in their respective home country capitals, governments of larger and wealthier countries

Alter-globalization protesters at World Trade Organization ministerial meeting, Hong Kong, December 2005

station trade experts in their embassies to countries that are major trading partners. Each WTO member country that can afford to do so also maintains a permanent mission to the WTO's headquarters in Geneva. Staff at permanent missions to the WTO are responsible for day-to-day relations with the WTO Secretariat and fellow WTO members, complying with the WTO's trade policy reporting requirements for their regularly scheduled country trade policy reviews, making complaints against and responding to complaints from fellow members over alleged WTO rules violations, and participating in ongoing WTO trade liberalization negotiations programmes. At one level below that of policy and negotiation, the consular staffs of foreign ministries in their foreign mission deal with more technical and routine issues surrounding international trade, such as customs documentation and enforcement.[5]

Although many governments conduct the bulk of their trade diplomacy at or under the auspices of the WTO, most governments engage in active bilateral and regional trade diplomacy as well. Regional trade organizations such as Mercosur in South America and the North American Free Trade Agreement (NAFTA) have some sort of permanent Secretariat that requires staffing by member governments, even if at relatively low levels, as well as periodic ministerial meetings that serve deliberative functions. Often the most substantive and difficult diplomatic work is done in preparing for ministerial meetings and then in engaging in negotiations at the meetings themselves, as these are the occasions for addressing the most contentious issues, whereas the permanent Secretariats tend to handle the more administrative aspects of the organization. By contrast, the Association of Southeast Asian Nations (ASEAN) organizes its cooperation largely through an intergovernmental structure consisting of annual deliberative ministerial meetings at head of government and foreign minister level and more frequent committee meetings addressing functional areas of cooperation such as trade, telecommunications, transport and tourism. Each of the cooperation programmes undertaken by ASEAN requires diplomatic staff based in home country foreign ministries, trade and commerce ministries and other agencies to prepare for regular meetings, attend and negotiate at the meetings, and fulfil commitments made when the staffs meet.

Another increasingly important aspect of trade diplomacy is export promotion and place branding, as was noted in the discussions of the promoter state (see chapter 3) and public diplomacy (see chapter 8) above. The commerce ministries of governments, often in cooperation with interest groups representing major domestic industries, such as the Confederation of Indian Industry (CII) in India or the US Chamber of Commerce in the United States, seek to disseminate as widely and effectively as possible promotional information about the range, availability, quality and price of goods and services produced in the home country. Trade promotion can be done through a number of channels for representation of and communication about a country's products to potential consumers. Putting up displays and making presentations at major international trade fairs, such as CeBIT, which showcases the latest information and telecommunications technologies each spring in Hannover, Germany, and the North American International Auto Show in Detroit, Michigan in the United States each winter. Other channels include direct marketing and advertising of products and more general nation-branding, in which the objective is to communicate to foreign publics a more general positive image of a country and thus the products exported therefrom. Whilst governments engage in nation-branding strategies to varying extents on their own, often they do it most effectively through public–private partnership organizations with business interest groups. The India Brand Equity Foundation (IBEF), a cooperative venture of India's Ministry of Commerce and the CII, is one of the most effective organizations dedicated to nation-branding (see chapter 8). The state-of-the-art IBEF website provides users with a sort of one-stop shop packed with information about India, its exports, and opportunities for inward investment in India (see below).[6]

Cross-Border Capital Flows (Investments)

The diplomatic management of relationships with respect to cross-border capital flows, which consist of portfolio investment and foreign direct investment ('FDI'), is less institutionalized than that concerned with trade, even if the investment-related issues that require diplomacy are just as politicized as trade-related issues. Investment flows and trade flows are intimately interlinked. In 1995 fully one-third of the $6.1 billion in annual global trade flows consisted of intra-firm trade: goods and services exchanged between a unit of a company in one country and another unit of the same company in a different country.[7] The primary question that arises is the extent to which foreign investors are treated equally to investors from the home country on the whole range of issues and disputes that arise, which extend from legal disputes with domestic parties to the all-important repatriation of profits. In the nineteenth century, conflicts between European investors and the governments of non-European states in which they were investing frequently occasioned diplomatic intervention by the investors' home governments and on several occasions (notwithstanding diplomatic engagement) resulted in armed conflict. In 1902, for example, British, German and Italian warships blockaded Venezuelan ports following the Venezuelan government's unwillingness to respond to an ultimatum from European diplomats. European governments demanded that Venezuela compensate European investors for damages sustained to property they owned in Venezuela during a recently ended civil war.[8]

In the contemporary period large global firms have found that the most effective means of pursuing their particular interests in making investments across borders has been to engage nation–state governments to represent them at multilateral organizations based on state representation. Hence firms have used their own diplomats to press governments to institutionalize and standardize protections for investors through multilateral

agreements. This has resulted in two negotiating processes, one more successful than the other. Signatory countries of the GATT agreed in the
Uruguay Round to a package of so-called 'Trade Related Investment
Measures' ('TRIMs'), which sought to apply to foreign investors the existing GATT principle of national treatment or non-discrimination in favour
of domestic firms. Among other things, TRIMs discouraged local content
requirements obligating firms to use locally produced inputs in their production processes and so-called 'trade balancing requirements' that limit
quantities of imported inputs and set targets for export volumes of finished
goods. The WTO, once it had begun to operate following the signing of
the Treaty of Marrakech, created a working group on Trade and Investment
at its Singapore ministerial meeting in 1996 to study the relationship
between trade and investment in the hope of helping member governments to consider possible future options regarding liberalization of cross-
border investment flows. Although an extension of TRIMs was originally
intended to be undertaken in the Doha Development Agenda, WTO
member delegations meeting at the Cancun ministerial meeting in 2003
were unable to reach agreement on modalities for negotiations to begin,
so the TRIMs agreement was dropped from the Doha agenda.[9]

Going beyond TRIMs, again largely at the behest of large firms with
cross-border investments, governments used the Organization for
Economic Cooperation and Development ('OECD') in the 1990s as a
venue to negotiate a more comprehensive agreement liberalizing national
regulations governing cross-border capital flows. The treaty, which was
to be known as the Multilateral Agreement on Investment ('MAI'), would
have mandated signatory governments to dismantle any national regulations that had the effect of discriminating against foreign investors in
favour of local investors. Civil society organizations concerned about
social protections feared that this type of mandate could be interpreted to
force governments that imposed, for example, environmental and labour
protection regulations that were more onerous than those of their neighbours to liberalize their regulations so as not to discriminate against firms
from neighbouring countries wishing to invest. Social forces seeking to
negotiate agreement on greater social protections envisaged the MAI as
facilitating a 'race to the bottom' in terms of social protections, so they
mobilized popular opposition to the MAI effectively using the internet.
Public pressure on industrial country governments, coordinated by civil
society organizations, resulted in the OECD suspending work on the MAI
in 1998.[10]

Monetary Cooperation

The principal need for diplomacy on monetary issues concerns maintaining stable exchange rates between currencies and orderly exchange rate adjustment. Monetary diplomacy has a long history in the nineteenth and twentieth centuries, undertaken with varying degrees of success. Governments have tended to find the idea of surrendering aspects of sovereignty concerned with managing their own monetary policy and currency to be among the most vulnerable to domestic political opposition. During an exceptionally hostile period in which competitive devaluations of currencies in the late 1920s and 1930s combined with tariff rises, international trade volumes collapsed. The effect was to stifle global economic growth for a decade and was widely perceived as contributing to the causes of the Second World War. As a result, diplomats of major economic powers meeting at Bretton Woods, New Hampshire, in 1944 agreed to create an International Monetary Fund (IMF) with the remit of managing an international monetary system based around fixed exchange rates. Member countries' currencies would be valued in gold, backed by real gold reserves, and member governments would need to seek the approval of the IMF prior to changing their currency's gold valuation. Hence, over the next quarter-century, much of the monetary diplomacy that took place did so at or under the auspices of the IMF. The Bretton Woods system was far from perfect structurally, however, in that IMF member countries were unwilling to allow the IMF to be the creator of sufficient additional liquidity in the international monetary system to facilitate the levels of global economic growth that took place in the 1950s and 1960s without significant dislocation.[11] The IMF also faced the dilemma that its largest and wealthiest member and shareholder, the United States, was not willing to submit to IMF rules regarding the running of persistent imbalances in its national balance of payments. These, among other factors, led to the breakdown of the Bretton Woods fixed exchange rate system from the late 1960s, and by 1973 a new international monetary system of 'managed floating' exchange rates had supplanted it.

Managed floating required a different approach to monetary diplomacy by national finance ministers and central bank governors. After the end of Bretton Woods, currencies initially floated freely against one another in an open market, meaning that a currency's value in terms of another was whatever currency traders agreed it to be at a given moment. However, currency markets needed streams of information about macroeconomic policy and monetary policy from governments in order to value currencies more effectively and avoid sudden and disorderly swings in exchange rates. Sudden currency movements tended to occur when new and different information entered the marketplace without warning, or when markets perceived that there was a lack of communication about coordinating monetary policy between governments of major currency countries, and between governments and central banks. For example, following the adoption of a contractionary monetary policy after over a decade of inflation by the Federal Reserve in the United States under newly appointed Chairman Paul Volcker in 1979, the value of the US dollar appreciated by 40 per cent against a basket of major currencies over a six-year period. It took a major international monetary policy summit in 1985 held at the Plaza Hotel in New York to stem the dollar's rise.[12]

Beginning in 1975, finance ministers began to meet at least annually, sometimes with central bankers, in an effort to agree on broad targets or trading ranges for major currencies such as the US dollar, the French franc, the Deutschmark, the sterling and the yen. This practice of multilateral diplomacy with the objective of ensuring monetary stability eventually became institutionalized as the G7 annual meeting of finance ministers of the seven major industrial economies: the United Kingdom, United States, Germany, France, Japan, Italy and Canada. Finance ministries and central banks of each member country committed themselves to act to the extent of their abilities to encourage their respective currencies to trade within ranges agreed at the meetings, even whilst recognizing that exchange rates were determined ultimately by the summation of the actions of many large and small traders in an open market. The principal instruments that had an impact on exchange rates during the early years of managed floating were statements by finance ministers and central bankers about their desired trading range for their currency, which held even greater credibility to the extent that they were in accordance with similar statements by finance ministers and central bankers of other major currency countries. Limited, measured interventions by central banks in currency markets could also be effective in some circumstances. By purchasing a certain quantity of sterling, deutschmarks and yen with dollars, for example, the Federal Reserve in the 1980s signalled seriousness in its intent to meet its commitment to see the dollar depreciate against the other currencies. Hence following the 1985 Plaza Accord, central banks made $10 billion in currency market interventions. The US dollar depreciated by 51 per cent against a basket of the other major currencies in an orderly, if relatively speedy, way until 1987, when finance ministers and central bankers assembled at another international monetary conference in Paris declared its decline to have been sufficient in the 1987 Louvre Accord.[13]

Coordinating monetary stability through multilateral diplomacy has become even more complex since the 1980s. The volume of international currency trading has accelerated so rapidly that the ability of even the largest central banks to have an impact upon exchange rates through any direct intervention in foreign exchange (forex) markets has been sharply curtailed. Between 1977 and 1995, the most conservative measure of the volume of forex transactions in the United States increased sixtyfold, according to the New York Federal Reserve Bank, whereas between 1980 and 1995 the value of US trade in goods and services 'only' tripled. The Bank for International Settlements reported that global forex transactions in traditional products increased by 80 per cent between 1992 and 1998 to $1.5 trillion per day.[14] In 2007 over $2 trillion in forex transactions took place daily. This has placed an added burden upon finance ministers and central bankers, and upon the heads of government and legislatures standing behind them making macroeconomic and monetary policies, to communicate clearly their objectives to their foreign counterparts. Global forex trading keeps the pressure on monetary diplomats to reach understandings and agreements on shared objectives regarding monetary stability and exchange rates that are transparent and credible to markets. The general management of international currency exchange rates today is conducted through a combination of regular consultations, led by the annual meeting of G7 finance ministers that now takes place simultaneously with the G8 annual summit (Russia is not included in the G7). Regular bilateral meetings are also scheduled between finance ministers and central bank governors of the United States, United Kingdom, European Union, Japan and other major currency countries such as, increasingly, China. The rôle of the IMF in multilateral monetary coordination today focuses primarily upon ensuring monetary stability in developing and middle-income countries, and, by doing so, protecting real economic growth from being eroded or wiped out by sudden currency collapses (see discussions of economic development and economic crises below).

Banking and Financial Markets

One of the features that distinguishes the contemporary global economy from that of earlier times is the sheer size and degree of integration of its financial markets. In January 2007 the market capitalization of companies traded publicly on global exchanges exceeded $50 trillion.[15] In 1980, foreign assets (investments) were estimated to be 25 per cent of global output, whereas by 2000 that figure was estimated to have increased to 92 per cent.[16] Severe financial market instability today has the capacity to pose as great a threat to the livelihoods, health and lives of the world's population as violent conflict and natural disaster. Hence one of the most critical and challenging tasks for diplomats of large and small countries alike is to maintain orderly markets and to prevent financial market instability, to the greatest extent possible, through communication and cooperation. When they are unable to prevent disruptive events from taking place, their mission is to act speedily and in a coordinated manner to mitigate the ensuing damage. This objective requires governments to work much more closely with different types of private actors, both domestic and transnational, than in many other projects of economic diplomacy. Stable, transparent, consistent and uniformly enforced rules across the banking and securities industries and the accounting profession, as well as rules to prevent particular countries or regions from becoming havens for money laundering and other financial transactions for transnational criminal organizations (TCOs), are needed worldwide to a greater extent than ever before. Information and communications technology has made it possible for financial problems in the 'weakest link' to be transmitted throughout the global financial system, sometimes faster than regulators are able to act to prevent damage resulting therefrom.

Perhaps the most important multilateral diplomacy to maintain orderly financial markets has been in the area of banking. In 1974 the Bank for International Settlements, since 1930 the central bank for the world's central banks, created the Basel Committee on Banking Supervision to promote best practice in bank supervision worldwide. The Basel Committee, comprised of central bank governors and heads of bank regulatory agencies in ten industrialized countries (known in this context as the 'G10'), has consulted regularly on ways to prevent weak bank regulation in one or more countries from making the global banking system vulnerable to collapse resulting from electronic transfer of funds. The 1991 collapse of the Luxembourg-registered Bank of Credit and Commerce International (BCCI), a bank funded extensively by Persian Gulf capital with a depositor base shielded from regulatory scrutiny and extensive loan exposure to the then economically precarious government of Pakistan, sent shock waves throughout the international banking system. Some smaller countries, often island nations such as Nauru (hence the expression 'offshore banking havens'), had begun to develop their economies by offering banking services in the international marketplace often with greater levels of anonymity and at more lucrative rates of interest than those available in large banking markets. One way to capture a share of the market by offering more favourable rates of interest was to maintain lower capital reserves than large banks in industrialized countries. Yet the cost of such a strategy was accepting a significantly higher risk of insolvency should events trigger a run on the bank, whether justifiably or not. Hence in order to counter this perverse incentive created by the global financial marketplace, the Basel Committee in 1988 negotiated the Basel Capital Accord, which established a voluntary framework for measuring the credit risk to which banks are exposed. The agreement established capital adequacy requirements based on a transparent metric of risk exposure, which all countries were encouraged to adopt for their banking systems. Whilst generally considered to be a success as a first step, the Accord was revised in 2006 to make it more nuanced and flexible.

Another issue for financial diplomacy affecting the global banking sector has been the need to combat money laundering, which is the use of financial transactions intended to conceal the source and utilization of funds. Money laundering has long been a common practice of transnational criminal organizations such as the Sicily-based Cosa Nostra (Mafia) and drug cartels based in Medellín and Cali, Colombia, but since the 1990s money laundering has received much more attention as it has become essential for the funding of terrorism. Money laundering has become much easier to accomplish technically as technology development has facilitated the electronic transfer of funds across borders. The main diplomatic strategy against money laundering has been a coordinated programme of intergovernmental action. Since the late 1980s a series of multilateral anti-money laundering (AML) agreements has been reached. In 1989 at the G7 Paris Summit, G7 members created the intergovernmental Financial Action Task Force on Money Laundering ('FATF'), which consisted of the G7, the European Union and eight other nations. By 2007 FATF's membership had grown to thirty-four nations. FATF began to study methods to combat money laundering. In 1990 they issued Forty Recommendations, an AML action plan ready for adoption by governments. In June 1995 a group of government agencies responsible for gathering financial disclosures from other government agencies and private institutions related to money laundering and terrorism financing met at the Egmont Palace in Brussels and formed the Egmont Group to study how they could share information legally to fight money laundering and block the financing of terrorism. The United Nations passed the UN Convention Against Transnational

Organized Crime, known as the Palermo Convention, in 2001 and the UN Convention Against Corruption, or Merida Convention, in 2005. The European Union adopted the Strasbourg Convention on Laundering, Search, Seizure and Confiscation of the Proceeds from Crime in 1990 and the Council of Europe Convention on Laundering, Search, Seizure and Confiscation of the Proceeds from Crime and on the Financing of Terrorism in 2005. The Basel Committee has also been active in using its supervisory remit to further AML objectives.[17]

Governments have not been the only diplomatic actors to engage in fighting money laundering. Cooperation between industry regulatory bodies and between global firms has also been significant. The International Association of Insurance Supervisors ('IAIS'), which facilitates multilateral cooperation between insurance regulatory bodies, issued a guidance paper on AML and combating terrorism financing. The Wolfsberg Group, which is comprised of the leading global banking firms, has met regularly in the 2000s to discuss common standards and approaches to combating money laundering and terrorism financing, and has issued a series of statements of principles since 2002 establishing standards to which its members have agreed to adhere, the most recent being the 2007 Wolfsberg Statement against Corruption.[18]

Multilateral financial diplomacy between private actors extends beyond the particularly pressing issues of combating money laundering and terrorism financing to more routine but increasingly essential cooperation to maintain and, if possible, expand the stability of the international financial system. This cooperation increasingly takes the form of agreeing upon and maintaining (through monitoring and enforcement) international standards for the key components of the financial industries: banking and insurance (as noted above), securities trading, and accounting. Financial regulatory bodies and exchanges alike have established venues or fora in which they communicate and take decisions to act on the global diplomatic stage in their collective interest. Perhaps the most significant of these bodies is the International Organization of Securities Commissions ('IOSCO'), which is a multilateral association of national securities regulatory agencies, such as the Securities and Exchange Commission in the United States and the Financial Services Authority in the United Kingdom. IOSCO's objective is to maintain consistent high international standards of securities regulation and to promote cooperation in the surveillance of international securities transactions.

The International Accounting Standards Board ('IASB'), which is comprised of national accounting standards agencies such as the Federal

Accounting Standards Board ('FASB') in the United States and the Accounting Standards Board ('ASB') in South Africa, performs a similar function for international accounting standards. The IASB has since the 1990s been at the centre of an ongoing rivalry between two different widely observed accounting systems: Generally Accepted Accounting Principles ('GAAP'), the recognized accounting system in the United States, and International Accounting Standards ('IAS'), an evolving internationally recognized system already in use in Europe and many other nations. The two systems differ in that GAAP is more of a 'letter of the law' system, whereas IAS is based more on general principles that allow room for interpretation. Although supporters of each approach agree that it would be advantageous for the international financial system to adopt a common global accounting standard, the spirited and often scholarly debate over the relative merits of the two approaches shows no sign of resolution at the time of writing. The major stock exchanges in the United States, the New York Stock Exchange ('NYSE') and the National Association of Securities Dealers' NASDAQ, require firms wishing to list shares on their exchanges to report their financial information according to GAAP, which can be problematic for firms in the rest of the world that prefer to observe IAS but nonetheless want or need to raise capital in what is still the world's largest capital market, the United States of America.

Economic diplomacy in the form of multilateral cooperation between securities exchanges themselves shares many objectives with cooperation between regulatory bodies, but has some different agenda items as well. Securities exchanges are expected to function as impartial venues for the trading of securities and yet often at the same time are operated as for-profit businesses in themselves, so in a sense they are competing against one another for the business of firms wishing to raise capital in global capital markets. Hence the managers of the exchanges find it in their interest to cooperate on matters of mutual concern. The World Federation of Exchanges counts amongst its members all the leading stock exchanges of the world, including NYSE Euronext (which owns the New York Stock Exchange and the European Euronext exchange), the NASDAQ, the London Stock Exchange, the Tokyo Stock Exchange Group, Hong Kong Exchanges and Clearing, the Singapore Exchange, the Shanghai Stock Exchange and the Bombay Stock Exchange. The World Federation of Exchanges cooperates with national and multilateral regulatory organizations to promote the maintenance of high standards of practice, ethics and transparency amongst its member exchanges, and also lobbies national legislative and regulatory bodies to address problems that its member exchanges face in doing business.[19]

Economic Development

Economic development differs somewhat from the other functional economic areas of diplomatic practice in that, beyond the usual categories of diplomacy involved with regime creation and maintenance, diplomats must devote a large amount of time and effort to the realization of specific projects and undertakings. Diplomats and their staffs must address a huge range of economic development needs, extending from development finance to monetary stabilization, capacities-building in governance and macroeconomic economic policy management. Multilateral diplomacy focusing on development issues takes place primarily through the venues of multilateral and regional intergovernmental bodies such as the World Bank and International Monetary Fund, the Paris Club of finance ministries of creditor countries, the G8, specialized United Nations agencies such as the UN Development Programme ('UNDP') and the UN Council on Trade and Development ('UNCTAD'), and regional development banks such as the African Development Bank ('ADB') and the Inter-American Development Bank ('IADB'). In addition to serving as venues for diplomacy between member countries, most of these organizations have come to function as diplomatic actors in their own right, at least to a certain extent (see chapters 2 and 4).[20]

In the period since the Second World War, the broad philosophical questions of how (and how much) economic development should be done, who should do it and who should pay for it have been among the most dominant of issues on which diplomats have spent their time, in industrialized and developing countries alike, both in multilateral venues and in bilateral consultations. Broad approaches to development questions are generally debated in the largest and most powerful multilateral venues for economic diplomacy: in the Bretton Woods institutions (World Bank, IMF and GATT/WTO), at the United Nations, and at G8 summits. Out of these often contentious discussions that regularly pit representatives of industrialized and developing countries against one another, broad policy approaches have emerged. For example, in 1964 members of the GATT agreed to adopt GATT Part IV, which allowed for developing countries to derogate from the founding GATT principle of liberal trade temporarily to the extent required to facilitate more rapid economic development. Thus the principle of 'special and differential treatment' ('S&DT') for developing countries in multilateral trade liberalization regimes was established. In 2000, the UN General Assembly agreed upon eight Millennium Development Goals, broad and ambitious objectives such as eradicating extreme poverty and hunger and ensuring environmental sustainability, with a strategy for achieving them by 2015.[21] At the G8 Gleneagles summit in 2005, G8 member governments committed themselves to doubling development aid to Africa to over $50 billion and to forgiving all the debt of eighteen of the most heavily indebted of developing countries, a group that has come to be known as the Highly Indebted Poor Countries ('HIPCs').[22]

Yet if economic development had been primarily a technical task, it might already have been completed by now, at least for the most part. What makes economic development often difficult is in large part the same set of problems of communication and representation that makes all diplomacy problematic. The diplomatic representation and communication functions needed to design, finance and bring to completion economic development projects are amongst the most challenging of tasks in diplomacy. The process by which a development project is realized involves many actors and negotiations and mediations, which have to take place over many iterations or rounds. A serious breakdown at any step can lead to failure of an entire project. Development needs are very diverse, with some countries needing far more, and far more types of projects, than others. A partial list of development needs includes infrastructure (transport, energy, housing, etc.), poverty eradication, environmental clean-up and preservation, transfer of capacities in governance (training, institutional development, policy advice), and monetary and currency stabilization. Ideas for development strategies and particular projects may originate from government, business or civil society actors in developing countries themselves, from member governments of the development banks, or from the bank staff themselves. Diplomats representing each actor must then prioritize strategies and projects and reach agreement on who will undertake which projects and how they will be funded.

Development banks play a pivotal rôle in this process. Senior management of the World Bank and regional development banks communicate with their boards of directors from their member countries regarding the course of the agency's overall development strategy and its strategy for each recipient country. This process varies slightly in the case of the operation of UNDP and UNCTAD. The senior staffs of these agencies have an input into the policy formation process. But once policies are set and funded by negotiation amongst all the actors, the agencies then become implementers of the policy, which includes apportioning the budgeted funds to competing project proposals. They then must mediate between government, business and civil society to contract a project and supervise its successful completion on time, on budget and with popular support and legitimacy. Development projects often involve numerous tiers of contracting and subcontracting organizations, public and private, transnational and sub-national. When conceptualized from the perspective of diplomacy, it is not hard to understand why the 'development business' is so difficult to do successfully and why it continues to be subjected to a barrage of political criticism both from countries that fund development and from beneficiary countries.[23]

Achieving and maintaining stability in the currency and monetary policy of developing countries is one of the hardest amongst the already challenging tasks for diplomacy, as unreliable or unstable monetary policy management and a volatile or plunging currency can undermine the effectiveness of all of the other types of development projects underway in a country. The International Monetary Fund continues to be the primary actor assuming responsibility for advising governments of developing countries on monetary policy and currency stability. The IMF provides credit to central banks and finance ministries of developing countries on the condition that they follow IMF policy advice.[24] The Paris Club, which is an informal gathering of representatives of finance ministries of nineteen creditor countries that meets regularly in Paris, communicates and negotiates with representatives of developing countries on their ability to repay their sovereign debt. The Club can take decisions to reschedule, reduce or forgive the sovereign debt of developing-country governments when they deem it to be in the collective interest of the international financial system to do so. Since its inception in 1956 the Paris Club has negotiated agreements with eighty-six debtor countries rescheduling debts valued at over half a trillion dollars.[25] The Paris Club confers with the IMF for advice in the course of taking its decisions. Since the 1990s the Paris Club has expanded its efforts to ease the debt burden of the Highly Indebted Poor Countries. In 2005 the Paris Club agreed to write off $17 billion in debt owed by Nigeria alone.

Non-state diplomatic actors such as the World Economic Forum also play a growing rôle in the diplomacy of economic development. Through its Davos Annual Meeting and regional summits, the Forum creates opportunities for business, government and civil society leaders in developing and industrialized countries alike to meet, exchange ideas, focus together on common problems, explore potential solutions and build networks on which they can draw throughout the year as specific ideas, opportunities and projects arise. More recently, other private projects such as the Clinton Global Initiative ('CGI'), a CSO established by former US President Bill Clinton in 2005, have acted as catalysts for bringing together private donors and public institutions in industrial and developing countries to facilitate development projects. The CGI reported on its website in early 2009 that its participants have made nearly 1,200 project commitments with a total value of $46 billion.[26]

Migration Issues

The ability of individuals to cross borders and to reside in another land under the governance of another sovereign is one of the oldest modes of diplomacy, as it is an embassy in itself, an act of representation that mediates estrangement between sovereign authorities. However, for a government to grant right of asylum to someone who is *persona non grata* in their home country is to make a diplomatic communication that may not be well received by that country's government. The regulation of movement of persons has long formed one of the core functions of foreign ministries: issuing of passports, visas and other travel documents, and the provision of consular services to one's citizens travelling or residing abroad. Diplomatic agreements between governments concerning the movement of persons and the rights of foreign persons to reside and work have been a major component of diplomatic relations between nation–states for over a century. Arguably the most important aspect of the treaties of European integration that have created the European Union is the right of citizens of any member country to reside and work in any other. Some bilateral agreements contain provisions allowing for certain numbers of each country's nationals to live and work in the other country on a reciprocal basis for a fixed period of time. However, migration has often posed greater threats and challenges for diplomats, as natural disasters, famine, war and systematic human rights violations have provoked large-scale migrations across borders. In recent decades, the increasing disparity of wealth between rich and poor nations has caused a rapidly increasing flow of economic migrants seeking to cross borders in search of work in foreign lands without official permission. Causes range from resource crises and economic collapse in developing countries to the basic desire to provide a better income and standard of living for families who stay behind in the home country.

As economic migration has grown, the issue increasingly has risen in importance on the security agendas for bilateral diplomacy between major powers. US–Mexican relations have had tense moments over the issue, even as border authorities have attempted to cooperate on an ongoing basis to maintain order and avoid human tragedies. The European Union has sought to address migration concerns with its neighbours to the south and east by negotiating regional institutional projects such as the Barcelona Process and the Union of the Mediterranean Initiative, offering financial incentives for cooperation to regulate migration to the EU across the Mediterranean Sea. Multilateral specialized agencies have come to play a greater rôle as venues for diplomacy on migration issues. The Office of the United Nations High Commissioner for Refugees ('UNHCR') was established in 1950 to manage migration questions resulting from emergencies. A year later, the International Organization for Migration ('IOM') was founded to promote and facilitate effective diplomacy and cooperation on the broadest range of migration issues and problems. Major CSOs that focus on poverty relief and humanitarian assistance also play significant rôles in addressing migration problems.

Crisis Management as Economic Diplomacy

As cross-border flows of goods, services, capital and labour have increased over the past two centuries, the risk of different types of economic crises originating in one location or country then spreading across borders and having a global economic impact has increased significantly. By the late nineteenth century, the international financial system was already sufficiently integrated that central banks and finance ministries of the major economies (Britain, France, Germany, United States) began to cooperate by making loans and lines of credit available to one another in the event of major bank failures, such as Barings in the UK (1890) and Knickerbocker in the United States (1907). Since the Second World War, governments, multilateral economic institutions and large global firms have all sought to avoid a repeat of the greatest ever failure of diplomacy to respond to a global economic crisis, when negotiators were unable to agree on a multilateral response to the financial market crashes of 1929. The resulting cycle of unilateral tariff increases and competitive currency devaluations led to a ratcheting up of political nationalism and hostility between governments and peoples. The transformation of technology facilitating electronic funds transfer in recent decades has made the need for multilateral cooperation in the event of crises much more urgent and has also made it necessary for authorities to communicate and act collectively within a much narrower time frame than ever before. Doubts amongst currency traders and speculators about the soundness of a developing country's ability to service its sovereign debt or the foreign exchange reserves of its central bank can result in the collapse of the value of its currency on foreign exchange markets in hours rather than weeks or months, as illustrated by the debt crises in Latin America in the early 1980s, Mexico in 1994, and East Asia and Russia in 1997. Sudden downturns in economic activity precipitated by, or occurring in conjunction with, specific events have undermined investor confidence. The 1987 stock market crash, the terrorist attacks of 2001 and the US subprime mortgage and credit crisis of 2007–8 have prompted swift coordinated responses by multilateral economic institutions, central banks and finance ministries of major economy countries to provide liquidity to international financial markets and reassure investors.

Financial crises are not the only type of economic crisis that increasingly requires a swift coordinated multilateral response. As industrialization has proceeded and global population has expanded, natural disasters increasingly have the potential to devastate national and regional economies and to contribute to an increase in political instability in afflicted regions. A particularly vivid example is the Indian Ocean tsunami that struck on Boxing Day 2004, which took over 350,000 lives in an arc of destruction that caused infrastructural damage to a dozen economies. Sri Lanka, Thailand and Indonesia were particularly severely affected. Multilateral institutions such as the UN, the World Bank and the IMF joined forces with major civil society organizations such as the ICRC and Médécins Sans Frontières, nation–state governments and large global firms to gather and distribute aid to injured and displaced persons and to coordinate the rebuilding of destroyed infrastructure. Another related type of crisis with similar potential to cause global economic damage is in the area of health and food safety. The outbreak of new pathogens with the potential to spread swiftly in the human population through the international transport network, such as the Ebola virus, SARS and avian influenza ('bird flu'), and the movement of bovine spongiform encephalopathy (BSE or 'mad cow disease') and equine foot and mouth disease have challenged governments and multilateral institutions. The policy and diplomatic challenge that they face is how best to craft and coordinate responses that are effective, affordable and at the same time do not sow the kind of fear amongst the general populace that itself can damage the vitality of economic life in affected countries. Health diplomacy has become more sophisticated and effective since the late twentieth century, although it is often hampered by conflicting interests. The World Health Organization cooperates with nation–state health authorities and major health CSOs to ensure rapid distribution of medications and, when necessary, to restrict cross-border movement of persons to prevent or slow the spread of new illnesses.

Many types of economic crises are able to be addressed through already-existing multilateral institutional structures that have been established in advance for dealing with potential problems and have already been tested. In the 1990s the International Monetary Fund drew on its experience in dealing with the 1980s debt crises to coordinate a response to the 1994 Mexican and 1997 Asian and Russian crises in which major central banks and major global commercial banks participated. However, the biggest challenges for effective diplomacy in responding to crises in a way that is timely and can address the full magnitude of an event are new types of crises, or crises with unanticipated dimensions. By definition, unexpected events are situations for which diplomats have not prepared responses in advance. The particular ways that some types of natural disasters affect national and regional economies fall into this category. The impact of the Boxing Day tsunami, for example, due to its location, size and the general infrequency of tsunamis in heavily populated areas, meant that organizations were ill prepared to respond rapidly and efficiently. Some non-state diplomatic actors, such as the World Economic Forum, have been experimenting with new approaches to developing communications networks that can mobilize and coordinate between public and private actors to respond rapidly and effectively to disasters. Following the 2003 earthquake in Gujarat, the Forum established its Disaster Relief Network, which consists of nation–state based networks of governments, civil society organizations and private firms ready to communicate in the immediate aftermath of a disaster so that the private sector can work closely with public officials on relief and recovery efforts.

The management of economic diplomacy in the late twentieth and early twenty-first centuries has become much more complex, even as it has become progressively more efficient. The number of agreements, and the number and type of actors participating in them, have increased dramatically. The number and type of structures or mechanisms for monitoring compliance with these agreements continue to grow. The increasing demand from the global public for transparency has made these monitoring functions more important and, at the same time, more demanding. Diplomats charged with negotiating agreements and communicating with their counterparts as part of the monitoring process not only have to be skilled practitioners of the core diplomatic functions of representation and communication. They also have had to increase their levels of competence in the particular technical areas over which they have assumed responsibility (trade, monetary policy, development, migration, health, etc.). The level of technical expertise required to be effective in these functions is all but certain to continue its increase. This in turn will make the ability to communicate with counterparts and with the public about complex and contested issues all the more essential. Once again, the skills and training of an actor's diplomats going forward will play a crucial rôle in whether that actor is able to use economic diplomacy effectively to mediate differences, understand others and achieve their own policy objectives.

10

Managing Military and Security Diplomacy

Introduction: Meeting Security Needs in the Nuclear Age

The success or failure of diplomacy in the domain of security and military relations in the nuclear age is arguably that on which the most is riding, in that failure could lead in the extreme to annihilation of civilization as we know it. Scholars of the classical approach to diplomatic studies have regarded the mediation of estrangement between nation–states that can lead to violent conflict as the most central and most important of diplomatic tasks. The diplomatic needs that were identified during and immediately after the Second World War, and the processes and practices that were devised to meet those needs, appeared to make the classical diplomacy scholars' case. The ability to mediate, manage and resolve conflict through communication and negotiation has been key to the survival of polities since the dawn of civilization, but what changed after the nuclear strikes on Hiroshima and Nagasaki in August 1945 was the relative significance of the consequences of failure to achieve the needed diplomatic mediation. Diplomacy intended to prevent future conflict has been the response to successive outbreaks of multilateral conflict with increasing severity since the eighteenth century. What has made the last two centuries different from the preceding period is that diplomats have sought to institutionalize the diplomatic mechanisms for representation and communication in a new and more formal way in order to facilitate regular consultation, mediation and, when required, negotiation to avoid or resolve conflict.[1]

By the end of the Second World War, the nineteenth-century Concert of Europe security system that developed following the Congress of Vienna in 1815, and its successor, the League of Nations, created in the Versailles Treaty in 1919 after the Great War (the First World War), could not be credited with having prevented the two largest wars in human history. Yet governments continued to believe that the development of institutions to facilitate security diplomacy had played a positive rôle in avoiding even more frequent and destructive conflict. Hence they set about negotiating the creation of the multilateral institutional structure for security diplomacy that prevails today, in which the United Nations Security Council occupies a central rôle, and in which regional collective security bodies such as the North Atlantic Treaty Organization ('NATO'), the Organization for Security and Cooperation in Europe ('OSCE') and the Commonwealth of Independent States' Collective Security Treaty Organization ('CSTO') are also prominent.[2]

The successful mediation of estrangement at the broader level, however, requires more than just an efficient mechanism through which diplomats can communicate with one another in the event of a prospective or actual crisis. The ability to communicate effectively requires that diplomats come to have a measure of familiarity with one another, and with each other's governments and their positions, even in advance of the need to address a particular bilateral or multilateral issue.[3] Direct communication between military officers of different nations is an equally important mode of security diplomacy for building familiarity, understanding and, eventually, trust. Senior foreign policy makers also need to be able to communicate effectively with their own senior military officers, who are responsible for creating and implementing military strategy about other states, their capabilities and their interests. Hence regular bilateral and multilateral meetings for the purpose of getting to know one another, and formal confidence-building measures – such as summits for heads of state and for high-level officers, visits to each side's military facilities and joint military exercises – can be just as important in avoiding conflict as institutional structures for communication themselves.[4] Modes of communication in bilateral security diplomacy have also evolved through establishment of dedicated channels, such as 'hotlines' between heads of government of traditional adversaries the Soviet Union and the United States, to ensure that unintended actions did not inadvertently signal the intention to initiate a conflict that would result in a nuclear Armageddon.

Security Diplomacy through the United Nations Security Council

The basic need for diplomatic mediation at the practical level between two or more states arises when a disagreement becomes so serious that their governments are unable to communicate and negotiate directly with one another so as to reduce tensions and avoid a heightened risk of economic or military conflict. In such circumstances, diplomatic mediation frequently requires the good offices of other parties. Institutions such as the Concert of Europe and the League of Nations were created expressly for this purpose. Yet the occasions for the commencement of both world wars of the twentieth century arose because the existing multilateral institutions for security diplomacy were not able to function as they were intended. In July 1914 Germany refused an invitation to a meeting of the Concert of Europe intended to avert war. In 1933 fascist governments in Japan and Germany both withdrew from membership in the League of Nations, followed by Italy in 1937, which contributed substantially to the inability of the League to prevent the outbreak of war in Europe in 1939. In neither case was the diplomatic negotiation that might have prevented conflict able to occur in the multilateral venue designed to facilitate it. Since the founding of the United Nations at San Francisco in 1945, the UN Security Council has become the dominant venue through which governments engage in bilateral or multilateral diplomacy to avoid, resolve and manage conflict. Whilst the Security Council has by no means always been successful in its mission, since it was created virtually all nations have felt obliged to seek its sanction for military action, or at the least to justify military action with reference to the statements and formal resolutions of the Security Council. This indicates that the UN founding signatories achieved their objective of the Security Council becoming a norm-setting and norm-maintaining institution for global security diplomacy. By signing the UN Charter, member states agree under Article 25 to abide by the decisions of the Security Council. The fact that most Security Council resolutions have elicited compliance over the organization's history has enabled its resolutions to command authority globally and has created the expectation that they will be enforced.[5]

In its mission to limit conflict through diplomacy, the Security Council is finely balanced in its structure between efficiency and fairness. That five UN member states (France, Britain, the United States, China and the Soviet Union / Russian Federation) were given permanent seats on the Security Council with the power to veto resolutions was a recognition of the rôle that the great powers have played in security diplomacy throughout the long history of the Westphalia nation–states system, and particularly through the nineteenth and twentieth centuries. By contrast, the ten rotating seats allowed for all UN member states to participate, at least to some degree, in what was thought to be the UN's most crucial work: keeping the peace. UN member states may bring complaints against other members and request the Security Council to act: to assist, to mediate or, in the absence of mediation, to seek the adherence of other members to their obligations under the UN Charter. As it goes about its work, the Security Council may invite the parties to a dispute and any other interested party to attend Council meetings on a non-voting basis. Ultimately, the Security Council may authorize the use of military force by UN members to enforce its resolutions if it deems it necessary, and it may call upon UN members to assist militarily in enforcement actions. One of the important aspects of the design of the UN's Security Council-led approach to conflict resolution is that it does not attempt to preclude the interests of member states in avoiding and resolving conflicts on their own or attempting to do so. Article 51 also expressly reaffirms member states' rights to act in self-defence, provided they report their actions to the Security Council.[6]

The Security Council faces two main challenges to its ability to achieve its broad conflict resolution objective. The first is opposition amongst Security Council member countries to a particular initiative, either because they have a partisan interest in the outcome or because they have a political reason to oppose it related to their own relationship with another member or members of the Security Council. These situations arise more often concerning the permanent members of the Council, because of their right to veto resolutions. Sometimes the permanent members have vetoed or otherwise blocked the passage of Security Council resolutions that they perceived as counter to their own proximate security interests, their military objectives or those of their immediate allies. US diplomats at the United Nations, for example, have used the threat of veto to prevent numerous Security Council resolutions concerning Israeli–Palestinian relations because of close US security ties to Israel. In other cases, US interests have prevented the Security Council acting to ensure implementation of resolutions passed. UN Security Council Resolution 242, which was passed in 1967 following the Arab–Israeli War of that year, called on Israel to withdraw from territories that its armed forces occupied during the war, and Security Council Resolution 338, passed after the 1973 Yom Kippur War, reiterated 242's directive, but the Security Council has never been able to take further direct steps to ensure implementation. This has resulted in the problem of Israeli control of Palestinian territories persisting into the first decade of the twenty-first century. With the backing of the United States, Israel has felt able to disregard its obligation as a UN member to adhere to Resolutions 242 and 338. This constitutes the Security Council's second main challenge: to be able to compel member states to abide by its rulings, in the absence of the threat of *force majeure* from some sort of UN standing army.

Yet, given this absence, this problem has not been nearly so great as might have been imagined. The felt need since the Second World War for a diplomatic mechanism such as the Security Council to mitigate conflict between states can be seen in the general willingness of UN member states to abide by its resolutions and cooperate in its undertakings. When the Security Council decides to act in a conflict situation, member states tend to observe its directives. It is more difficult to convince non-state actors in conflict zones to adhere to Security Council rulings. For example, the Security Council has been engaged in efforts to bring peace to, and keep the peace in, the region of central Africa stretching from the eastern Democratic Republic of Congo (DRC, formerly known as Zaïre) into Uganda, Rwanda and Burundi through close monitoring, a series of resolutions, imposing an arms embargo on the region and authorizing the deployment of a UN peacekeeping force, MONUC, in 2003. Throughout this difficult mission, which has taken several years to begin to bear fruit, the Security Council has been able to work with the governments of the DRC, Uganda, Rwanda and Burundi much more easily than with rebel militia organizations such as the Democratic Forces for the Liberation of Rwanda and the Interahamwe.[7]

Bilateral, Regional and Multilateral Security Treaties and Relationships

The bilateral security alliance between two states is the most classical and traditional of diplomatic relationships that goes beyond basic diplomatic relations, although the context in which such alliances are situated has been shifted by the advent of the United Nations. In the post-World War II era, these agreements have almost always been articulated in the context of the obligations of both countries as UN members. This shift is significant, in that, by signing the UN charter, member states are committing themselves to a set of norms of diplomatic conduct that would preclude certain types of bilateral alliances, such as secret alliances directed against third countries. The 1939 Molotov–Ribbentrop Pact between the governments of Nazi Germany and the Soviet Union, which was directed against Poland, is probably the most notorious of alliances containing secret provisions in recent times. A bilateral security alliance usually takes the form of a treaty in which the two states articulate a set of common security objectives and that commits each state to come to the aid of the other if the other is attacked by a third party. Bilateral agreements generally function without the establishment of a Secretariat or organization that operates on a permanent basis. They generally take the form of an agreed set of policies and procedures that govern ongoing diplomatic communication and guide how each side will act under specified circumstances, such as an attack on one or both parties. Such agreements almost always provide for the sharing of military intelligence between the two armed forces, and some agreements also call for varying degrees of joint military training, exchange of officers, and certain shared defensive missions. One particularly successful bilateral alliance has been the Mutual Security Treaty signed in 1953 between the Republic of Korea (South Korea) and the United States. Under the agreement the United States has kept troops permanently stationed in South Korea, to help ensure stability on the Korean peninsula, for over half a century since the ceasefire in the Korean War, and, more recently, South Korea has contributed over 3,000 troops to multilateral peacekeeping missions in Iraq and Afghanistan. Another more recent example is the Russia–Belarus security alliance. In 1995, the Russian Federation and Belarus negotiated a bilateral security treaty along with a series of other bilateral cooperation agreements, including a customs union, that reflected the close political relationship that developed between the two post-Soviet states from 1993.

Regional and multilateral security alliances resemble their bilateral analogues, only with three or more members. One example is the Australia, New Zealand, United States Security Treaty ('ANZUS'), which was signed in 1951 as a mutual security agreement amongst the three countries. Its structure was modified in 1984 when the United States withdrew from its alliance commitments to New Zealand after New Zealand banned port visits by naval vessels carrying nuclear weapons. This left the alliance as a two-legged agreement between Australia and New Zealand and between Australia and the United States. On other occasions, bilateral security alliances evolve into regional or multilateral agreements after a third state petitions to join. In turn, because by their nature regional and multilateral alliances are likely to require a degree of multilateral diplomatic cooperation and military coordination, they may morph into regional security organizations. The eight-member Commonwealth of Independent States (CIS), for example, signed a Collective Security Treaty in 1993 committing some of the member states of the former Soviet Union to defend one another in the event of an attack from outside. In 2002, six CIS countries met to transform the Collective Security Treaty into the Collective Security Treaty Organization (CSTO), a collective security organization patterned after NATO with a governing Secretariat, joint training exercises and shared military procurement pricing.[8]

Multilateral Regional and Collective Security Processes

Regional and multilateral collective security organizations play a critical and complex rôle in security diplomacy, in that they serve both as vehicles for coordinating action amongst several states in the security arena and, at the same time, as venues for the diplomatic processes of making, implementing and enforcing security policy. Whilst these organizations are important as diplomatic venues and actors in themselves, the focus in this chapter is on how security diplomacy is practised through them. In many of these organizations, such as the North Atlantic Treaty Organization ('NATO'), there are separate venues in which military leaders and civilian leaders meet and consult, even though the *raison d'être* of the organization is about seamless coordination of civilian and military security policy. The North Atlantic Treaty Organization is by far the largest and oldest of these institutions, but other institutions such as the Organization for Security and Cooperation in Europe ('OSCE'), the Economic Community of West African States ('ECOWAS') and, more recently, the European Union ('EU'), the African Union ('AU') and the Shanghai Cooperation Organization ('SCO') are also multilateral organizations that implement significant security alliances. Unlike other organizations, the OSCE evolved from a multilateral conference, the Conference on Security and Cooperation in Europe ('CSCE'). The CSCE, also known as the Helsinki Process, was itself a part of the diplomatic process known as détente, which thawed frozen East–West relations during the 1970s.[9]

NATO and the Warsaw Treaty Organization, or Warsaw Pact, were founded as regional defensive alliances in 1949 and 1955 respectively, each with the intent of deterring attack upon its members by states in the other alliance. The core principle of each alliance was that an attack on one member was to be treated as an attack upon all. Hence it was the initial diplomatic negotiation of the institutional design of the two agreements that made them the effective security structures to keep the Cold War from going 'hot'. Throughout the Cold War period, the most important diplomatic issues that arose for each organization surrounded membership, with the German Democratic Republic joining the Warsaw Pact in 1956 and Albania leaving in 1961, and several countries joining NATO, beginning with the Federal Republic of Germany in 1955. Both agreements created institutional structures for mediating and coordinating relations between, and joint operations of, their respective member states. In each case this took the form of a political committee and a joint military command structure. The political side of alliance cooperation required ambassadorial representation at alliance headquarters (NATO in Paris and later Brussels, the Warsaw Pact in Warsaw), as well as the permanent staffing of the headquarters by diplomats and other experts who are either part of the member state delegations or else in the employ of NATO itself. The primary venue at which NATO diplomacy is conducted is the North Atlantic Council ('NAC'), at which each NATO member has a seat. Chaired by NATO's Secretary-General, the NAC meets weekly at the level of member governments' permanent representatives (ambassadors) to NATO, twice annually at the level of member state foreign ministers, and occasionally at the head of government level. The NAC is empowered to take on behalf of the alliance all decisions permitted under the 1949 North Atlantic Treaty, which created NATO. Crucially, the NAC takes decisions by consensus, which means that each member state has an effective veto, but which also means that when NATO acts, the message it sends to its interlocutors is understood as based upon unanimity, with all the persuasiveness that unanimity accords. The NAC has created a number of committees to advise it on an ongoing basis. Much of the diplomatic work that goes on daily at NATO headquarters in Brussels is conducted by committees reporting to the NAC. Of these committees, the Military Committee is the most significant, as it serves as the highest-level military advisory body to NATO's civilian authorities.[10]

The NATO Military Committee is the linchpin between alliance political and military decision making. Meeting weekly, on the day after the NAC meets, the Military Committee's main rôle is to organize the military cooperation required to implement NAC decisions. Usually comprised of senior officers from each member state's armed forces, the Military Committee meets several times each year at the level of ministers of defence. The realities on the ground of the joint military command structures required much more thoroughgoing, integrative aspects of diplomacy than negotiating treaties and cooperating to undertake strategic defence planning. In this regard, NATO military cooperation is also diplomatic in a way that renders it essentially different from the military command structure and defence planning process within the armed forces of a single state. For the armed forces of different countries to learn to work together effectively, a huge range of estrangements needed to be mediated, protocols of representation established and channels of communication made familiar. Forces training together and, when required, fighting together successfully demanded agreement on every issue from what language would be used in which situations to who would outrank whom and who would take orders from whom in each non-combat and combat situation. These were engagements of diplomacy very different from, but no less important than, the *haute politique* diplomacy that traditional scholars of diplomatic studies usually associate with security diplomacy. The fact that alliance member governments and their armed forces engaged in this hands-on level of security diplomacy changed the relationships between these states significantly in ways that were not planned or anticipated when the alliances were created.

Despite the structural similarities between NATO and the Warsaw Pact, the distribution of power within each alliance was different enough from the other to affect substantially the practice of diplomacy within them over time. From its beginning in 1955 until its dissolution in 1991, the Warsaw Pact effectively served as an institutional conduit for the exercise of power by the Soviet Communist Party and military authorities over their Warsaw Pact allies. NATO, by contrast, evolved into a more effective venue for diplomatic negotiations between its member countries. NATO mediated a series of contentious issues that persisted throughout the Cold War, ranging from the differing security priorities of NATO members on each side of the Atlantic to questions of military strategy. The respective interests of Europe and North America in détente with the Soviet Union were more often out of sync than aligned at any given time, for example. West Europeans perceived the development of US President John Kennedy's 'Flexible Response' strategy in the United States in the early 1960s as raising significantly the threat of an invasion of Western Europe by the Warsaw Pact using conventional forces. American political and military leaders in turn were suspicious of West German Chancellor Willy Brandt's resulting *Ostpolitik* diplomatic opening to the Soviets. Western Europeans then feared that US President Richard Nixon's détente, which produced the Strategic Arms Limitation Treaty ('SALT') in 1972 (see below), would lead to decoupling of US from West European strategic interests in European security. Whilst NATO diplomacy failed to prevent France from withdrawing from NATO's integrated military command structure in 1966, France remained committed enough to the alliance and its institutions to continue as a member and to participate in NATO's

French President Nicolas Sarkozy congratulates former Danish Prime Minister Anders Fogh Rasmussen on Rasmussen's selection to be NATO Secretary-General at NATO summit, Strasbourg, April 2009

political structure and finally, in 2009, rejoined NATO's military command structure as well.

The political and military channels of representation and communication that NATO developed during the Cold War facilitated NATO's transformation after the Cold War from a regional security organization into a collective security organization with an increasingly global reach. Even as NATO has struggled at times in the post-Cold War period to re-imagine and redefine its 'strategic concept' or principal mission, it has proven remarkably adept at the core diplomatic functions of representation and communication, and the objectives at which those functions are targeted: negotiation, and mediation of estrangement between alienated actors in the broadest sense. NATO began this process by taking seriously the imperative to embrace its former adversaries. Starting with the German Democratic Republic, which was absorbed into an existing NATO member, the Federal Republic of Germany, at the time of German reunification in 1991, many former member states of the Warsaw Pact have joined NATO.

NATO created the North Atlantic Consultative Council ('NACC') in 1991 to institutionalize cooperation between NATO and its former Cold War adversaries. Three years later, NATO initiated its Partnership for Peace ('PfP') programme, which offered to all non-NATO members in Europe and the former Soviet Union individually tailored bilateral cooperation agreements. PfP agreements include generic features such as commitments by signatories to norms of human rights and peaceful resolution of disputes, in return for NATO assistance in resolving threats to the security of PfP members. In addition, PfP agreements contain a degree of military cooperation of the signatory's choosing, which can include joint military training, assistance with modernization of a signatory's armed forces, participation in NATO security operations, and a path of preparation for NATO membership. In 1997, NACC became the Euro-Atlantic Partnership Council ('EAPC'), under which NATO's twenty-six members and twenty-four partner countries – comprised of the European states and former Soviet republics that are not NATO members – meet regularly on a formal basis to discuss security issues of common concern. Most EAPC partner countries have established diplomatic representative offices at NATO's headquarters in Brussels.

Beginning in 1997 NATO institutionalized the special and unique relationship that was emerging with the Russian Federation, the successor state to its former prime Soviet adversary, by signing the NATO–Russia Founding Act on Mutual Relations, Cooperation and Security. Russian peacekeeping forces had begun serving alongside NATO counterparts in Bosnia from 1996. The 1997 agreement created a Permanent Joint Council ('PJC') in which NATO's plenary assembly, the North Atlantic Council ('NAC'), met on a regularly scheduled basis with a Russian representative on a bilateral, one-to-one basis. Under the agreement, Russia established both political and military representation at NATO's headquarters in Brussels. Two years later, NATO and the Russian Federation deployed troops jointly to protect ethnic Albanian Kosovars from attacks by Serb nationalist forces in the Serbian province of Kosovo. Whilst not without considerable disagreement between NATO and Russian commanders over the remit of the international force in Kosovo, the deployment can be seen as emblematic of the success of NATO's security diplomacy in mediating the estrangement with what was once its greatest adversary and establishing not only representation and communication, but an established institutional format for security cooperation on an ongoing basis. A revision to the 1997 agreement in 2002 turned the PJC into the

NATO–Russia Council ('NRC'), in which Russia and the twenty-six NATO members meet monthly at ambassadorial level as a council of twenty-seven, to discuss issues of mutual security interest, with semi-annual meetings at the foreign and defence minister level and occasional head of government summits.[11]

NATO's wide range of forms and degrees of cooperation has extended well beyond its traditional adversaries and other immediate European neighbours. The organization established the Mediterranean Dialogue with seven states around the Mediterranean basin to address issues of common concern. Although the thrust of the Mediterranean Dialogue has been to improve communication between NATO and partner countries, forces from Egypt, Jordan and Morocco have also served with NATO forces in Bosnia and Kosovo. NATO has also established close relationships with the governments and armed forces of like-minded countries in the Asia-Pacific region, which is outside of NATO's traditional area of operations: Japan, Australia, South Korea and New Zealand. NATO officials began to meet with their Japanese counterparts as early as 1990. What began as political cooperation has evolved into more applied projects, in which Japan has contributed valuable support to NATO undertakings in the Balkans and Afghanistan. Australia now maintains a representative at NATO headquarters in Brussels to facilitate practical cooperation on projects such as counter-terrorism, and Australian forces are deployed alongside NATO troops in NATO's International Security Assistance Force ('ISAF') mission in Afghanistan.

In what is perhaps one of the greatest tests of NATO's institutional and political adaptability, the European Union has begun to develop its own identity as a security actor through its European Security and Defence Policy (ESDP) with NATO's cooperation since 2001. Under ESDP, the EU is able to take decisions on military actions in which the United States and Canada do not choose to participate, using NATO's forces and command structures but without American and Canadian participation. For different historical reasons, not all EU members have joined NATO, but, since 2004, nineteen of the twenty-seven EU member states (as of 2009) have been members of NATO as well. In 2003 NATO and the EU reached agreement on the 'Berlin Plus' arrangements, which allow the EU access to NATO resources for EU-led operations under the command of NATO's Deputy Strategic Allied Commander Europe ('SACEUR'), a post always filled by a European. One of the indications of how important NATO considers its own transformation to be, and of the importance it ascribes to the ability to communicate the meaning of its transformation to the rest of the world, is the expansion of NATO's public diplomacy activities and staff (see chapter 8). NATO has recognized the extent to which a broader global understanding of its mission has contributed to its ability to achieve its objectives, and in recent years it has shifted its own diplomatic resources to undertake this function more effectively.[12]

Arms Control Diplomacy

As the capacity of weaponry to wreak destruction upon civilian populations as well as military forces mushroomed over the course of the twentieth century, diplomats have focused increasingly on negotiating to limit the use of arms and their impact upon non-combatants. The effects of the use of mustard gas in the Great War (the First World War) shocked civilian populations and governments alike, which led to popular pressure on governments to negotiate the Geneva Protocol of 1925 (Protocol for the Prohibition of the Use in War of Asphyxiating, Poisonous or Other Gases, and of Bacteriological Methods of Warfare), which banned the use of toxic gases and bacteriological weapons in warfare. Arms control diplomacy has been pursued in several, often complementary, directions, but with a distinct shift in focus in the years since the end of the Cold War towards multilateralism and non-proliferation. Diplomacy has risen to the task to the extent that an ever wider array of treaties constraining the behaviour of governments in war has been agreed, and compliance with the emerging regimes has been substantial, if not complete. Yet even amidst the successes of arms control diplomacy, the need for more of it remains constant, owing to the continued development of arms technologies and the profusion of new types of non-state actors with whom it is not easy for diplomats of nation–state governments and multilateral organizations to communicate according to customary diplomatic procedures.[13]

The oldest approach to arms control diplomacy has been to negotiate multilateral agreements establishing the rules of war, which, amongst other objectives, sought to preclude combatants from using weaponry in strategies intended to harm civilians. These efforts began in the nineteenth century under the auspices of the Concert of Europe and accelerated in the twentieth century in response to the emergence of new weapons technologies. For example, the 1899 Hague Declaration on the Use of Projectiles the Object of Which is the Diffusion of Asphyxiating or Deleterious Gases committed combatants not to use newly developed ballistic missiles and rockets to attack their enemies with toxic gases. A second approach has been to negotiate agreements limiting or banning outright the use of types of weapons that intentionally or otherwise are bound to cause widespread collateral damage to civilian populations, such as chemical and biological warfare ('CBW'). The 1925 Geneva Protocol was followed over sixty years later by a multilateral Chemical Weapons Convention (Convention on the Prohibition of the Development, Production, Stockpiling and Use of Chemical Weapons and on their Destruction), which was agreed in 1992, entered into force in 1997 and by 2007 had at least 183 nation–state signatories. The Convention obliges signatories to disarm existing stocks of chemical weapons and refrain from acquiring new ones.

A third form of arms control diplomacy, the negotiation of arms limitation and reduction treaties, arose during the Cold War specifically on a bilateral basis between the United States and the Soviet Union, as a result of the nuclear 'arms race' competition between the two countries to outbuild the other's nuclear arsenal. The major agreements of this type were the two Strategic Arms Limitation Treaties, SALT I, signed by US President Richard Nixon and Soviet Communist Party General Secretary Leonid Brezhnev in 1972, and SALT II, signed by Brezhnev and US President Jimmy Carter in 1979. SALT I froze the two countries' intercontinental and submarine-launched ballistic missile launchers at existing levels, whilst SALT II mandated the first cuts in numbers of launch vehicles and limited the introduction of new missile systems. Subsequently, two Strategic Arms Reduction Treaties ('START' I and II) were signed, in 1991 and 1993 respectively, the latter between the United States and the Russian Federation. The first START Treaty cut numbers of warheads, missile launchers and intercontinental bomber aircraft substantially, whilst START II banned the use of Multiple, Independent Re-entry Vehicles ('MIRVs'), a technology allowing for several warheads to be fired at different targets from the same launch vehicle (missile). A further agreement, the Strategic Offensive Reductions ('SORT') Treaty, or Moscow Treaty, signed by Presidents Vladimir Putin and George W. Bush, committed the Russian Federation and United States to reduce their number of operational warheads to between 1,700 and 2,200 each by 2012.[14]

A fourth approach, the negotiation of non-proliferation agreements, also began during the Cold War as an attempt by the then very small family of nuclear powers (Soviet Union, United States, Britain, France and People's Republic of China) to prevent other states from acquiring nuclear weapons. Since the Cold War ended, this form of arms control diplomacy has become the most important of all the approaches. It has become progressively more multilateral, as existing nuclear powers and small states fearing the effects of nuclear weapons proliferation are joined by the newer members of the club of nuclear-armed nations. Yet non-proliferation as a multilateral diplomatic objective appears to fall progressively shorter of its objective, as another half-dozen countries have acquired nuclear weapons or the capacity to build them. Another handful of states are close to that capacity. The Soviet Union and United States attempted to limit proliferation of weapons systems using a different psychology by negotiating the bilateral Anti-Ballistic Missile ('ABM') Treaty, also in 1972. The ABM Treaty prohibited the two sides from building a ballistic missile defence system against incoming missiles. The theory was that such an agreement would encourage military planners in both countries not to think in terms of planning to be able to survive a full nuclear exchange in war. The US government of George W. Bush withdrew the United States from the ABM Treaty in 2002 over strong Russian objections. The Bush administration's reasoning was that, in a post-Cold War world, it was in the interest of the United States to collaborate with other nation–states in constructing a ballistic missile defence system to protect against attacks from rogue states and non-state actors employing terrorist tactics. Russia's government has remained sceptical of this shift in strategy, and the future of ballistic missile defence remains uncertain.[15]

Beyond the challenge of negotiating and implementing arms control agreements successfully lies the further challenge of ensuring continuing compliance by all of the signatories. Negotiators understand that in many cases it may be in the interest of a government that signs an arms control treaty to cheat, if it can do so without being detected, especially if that government is legitimately fearful that the other party or parties to an agreement would be inclined to do the same thing. Hence the objective for negotiators is to build into the treaty language procedures for monitoring, inspection and verification of treaty commitments: evidence of dismantling of weapons systems, levels of armaments in place at particular locations, quantities of nuclear fuel in storage, numbers of troops on payrolls. Monitoring can be done through self-reporting or through a multilateral auditing procedure conducted by all treaty signatories. Inspections of missile sites can be passive if conducted by remote surveillance or active if conducted through on-site visits. They can be scheduled or conducted on a surprise basis. The main objective for diplomats negotiating an arms control agreement is to agree on a compliance system that creates norms that reduce or minimize the incentive to cheat.

Security Diplomacy with Non-State Actors

One of the major challenges that diplomats face in dealing with a security crisis is how to represent themselves to and communicate with non-state actors that are dissimilar to themselves and that may not have established procedures for conducting diplomacy. It raises the broader question of how non-state diplomatic actors represent themselves and communicate about security issues. Amongst the least problematic in this area of diplomatic practice are the interactions between governments, multilateral organizations and global civil society organizations that arise when humanitarian relief is needed, either in war zones or in natural disaster situations. Channels for communication between foreign and defence ministries and CSOs that often participate in relief efforts are usually well established. The United Nations plays a leading rôle in facilitating these communication channels. Many CSOs send permanent representatives to the UN to be ready to coordinate relief efforts when situations arise. In recent years the World Economic Forum has also facilitated this communication capacity by creating its Disaster Relief Network, through which governments, CSOs and global firms wishing to participate in disaster relief efforts can communicate rapidly to coordinate swift aid distribution following earthquakes, typhoons, tsunamis and other natural disasters.

Other types of non-state actor present far greater challenges for security diplomacy because often the cause of the security crisis requiring diplomacy is the reason for, or the fact of, the non-state actor's existence. Rebellious territories or breakaway regions that are attempting to secede from sovereign nation–states often establish relatively functional governments, complete with foreign ministries and at least a minimal capacity and a strong willingness to engage in diplomacy with other governments and multilateral organizations. South Ossetia and Abkhazia, regions which have attempted to break away from the Republic of Georgia, are highly visible examples of such polities in the first decade of the twenty-first century. The difficulty arises in that, often, other governments are precluded politically from being able to engage in official diplomatic representation and communication with such entities, as to do so would be too damaging to their ongoing diplomacy with the state from which the entities are attempting to break away. Negotiations are thus often forced to be unofficial and are frequently conducted 'underground', in secret, or through the good offices of a third party. For states whose recognition is controversial and that are recognized by only a limited number of other states, such as the Republic of China on Taiwan and the Turkish Republic of

Northern Cyprus, diplomatic representation and communication can be conducted more openly, but nonetheless preserving the fiction, and accompanying protocol (or lack thereof), that diplomatic relations are not 'official'. The Republic of China government in Taipei is represented in the United States by the Taipei Economic and Cultural Representative Office, and the US government is represented in Taiwan by the American Institute in Taiwan, two unofficial, private bodies whose mission is to perform all the diplomatic and consular functions normally conducted at embassies and consulates. Official channels of communication between Washington and Taipei are no less open than those between Washington and Beijing. Significantly, notwithstanding the lack of official diplomatic relations, the United States government remains committed to the security of Taiwan against external attack.

Security diplomacy with a third category of non-state actor is even more problematic. Organizations employing 'terrorist' methods ('OTMs'), transnational criminal organizationss (TCOs) and 'warlords' controlling territory, population and resources within states are problems for diplomacy often precisely because these types of actors frequently choose not to communicate with other diplomatic actors (see chapter 6). OTMs like al-Qa'eda choose to engage in their own form of public diplomacy through releasing video and audio recordings sporadically to putatively sympathetic media networks like al-Jazeera. Yet no government or multilateral organization has a diplomatic representative to al-Qa'eda, and there are not even unofficial channels of communication available when the need arises. Hence, the only diplomatic communication that can mediate estrangement between al-Qa'eda and the rest of the world must be filtered through the global media, with all the challenges that such an indirect form of communication poses. Whilst transnational criminal organizations and warlords may at times choose to engage in communication with government interlocutors in an effort to achieve objectives of their own, it cannot often be understood as diplomacy in the normal sense, in that some of the behavioural norms that underlie diplomatic culture, such as durable structures of representation and preservation of the safety of negotiators, cannot be assumed. Moreover, although the need for ongoing communication may be great, ongoing representation between such actors and governments is not possible because neither governments nor OTMs, TCOs and warlords acknowledge the fundamental legitimacy of the others as actors. Without being able to get beyond this basic diplomatic necessity of accreditation, any communication can be at the very best highly provisional and ad hoc.

Broadening the Security Diplomacy Issue Agenda

Perhaps the greatest challenge for understanding how to manage military and security diplomacy in the contemporary period is the difficulty of grasping where security ends, or rather how so many other diplomatic issues are increasingly inseparable from security questions. As traditional armed conflict between nation–states as an instrument to resolve conflict over territory and populations becomes less common as a result of the successes of multilateral security diplomacy, the importance in the security diplomacy agenda of combating poverty, domestic violence, genocide, devastation from natural disasters, environmental degradation and climate change is rising. As armed forces increasingly are called upon to prevent genocides and engage in disaster relief, negotiations to set and implement viable policies become a more critical mission for contemporary diplomacy. On the agenda of security diplomacy considered in this broader sense, the environment and global climate issues perhaps rank highest in importance. The UN-sponsored Law of the Sea conferences were one of the first major multilateral endeavours in the area of environmental diplomacy. At the Third Law of the Sea Conference in the early 1970s, negotiators reached agreement on a UN Convention on the Law of the Sea, which set rules for the environmental protection of the seas and for commercial development of seabed resources. Negotiators sought to balance business interests of large firms in industrialized countries with the need to harness seabed resources to create wealth for developing countries. The treaty created multilateral bodies, the International Seabed Authority and the International Tribunal for the Law of the Sea, to enforce and implement treaty provisions.[16] Despite opposition from some United States administrations to a number of the Law of the Sea Convention's key provisions, this first major product of environmental security diplomacy has proved moderately successful thus far in terms of seeing its agreed norms established and observed by the global community.

The Kyoto Process for Mitigating Climate Change, in which a growing range of governments and non-state actors are participating, is indicative of the direction in which environmental diplomacy is evolving. The UN Framework Convention on Climate Change was adopted in 1997 at a UN conference in Kyoto, Japan, entered into force in 2005, and by 2009 over 180 governments had become signatories. In the Kyoto Process, nation–state governments are committing themselves and private firms operating within their borders to reduce emission of potentially harmful greenhouse gases into the atmosphere. The Kyoto Process has generated its own particularly complex diplomacy in which representatives of global firms and environmental CSOs are negotiating with one another, with sub-national and nation–state governments and with multilateral organizations. Unusual diplomatic alliances have emerged between unlike actors with seemingly disparate interests, resulting in negotiators proposing and developing new mechanisms for achieving greenhouse gas reductions. The still controversial market-based 'cap and trade' scheme for trading carbon emissions is one result of these processes. Only time will tell how effective this particular diplomatic process, and the agreements that flow from it, will be.[17] That environmental diplomacy is a security issue is beyond question, given the potential for failure to reverse or mitigate climate change to cause natural disasters and military conflict on a global scale. Equally, security for and protecting access to natural resources such as water have already risen in prominence on the security diplomacy agenda and are likely to rise higher still in years to come.

The major transformation that has occurred in security diplomacy since the Second World War has been the rise of effective multilateral security organizations like the United Nations and the North Atlantic Treaty Organization. This transformation has resulted in part from the dramatic increase in the risk of failure to preserve the peace in an era in which technology has permitted the development of weapons of mass destruction. Negotiation of security agreements, as well as their monitoring and enforcement, has been facilitated immeasurably by the advent of multilateral security bodies, each of which has contributed immeasurably to the process by developing a diplomatic culture of its own. These dense webs of familiarity, understandings and personal relationships do much to lower the security risk generated by one actor's uncertainty about how the other is likely to behave in a crisis situation. Multilateral and regional security diplomacy has by no means displaced more traditional bilateral security diplomacy. Yet multilateral bodies are helping nation–state governments to keep up with the diplomatic communication and negotiation required to address the emergence of threats from new types of actors, such as TCOs and OTMs, and new security challenges such as the environment and climate change, natural disasters and poverty. As in the management of economic diplomacy, security diplomats must be able to combine traditional diplomatic skills with an increasing level of technical expertise. The extent of each actor's skill set will contribute significantly to their ability to function more or less effectively than their interlocutors and rivals.

11

Managing Cultural Diplomacy

Introduction: Mediating Differences between Cultures

Culture is both a leading cause of the need for diplomacy to mediate estrangement between nation–states and an important diplomatic vehicle for mediating that estrangement. Culture is one of the prime causes of difference between peoples, governments, firms and other organizations. People often find cultures that are different from their own to be alien and, in many cases, threatening. Cultural diplomacy is primarily about how governments use the culture of their nation–state or place to communicate to others about themselves as a means of overcoming alienation from others. Global firms also can be said to engage in forms of cultural diplomacy to promote global acceptance of their particular brand and corporate culture. Multilateral organizations such as the United Nations have at the core of their mission the overcoming of cultural alienation amongst the world's peoples. Yet culture is probably most problematic in the context of relations between states. Conflicts between the cultural norms of societies and states can be exploited by governments and political leaders in situations in which political and diplomatic estrangement already exists between states. Controversies such as the issuing of a *fatwa* by Iranian Ayatollah Ruhollah Khomeini against Indian-British novelist Salman Rushdie following the publication of his novel *The Satanic Verses*, and the more recent controversies surrounding the wearing of Islamic headscarves by girls in French and Turkish schools, illustrate the power of estrangement resulting from cultural differences. In a particularly extreme example of cultural alienation, in early 2008 an Islamist Sudanese government jailed British schoolteacher Gillian Gibbons, who had permitted her class of seven-year-old schoolchildren to name a teddy bear 'Muhammad', for blaspheming against the Prophet. Gibbons was pardoned by Sudanese President Omar al-Bashir only following petitions from Muslim members of Britain's House of Lords.

To share aspects of one's culture with another state and people builds familiarity and a level of comfort on each side that is grounded in greater knowledge of how the other side's government and people might be likely to act or react in a given situation. Cultural diplomacy is often, although not always, accomplished through some form of cultural exchange between two (or more) states: educational exchange, dance troupes, football (soccer) teams, prizewinning novelists, to name a few. Hence the process of building familiarity and comfort is often intended to be explicitly reciprocal. Although cultural diplomacy is closely related to public diplomacy, cultural diplomacy differs in that it is not generally crafted to have an issue-specific message focus. Cultural diplomacy between peoples can be conceived and carried out by civil society organizations without any significant participation by a government. In other cases when a government sponsors cultural diplomacy, the audience involved in cultural diplomacy may not be the public at all, but another government or its leader. Cultural diplomacy can form one part of a broader public diplomacy strategy. Whilst culture is an important tool to use in communicating to a foreign public, public diplomacy uses a much wider range of communicative tools than culture alone. Hence cultural diplomacy and public diplomacy should be considered very distinct, even if overlapping, spheres.

The management of cultural diplomacy differs substantially from the management of economic and security diplomacy in that the rôle of multilateral institutions and other established regimes and arrangements for managing relationships is smaller and tends to be more specialized or functionally specific. Some multilateral diplomacy falls under the rubric of cultural diplomacy at a broad level. Institutions such as the United Nations Educational, Scientific and Cultural Organization ('UNESCO') play an active rôle in promoting and defending global cultural diversity. One of UNESCO's primary ways of protecting and revitalizing cultural diversity is to promote inter-cultural dialogue, which it does through such approaches as bringing together experts on the histories of different religions to promote inter-religious understanding. The United Nations more broadly undertook an initiative called the Alliance of Civilizations, beginning in 2005, stretching across several of its functional organizations (including UNESCO), which is intended to build inter-cultural understanding as a bulwark against polarization and extremism. Some large private civil society organizations, such as the World Economic Forum, provide venues for cultural diplomacy (see below). In the functional areas of education, sport and religion, specialized civil society organizations such as the English-Speaking Union, the International Olympic Committee ('IOC') and the World Council of Churches provide funding and, in some cases, organizational assistance for cultural exchange programmes. Notwithstanding the activity of multilateral institutions and civil society organizations, much of the management of cultural diplomacy remains in the hands of nation–state governments, as the discussions of practices and functional areas that follow illustrate.

Ceremonial Visits and Culture

At the outset, it should be noted that one of the oldest forms of diplomatic communication, the visit of one head of state to another, often has a significant component of cultural diplomacy. State visits, according to traditional diplomatic protocol, are treated as the most formal of personal exchanges between two nation–states. Particular rules of protocol governing much of the form and content of such visits are generally observed, ranging from the manner in which the visiting head of state is received upon arrival in the country visited to the forms for the customary state dinner held in honour of the visiting leader. A state visit is primarily cultural in content, particularly when at least one of the heads of state involved in the visit leads a country with a political system in which the head of government and head of state are separate offices. In such instances, the main function of the visit is not to negotiate or sign agreements of a political character, as is often the case when two heads of government meet. State visits involving a ceremonial head of state, such as a constitutional monarch (e.g. in the United Kingdom, Japan and the Netherlands) or an elected President in a parliamentary system (e.g. the Republic of Ireland, Israel and the Federal Republic of Germany), generally serve a different function. The visiting head of state will participate in activities and engage in discussion with his or her host and, during the rest of the visit, either share aspects of culture that are unique to one nation or the other or else emphasize shared cultural interests. The exchanging of gifts (see below), cultural performances arranged for the two heads of state, and even the foods served at the state dinner fulfil the former function. In an example of the latter, when HM Queen Elizabeth II of the United Kingdom made a state visit to the United States in 2007, she travelled to Louisville, Kentucky, to attend the running of the Kentucky Derby at Churchill Downs. By doing so, Queen Elizabeth recognized the shared cultural interest in horse racing and breeding in the United States and the United

Kingdom, in addition to the long-established business ties between the horse industries in the two countries. She also was able to share her own family's deep love of horse racing with fellow enthusiasts in Kentucky, the heartland of US horse racing culture.[1]

The Giving and Receiving of Gifts

One of the oldest and most traditional forms of cultural diplomacy, but one that is no less important today as a means of mediating estrangement between two governments or peoples, is the exchange of gifts that are in some way emblematic of the nation or state as cultural tokens and symbols of friendship. The gift of two giant pandas, Hsing-Hsing and Ling-Ling, by Chinese Communist Party Chairman Mao Zedong to US President Richard Nixon as a present from the Chinese people to the American people in 1972 was one of the most powerful tokens of the diplomatic thawing of previously complete alienation between two countries in contemporary times. Despite the reality that giant pandas are extremely shy and not at all easy for humans to approach, their image as cute and cuddly creatures did much to elevate the popular image of China, which had been viewed by many in the United States as mysterious, forbidding and even threatening, in the 1970s. The Washington National Zoo built a special home for the new arrivals, which included both indoor and outdoor viewing areas, as well as secluded zones into which the pandas could retreat for privacy. The two pandas lived out their natural lives at the Washington National Zoo, remaining the park's most popular attraction for both Washingtonians and visitors alike. The pandas' enduring popularity was so great that after both Hsing-Hsing and Ling-Ling had passed away, the Chinese government agreed to provide another pair of the rare beasts for the people of Washington to enjoy.

The giving of diplomatic gifts is often much more prosaic, accompanying most official visits between heads of state. Yet such giving is no less important for being routine, as each gift received in some way embodies an element of the culture of the giver that the giver wishes the recipient to remember long after the visit or meeting is past. When HM Queen Elizabeth II and HRH the Duke of Edinburgh visited President George W. Bush and First Lady Laura Bush at the White House in Washington in 2007, the Bushes presented the Queen with a bronze replica statuette of an original life size statue entitled *High Desert Princess*, which stands in

Giant pandas Tai Shan and Mei Xiang, National Zoological Park, Washington, DC, February 2006

front of the National Cowgirl Museum and Hall of Fame in Fort Worth, Texas, and gave the Duke of Edinburgh a sterling silver Tiffany & Co. box with an engraved inscription. The President and First Lady also gave the royal couple a leather presentation box containing documents from the National Archives, including a copy of a 1938 letter from President Roosevelt to King George VI, photos from previous royal visits, and a DVD of the footage from the Queen's first visit to the United States (as Princess Elizabeth) in 1951. The royal couple in turn gave the President and First Lady a sterling silver oversized plate with the Presidential seal, the Royal seal and a centre seal with the star of Texas surrounded by roses, and to Laura Bush a gold and crystal clock with the Royal seal, both made by elite British jeweller William & Son.[2] Different governments have different regulations governing whether the recipients of diplomatic gifts may keep the presents as their personal possessions. Many states require that gifts of any significant value become the property of the state or its people.

The Arts

The main vehicle for cultural diplomacy that reaches a wider audience is the exchange of artistic and creative output. Culture as represented by the arts is perhaps the greatest single source of the impressions that people abroad form of a nation–state; from early in their school careers children learn to differentiate between other countries by cultural features such as music, paintings, national costume or dress, and famous buildings and structures located in particular places. Arts tend to communicate an image or impression that is not politicized and is associated with authenticity and quality or excellence. Former US Ambassador to the Netherlands Cynthia Schneider commented that she found that the staging of jazz performances was one of the most effective ways to communicate about the United States and its people in a positive light, even to audiences not predisposed to have a high opinion of the United States.[3] Arts exchange is done in a variety of ways, ranging from tours by musical and dramatic artists and writers, to exhibitions of visual arts, design and dress, to the staging of elaborate multimedia festivals featuring several different artistic media of a country at the same location. Another approach taken by some countries is the construction of permanent cultural centres in major cities abroad or siting of dedicated cultural facilities within embassies and consulates, which can host cultural events representing the home country on an ongoing basis. Arts exchanges play different functions at different stages of a diplomatic relationship. In a period in which a diplomatic relationship between two states either is being established for the first time or is in a 'thaw' after an extended period of tension or alienation, arts exchanges can be an essential precursor to communication and negotiation about more substantive issues in contention. In a more established relationship, arts exchanges can perform the no less important maintenance function that contributes to sustaining mutual understanding between two peoples and governments. As successive generations of children in each country come of age, there is an ongoing need for their socialization into diplomatic relationships that are founded upon familiarity between peoples and cultures.

The use of cultural exchange in a phase of opening or thawing a diplomatic relationship generally involves a tour by high-profile and highly regarded artists, who travel often without any high-ranking diplomats or political officials. The February 2008 concert by the New York Philharmonic in Pyongyang, North Korea (Democratic People's Republic of Korea), illustrates this phenomenon particularly well. North Korea's agreement in six-party talks in 2007 to abandon its nuclear enrichment programme in return for international assistance in developing nuclear power generation cleared the way for a potential improvement in diplomatic relations between two countries that have never signed a peace treaty since the armistice ending the Korean War in 1953. Many scholars have taken the view that multilateral efforts to reach a deal on North Korea's nuclear programme were complicated by the high level of mutual suspicion and distrust between the American and North Korean governments. Each distrusted the other's motivations and objectives. The Philharmonic's visit to Pyongyang by all accounts began to break down that diffident environment. In the concert hall, both the North Korean and American flags were prominently displayed. The orchestra opened the concert by playing the US national anthem, 'The Star-Spangled Banner', included such American classics as George Gershwin's 'An American in Paris', and concluded by playing a traditional Korean folk song, 'Arirang', that is regarded by Koreans as articulating a longing for reunification of the Korean peninsula. The concert was broadcast live throughout North Korea, reportedly to a large audience, and according to news reports many North Koreans were deeply moved by the performance. According to former US Defence Secretary William Perry, who attended the concert, 'what's holding us back is mistrust built up over the decades. Then something wonderful happened – the New York Philharmonic gave a performance in Pyongyang, and the American people and the North Korean people made a connection, talking in a language that needs no translation. It has the potential of transforming the mistrust that has been holding us back.'[4]

Arts exchanges between countries with established relations may reach a broader audience over a longer period, even if they attract less media attention than groundbreaking events such as the Philharmonic's visit to Pyongyang. India and the United States have both operated cultural centres in a number of locations around the world, although the US cultural centres have been reduced in recent years owing to budget cutbacks.[5] In recent times India has also staged 'Festivals of India' in numerous countries, such as Britain. Under the aegis of these festivals, the Indian government has coordinated tours of performing artists ranging from yoga and classical dance troupes to Bollywood stars and popular music acts, exhibits of visual arts, culinary and fashion events, and marketing drives for Indian products and tourism in India.

Arts exchanges can be effective even when aimed at much smaller audiences, if the audiences are elite target groups of opinion leaders. Entertainment at events such as the World Economic Forum's Davos Annual Meeting and regional summits serves as a platform for sharing culture with an assemblage of global elites from business, government and civil society whose perceptions and opinions may be particularly influential when they return home to their own countries. At the Forum's Davos Annual Meeting in 2007, the Bern Symphony Orchestra played a concert for the delegates on the last evening of the meeting, representing the host country, Switzerland. At the Forum's India Regional Summit in Delhi in November 2005, India's commerce ministry hosted Forum delegates to an evening of traditional and modern Indian musical and dance performances under the stars, backlit by the silhouette of the Purana Qila, an historic fortress, which was followed by fine dining on Indian regional cuisines under marquees in a sprawling garden setting.[6]

A long-established multilateral venue for cultural exchange in the area of popular music has been the Eurovision Song Contest. Founded in 1956, the contest is a widely televised annual competition between European pop singers nominated through different processes in their respective nation–states. European eligibility is defined broadly, extending from Iceland to Azerbaijan and Israel. For the final round of the competition, all the finalists converge with their fans and supporters on the city selected to stage the finals, which rotates amongst participant countries each year. A live audience and millions of television viewers are able to contrast and enjoy different pop styles originating in over 50 countries. Particularly smaller country participants and states that have become independent more recently attach importance to the event as a way for the broader European public to come to know their identity and culture. The Eurovision Song Contest forms part of a fabric of cultural exchange that serves to mediate estrangement across Europe, broadly defined, by helping citizenries to know better the cultures, and thus the peoples, of other states. In some situations this mediation rôle can be more important than others. In May 2008, for example, the finals of the Eurovision Song Contest took place in Belgrade At that particular time, Serbia had been placed in a difficult political position with respect to the European Union following the unilateral declaration of independence of one of its provinces, Kosovo, and the recognition of that declaration by eighteen out of twenty-seven European Union member countries.

Education and Language Study

Like arts exchanges, the exchange of students at all levels of education for learning about the cultures of host countries and for learning together with students in the host countries is a core component of cultural diplomacy. Annual transnational flows of students are substantial. For example, in academic year 2005–6, the United States received over 564,000 international students and sent over 223,000 US students to study abroad.[7] Learning about another country directly from its own teachers *in situ* permits a more direct mediation of estrangement than may be possible through study of a place at a distance. Studying with students from another country in their own land creates what Jürgen Habermas calls a *Lebenswelt* or 'lifeworld' between the students, which is a network of shared meanings and understandings that results from working closely together on a common task with a common objective. Many students who study abroad form close friendships that they retain throughout their lives. Moreover, studying in another country enables students to learn about the country and its people through all the daily aspects of living there, over and beyond whatever academic subject they are studying. Secondary school students, as well as some undergraduates, often have a homestay component of their exchange programme, in which for all or part of their study abroad they live with and participate in the life of a host family, which may have children of similar age to the visiting exchange student. The homestay can be a particularly important part of exchange programmes in which language study is part of the objective (see below).

Many nation–state governments have created specific agencies or departments dedicated to promoting educational exchange. In the United Kingdom the British Council fulfils this function. The British Council funds many exchange programmes of its own and also serves as a clearinghouse for information on sources of funding for students seeking to study in the United Kingdom. Many governments operate particular funding programmes to promote exchange of secondary school, undergraduate and postgraduate university students for periods ranging from short study tours (in the case of secondary school students), to one term or year abroad programmes (for secondary school and undergraduate students), to funding for entire postgraduate degree programmes. In 1979, for example, the British government established the Overseas Research Students Awards Scheme ('ORSAS') to attract the best non-UK and non-EU students to British universities to pursue postgraduate research degrees. Winners of the awards have their annual university fees reduced from the fee paid by 'overseas' students to the much lower fee paid by home and EU students. Depending upon the particular degree programme, winning an ORSAS award can save a student up to £10,000. The European Union, early in its institutional development, established as a policy priority that education could be used as a tool to build support for European integration. In 1987 the EU established the Erasmus programme, which funds exchange between university students across the EU, the European Economic Area and Turkey. The programme is administered primarily by networks of academic departments in different EU countries with the objective of enabling students to spend a term or a year in a university in another European country, for which they are to receive full credit towards their degree at their home institution. Since 1987 over 1.5 million students have benefited from Erasmus funding. In the 1990s the programme became part of a wider system for funding student and faculty exchange from secondary school to postgraduate level called Socrates, and in the mid-2000s the EU's student exchange objectives have been broadened further under the aegis of a programme to be known as Lifelong Learning. The objective is clear, and the results have already proved successful: students from EU countries who study in another European institution develop better understandings of another European culture and thus of similarities, as well as differences, between European cultures. As a result they tend to be more supportive of the European Union generally, and of further European integration, than students who have not had the same opportunity.

The Fulbright Program is a particularly interesting case of bilateral cooperation to fund educational exchange. This unique exchange scheme was founded in 1946 through the initiative of US Senator J. William Fulbright and is administered by the US State Department's Bureau of Cultural and Educational Affairs. The programme is funded jointly by the US and other governments, primarily through 50 binational commissions but also through direct relationships between US embassies and counterpart foreign ministries and education ministries, to facilitate international exchange of postgraduate research students and teachers between the United States and over 100 countries. Those selected for Fulbright grants go abroad to participate in a wide range of educational undertakings, including teaching, studying and engaging in independent research. Over 286,000 participants have received Fulbright awards over the life of the programme.

Nation–state governments are not the only actors engaged in the cultural diplomacy of educational exchange. Many civil society organizations exist for the purpose of facilitating exchange between students. Charitable foundations such as the Rhodes Trust, the Winston Churchill Foundation, and the German Marshall Fund of the United States fund student exchange in university-level education. Many such institutions have come to be either as a result of a single individual's vision of and commitment to transnational cooperation through education or else through transnational coalitions of individuals committed to the same. The Rhodes Trust, an organization that provides scholarship funding for students from Commonwealth countries, the United States and the European Union to study at Oxford University in the United Kingdom, was established through the bequest of Cecil Rhodes, an Oxford graduate who emigrated to South Africa in 1870 and was later Governor of Cape Colony. Rhodes was committed to building and sustaining cultural bonds between the British Empire and the other Anglo-Saxon peoples of the world through higher education. The Winston Churchill Foundation, founded in the United States in 1959 by authority of Sir Winston Churchill, established a scholarship programme in the 1960s to enable American students to pursue postgraduate study at Cambridge University in the UK. The German Marshall Fund was established in the United States in 1972 through a gift from the government of the Federal Republic of Germany in recognition of US post-World War II Marshall Plan economic reconstruction and development aid to Germany. The organization funds transatlantic cooperation between US and European university students and between policy makers and journalists. Other private foundations, such as American Field Service ('AFS') and Youth For Understanding, fund and operate exchange programmes in many countries for secondary school students.

Yet another mode of educational exchange that has emerged in recent years is the creation by universities of satellite overseas branches or campuses to which their own students can go on exchange and at which, in many cases, students of the home country may also enrol. US and UK universities have been leaders in this trend. Beginning in the 1950s the US-based Johns Hopkins University established branches of its graduate school for international affairs, the School of Advanced International Studies ('SAIS'), in Bologna, Italy, and later Nanjing, China. The UK-based University of Kent in the late 1990s created its Brussels School of International Studies ('BSIS') to be a centre for the English-language study of International Relations and conflict resolution in the capital city of the European Union. Other British universities have established satellites in Japan, and several US institutions are opening campuses in the Persian Gulf region.

Within educational exchange, studying abroad for the purpose of learning another language is significant and distinct. Studying a foreign language is a primary vehicle for learning about the culture or cultures in which that language is situated. In many countries, institutions have been founded specifically to promote education about their own culture through the teaching of their language. Some receive government funding, whilst others are funded privately. The Goethe-Institut, which was established to promote knowledge of German culture through the teaching of the German language, is funded primarily by Germany's Auswärtiges Amt (Foreign Office) and Press Office. The Goethe-Institut maintains 147 centres in 83 countries for teaching German language and culture and promoting inter-cultural exchange. La Maison Française, funded by the French government, is a network of French language and cultural centres on university campuses around the world. The Alliance Française is a civil society organization that receives a subsidy from the French government to promote teaching of the French language through a global network of satellite franchises in over 130 countries. The English-Speaking Union ('ESU') was founded after the First World War as a private international charitable foundation to promote international understanding through learning and use of the English language. Under the patronage of HM Queen Elizabeth II, the UK-headquartered ESU operates in over 50 countries, funding international debating and public speaking competitions in English, in addition to promoting and funding student exchange at secondary school and university level. More recently, the People's Republic of China's government launched the Confucius Institute, an ambitious programme to promote the learning of the Chinese language globally. Founded in 2004, at the time of writing there are over 320 Confucius Institutes operating in over 80 countries, well on the way towards the Beijing government's objective of opening 1000 institutes by 2020.

Sport

International sporting competition has long served as an effective mechanism for the mediation of estrangement between peoples, and consequently their governments, and for promoting inter-cultural understanding and cooperation. From the time of the original Olympic Games in ancient Greece, individuals and teams have represented their countries in competitions that have functioned as substitutes for armed conflict between states. By their nature, sporting competitions call upon both competitors and their supporters and fans to observe the rules of the game, to play fairly and to accept a win or loss as a fair outcome. Participating in a sport is a common culture that participants share, irrespective of their nationality. Competitors and teams share a bond with their opponents in their mutual love of and dedication to the sport, which they often have a chance to develop through personal contact before and after a match or competition. Spectators at the event and fans viewing on television form a similar virtual community with spectators on the opposing side. Oftentimes heads of government, heads of state and other senior officials assume the rôle of chief spectators at international sporting events, viewing a match or competition together, even as they cheer for their respective side, and using the occasion for an informal meeting to discuss issues and resolve disagreements. The rôle of international sporting competition today is complicated by the fact that it has become a highly lucrative global business. Through media, sponsorships and other marketing relationships, global firms have become significant actors in sporting diplomacy.

In recent times, bilateral sporting diplomacy has played a significant rôle in thawing frosty relations between countries, often in situations in which official diplomatic relations may not even exist. Sometimes governments may decide to agree to a sporting event with a nation with which relations are adversarial as a precursor to beginning diplomatic interaction that could result in closer relations. Sporting competition can prepare a domestic population to view in a more favourable light another nation hitherto portrayed by official statements and domestic media as hostile. Often the resulting shift in how a domestic public views a state and people previously regarded as hostile itself becomes a driver that presses the home government to accelerate diplomatic contact with the other side.[8] The most interesting recent example of this phenomenon is the 'cricket diplomacy' between India and Pakistan, commencing in 2004, following a period of heightened military tension between the two powers in spring and summer 2002 over cross-border terrorist activity in Kashmir. India's national cricket side were invited for their first tour of Pakistan in fourteen years beginning in the week of 8 March 2004. The cricketers on both sides were sensitive to the rôle that they were being asked to play in the diplomacy between their two nations. Rameez Raja, the Chief Executive of the Pakistan Cricket Board, said 'I'm absolutely delighted and thrilled that this thing is happening and that cricket has been given a great deal of importance in this set-up, because not only our cricketing relations will improve but also cricket has been made part of our bi-lateral talks, so from that point of view I am very, very happy.' India's Captain, Sourav Ganguly, commented similarly: 'whenever we travel, we travel as ambassadors for the country'. At the same time Raja warned that sportsmen should not become involved in the political process: 'We cricketers come from a certain background and we should put politics on the back burner.'[9] The tour was received with huge enthusiasm by both the Indian and Pakistani publics, a significant number of whom still have family members living on opposite sides of the 1947 partition line. Pakistan's national cricket side staged a return visit to India the following year that was received with equal approbation. Observers generally agree that 'cricket diplomacy' helped to pave the way for the warming of Indo-Pakistani diplomatic relations, which had moved forwards significantly by the latter years of the decade.

In other cases, contacts forged between sporting competitors themselves function as the initiators of bilateral competitions that then pave the way for an improvement in diplomatic relations. The most striking example of this chain of causality was the 'ping pong diplomacy' between the People's Republic of China and the United States in the early 1970s. At a ping pong (table tennis) competition in Japan in 1971, world champion Zhuang Zedong spoke to US team member Glenn Cowan, who was hitching a ride on the Chinese team's bus after his own team's bus left without him. Zhuang befriended and exchanged gifts with Cowan and suggested a match between the Chinese and US teams at a time when there were no diplomatic relations between the two countries. The US ping pong team visited China in April 1971, where they met with an enthusiastic reception, and the Chinese team made a return visit to the United States a year later.[10] The thaw in relations between the two peoples helped to facilitate the initiation of high-level diplomatic contact between the two governments. US Secretary of State Henry Kissinger visited China in October 1971, which was followed by President Richard M. Nixon's historic visit to China in February 1972, an event later memorialized culturally through a different medium by US composer John Adams's lyric opera *Nixon in China*.

Multilateral sporting diplomacy functions along different lines from bilateral diplomacy because it is regular, institutionalized and organized by permanent, multilateral civil society organizations that administer the rules of the sport and adjudicate disputes. These organizations manage the calendar of international competition, sanction and facilitate competitions, and, in some cases, host the competitions themselves. But as with other forms of cultural diplomacy, these multilateral bodies and the international competitions that they sponsor can be both causes of cultural alienation and important vehicles for resolving it. Among the biggest and best-known of these institutions are: the Fédération Internationale de Football Association ('FIFA'), the governing international body for association football (soccer) that hosts the quadrennial football World Cup, which is the largest and most viewed global competition in a single sport; the International Cricket Council ('ICC') and the International Rugby Board ('IRB'), which organize the World Cup competitions of cricket and rugby union respectively every four years; the International Tennis Federation

('ITF'), which is comprised of 205 national federations (reportedly more than any other sport), and the Fédération Internationale du Ski ('FIS'), each of which organizes an annual international tour of competitions for individuals, as well as competition at the nation–state level. Most other sports that attract significant international participation, including athletics (track and field), golf, ice skating, swimming, motor racing and, more recently, baseball, have similar multilateral organizations that govern and sponsor international competition. Many multilateral sporting organizations receive a significant portion of their funding from global media and retailing firms, which requires them to take the interests of their sponsors into account as they play their rôle in sporting diplomacy. This poses a further diplomatic challenge to the leaders of international sporting organizations as they perform their management function but generally does not interfere with their ability to achieve their objectives.

The major multilateral sporting bodies are conscious of their ability to play a rôle in overcoming cultural alienation, and it shapes how they construct their missions. For example, FIFA's mission statement on its website mentions the following:

> The world is a place rich in natural beauty and cultural diversity, but also one where many are still deprived of their basic rights. FIFA now has an even greater responsibility to reach out and touch the world, using football as a symbol of hope and integration . . .
>
> We see it as our mission to contribute towards building a better future for the world by using the power and popularity of football . . .
>
> Football is no longer considered merely a global sport, but also as unifying force whose virtues can make an important contribution to society. We use the power of football as a tool for social and human development, by strengthening the work of dozens of initiatives around the globe to support local communities in the areas of peacebuilding, health, social integration, education and more . . .[11]

FIFA Chairman Joseph Sepp Blatter writes at the bottom of the mission statement, 'We see it as our duty to take on the social responsibility that comes hand in hand with our position at the helm of the world's most loved sport.'[12] The ICC mission statement takes a similar tone: 'As a leading global sport cricket will captivate and inspire people of every age, gender, background and ability while building bridges between continents, countries and communities.'[13]

Above and beyond the individual multilateral sporting organizations and the competitions that they host are the modern Olympic Games and the organization that sponsors them, the International Olympic Committee ('IOC'). The modern Olympic movement, begun in 1896 by Pierre de Coubertin, was intended specifically to promote world peace by mediating estrangement between states and peoples. The ancient Olympic Truce or *Ekecheiria*, under which athletes and their families were permitted to travel to and participate in the ancient Games and return home safely, was agreed by three Greek kings in the ninth century BC and was announced throughout participating countries by heralds. The IOC revived and expanded the idea of the Truce in an effort to achieve the following objectives:

- raise awareness and encourage political leaders to act in favour of peace;
- mobilize youth for the promotion of the Olympic ideals;
- establish contacts between communities in conflict;
- offer humanitarian support in countries at war;

and, more generally:

- to create a window of opportunities for dialogue, reconciliation and the resolution of conflicts.[14]

Beginning in 1992, the IOC undertook a series of peace initiatives in close cooperation with the General Assembly of the United Nations, under which the model of the Olympic Truce would be used to promote the reduction of tensions between states in conflict, and space for communication and negotiation could be created. The UN General Assembly has taken on the rôle of the ancient Greek heralds in proclaiming the Olympic Truce to the world every two years, one year before each Olympiad commences, and inviting the nations of the world 'to seek, in conformity with the goals and principles of the United Nations Charter, the peaceful settling of all international conflicts through peaceful and diplomatic means, and recognizing the importance of the IOC initiatives for human well-being and international understanding.'[15] In 1992 athletes of the former Republic of Yugoslavia, which had collapsed amidst violent conflict shortly before the summer games at Barcelona commenced, were permitted to participate under the Olympic flag. In the 2000 summer games at Sydney, athletes of the two estranged Korean states paraded together under a common flag of the Korean peninsula. The August 2008 invasion of the Republic of

Georgia by Russian Federation forces as the Beijing Olympiad began cannot be seen as in keeping with the spirit of the Olympic Truce.

The fact that the modern Olympic movement and the games that it has hosted have been regular sites of diplomatic controversy attests to the global cultural significance attributed to the games. Adolf Hitler sought to showcase the achievements of Nazism in the German Reich at the 1936 Olympiad held in Berlin. Several Western nations, including the United States, boycotted the 1980 Olympiad in Moscow on account of the Soviet Union's 1979 invasion of Afghanistan. More recent controversies involved the process by which the IOC makes its sometimes lucrative award to a city of the right to host the games, and problems concerning the screening of competitors for doping. Overall, the controversies that the Olympic movement has faced have tended to be similar to those faced by other major multilateral sporting organizations and events. The primary questions over which nations, their national sporting organizations, and competitors have found themselves at odds have been issues of accreditation and legitimacy and of fairness, all questions that are essentially diplomatic in nature and requiring of mediation through processes of representation and communication. The question of accreditation, which arises in the Olympics as the issue of which states are entitled to participate and which are not, serves as a proxy for the broader diplomatic issue of recognition of governments by one another. Following the sudden dissolution of the Soviet Union in 1991, the former Soviet Olympic team competed in the 1992 Barcelona summer games as the 'Unified Team'. Four years later, each successor republic fielded its own team. Sometimes governments cannot agree about which states should be eligible to compete in the Olympics. Yet in the common search to allow maximum participation in sport, the Olympic movement often finds modes of compromise that in some cases could serve as models for the resolution of the broader political dispute underlying the recognition question. For many years the Republic of China on Taiwan was not permitted to compete, due to the insistence of the government of the People's Republic of China in Beijing that only one China existed and thus only one team could compete using the name 'China'. The Beijing government were equally opposed to the use of the name 'Taiwan' and the Republic of China's flag, as its acceptance and visibility in the international community appeared to confer a measure of legitimacy on Taiwan's independence. Yet the governments in Beijing and Taipei came to an agreement with the IOC that finessed questions of sovereignty and naming and allowed Taiwan to compete under the name

'Chinese Taipei' and fly the flag of the Olympic movement (five coloured circles on a white background).

Fear of being excluded from international sporting competition, another mechanism of diplomatic accreditation through sport, can serve as a significant motivator for governments to adhere to international norms of state behaviour. Sporting boycotts are rare, and as such are perceived as drastic actions. The decades-long sporting boycott of South Africa's white minority government and the international ostracism that the boycott conferred are credited with playing a rôle in encouraging the South African government eventually to end its apartheid policy and move to democratic majority rule. International sporting bodies take the lead in deciding whether boycotts are appropriate and in enforcing them. In 2002, the International Cricket Council warned England's national cricket side that they would be penalized in the international cricket standings for refusing to participate in World Cup matches in Zimbabwe on account of their opposition to policies of Zimbabwe's President, Robert Mugabe, notwithstanding UK Prime Minister Tony Blair's stated opposition to the English team's competing there. In this case, the ICC upheld the generally accepted norm that in most cases the importance of all sides being permitted to compete should trump the use of sporting participation as a tool in diplomatic and political disputes.

Religion

Religion, like other forms of culture, is both a cause of and a vehicle for mediating estrangement. Many religions are transnational in nature, having believers and followers in many lands. The institutional structure of organized religions varies enormously, however. Some religions are organized predominantly at the local level, whilst others are organized nationally within nation–states, and others yet possess a transnational institutional structure. Transnational religious organizations often function as global civil society actors that can serve as cultural bridges between estranged peoples and governments. The relationship between religious organizations and governments of nation–states also varies significantly, from states in which the government has no relationship to any religious organization to states that have an established or state 'church' and in which government officials play a direct rôle in selecting religious leaders. In nation–states with an established religion or church, senior religious figures can play a cooperative rôle in the government's diplomatic communications. For example, the Church of England's bishop for its diocese of continental Europe is in a position to be able to communicate to other senior religious leaders across Europe about matters spiritual and temporal. In the 2000s, the Rt Revd Geoffrey Rowell, bishop for that diocese, was able to serve as a useful conduit for information between the British government and a range of political and civil society interlocutors across Europe and the former Soviet Union. As such, Rowell was often accorded quasi-diplomatic status by UK government diplomats on his European travels.

Only in rare cases are religious organizations and governments actually coterminous. The Holy See is anomalous in that it is both the remnant of a nation–state, with its own government, and the headquarters of a global civil society organization comprised of over 1 billion practitioners (to varying degrees) of the Roman Catholic form of the Christian religion. Although Israel sees itself as a religious state, its government does not claim religious authority over Jews either in Israel or abroad. Since the formal abolition of the Islamic Caliphate in 1924, no official transnational Islamic religious organization has existed, which has permitted powerful religious and political leaders in Islamic states such as Iran, Saudi Arabia, Indonesia and Malaysia to claim to speak to and for Muslims on a more global basis. The Organization of the Islamic Conference is a multilateral organization of governments of nation–states with large Muslim populations.[16]

Religions by their nature tend to be committed to peaceful coexistence as a value or virtue in principle if unfortunately not often enough in practice. Hence religious organizations and their leaders regularly play a rôle in diplomatic mediation of conflicts and facilitating communication between actors that are estranged. Religious leaders, if respected, are generally perceived to have a degree of credibility and good intentions with which governments at odds may not be ready to credit diplomats of adversary governments. The Aga Khan, for example, leader of the world's Nizari Isma'ili followers of Shia Islam, has been an active promoter of religious tolerance between faiths throughout his life. The American Protestant Christian minister Jesse Jackson has travelled on numerous occasions to countries with which the United States has no or poor diplomatic relations to achieve objectives such as the release of hostages.

Religious leaders can also be perceived as politically divisive for taking partisan stands on political issues involving the state in which they reside and its relationships with other states. Pope Pius XII, who was elected to the papacy in 1939 during the fascist rule of Benito Mussolini, after having served as Cardinal Secretary of State for the Holy See under his predecessor

Pius XI, was criticized widely for signing concordats (treaties) with Mussolini, the fascist Ustashe government of Croatia and Hitler's German Reich, and for doing little to protect the Jews of Rome when Nazi armies eventually occupied that city briefly in 1944.[17] The Dalai Lama, spiritual leader of Tibetan Buddhists and living in exile in India since China's annexation of Tibet in 1959, is perceived as divisive by the Beijing government and others for his political advocacy of autonomy for Tibet. Ayatollah Ruhollah Khomeini, whilst serving as the religious and formally temporal leader of the Islamic Republic of Iran, was excoriated by the international community in the late 1980s for issuing a *fatwa*, or religious edict, that called for Muslims around the world to kill novelist Salman Rushdie.

Broadly speaking, culture in global society is both a cause of alienation and estrangement between the world's peoples, governments and organizations, and an effective vehicle for overcoming that estrangement. Cultural diplomacy can be employed by governments, multilateral institutions, global firms and civil society organizations to build understanding and familiarity between different peoples and states. Since the Second World War, diplomacy has contributed substantially to reducing the incidence of military conflict as a means of resolving international disputes, and more recently diplomacy has been focused on reducing global poverty and inequality and the conflict that flows therefrom. The likelihood that cultural differences will increase in importance as a cause of international conflict suggests the need for more cultural diplomacy and more effective management of cultural diplomacy efforts. Cultural diplomacy need not be directed by governments to be effective, but management of cultural diplomacy is likely to be more effective to the extent that governments, multilateral organizations, firms and CSOs are able to coordinate their undertakings.

12

Conclusions: Contemporary Diplomatic Practice and Theory Looking Ahead

Introduction: Contemporary Diplomacy in Practice During the 2008 Financial Crisis

The global financial turbulence of summer and autumn 2008 began with a crisis in the subprime mortgage market in the United States, which led to the inability of financial markets to price complex debt securities held by major financial institutions across the globe. This in turn caused a freeze in global credit markets, a steep tumble in equities markets around the world and a sharp recession in the non-financial global economy. The diplomatic processes that took place as all the actors involved sought to cooperate (in most instances) to resolve the crises, prevent a collapse of the global financial system and restart economic growth around the world serve as a tableau that illustrates vividly all of the themes emphasized in this book. As global credit markets seized up, finance ministers and central bank governors of the major powers conferred with one another frequently using remote technology and in person. They communicated and met in person with CEOs of major global financial firms such as Citigroup, Royal Bank of Scotland, Goldman Sachs, Morgan Stanley and Lloyds HBOS. Central banks coordinated interest rate cuts, injections of liquidity into the global economy and increased borrowing facilities. Finance ministries of major powers such as the United Kingdom and United States agreed to recapitalize major financial institutions by taking equity stakes. Transnational bodies such as the European Union and the International Monetary Fund served as venues for multilateral consultations on a coordinated approach to stimulating the economy. The IMF agreed to act as a vehicle for creating additional liquidity for the international monetary system. Central bank governors and finance ministers were called to account for their diplomacy by elected legislatures in their home countries and asked to justify their actions. As developing countries were pulled into the deepening global recession, governments and civil society organizations in developing countries called for concessions by developed countries swiftly to conclude the World Trade Organization's Doha Development Agenda of multilateral trade liberalization.

This chapter seeks to apply the ways of thinking about contemporary diplomacy articulated in the preceding chapters to problems and challenges like the 2008 financial crisis that diplomats are likely to encounter in the near future. One key methodological question to be asked is whether it makes sense to go beyond our survey of continuity and change in contemporary diplomatic actors, processes and practice to theorize about diplomacy in a more organized way. The next section reflects more specifically upon the relationship between practising diplomacy and theorizing about diplomacy in light of contemporary changes (as well as continuities) in diplomatic practice. It ends up being not as easy as one might think to separate diplomatic theory and practice. Then follows a review of the themes of the book in the context of the challenges faced by diplomacy going forward.

Theorizing and Practising Diplomacy

What does it mean to theorize about diplomacy? Theory of diplomacy can serve a number of purposes: to analyse and understand better what diplomacy is and what diplomats do, to serve as a guide to best practice, and to understand the rôle of diplomacy in the broader range of global interactions that fall under the rubric of 'international relations'. As has been noted earlier, diplomacy really only became a distinctive subject of study for scholars between the two world wars, and not until after the Second World War did the notion of theorizing about diplomacy become accepted. Prior to the twentieth century, diplomacy, like much of politics and international relations, was studied as a part of the discipline of history. Classical texts of diplomacy written by professional diplomats such as Sir Ernest Satow were often in the form of memoirs, as in Satow's memoir *A Diplomat in Japan*.[1] Since World War II, two broad approaches to theorizing about diplomacy have emerged: the first a generally positivist way of placing diplomacy in the context of interstate security relations, and the second a post-positivist view of diplomacy as encompassing a broader range of actors and processes. The first approach conceives of the relationship between theory and practice of diplomacy very differently from the second.

Scholars in the first camp have in effect constructed our contemporary idea of diplomacy through their theorizing about diplomacy. In the process they developed a field of study or sub-discipline known as diplomatic studies. Adherents of this 'classical' view of diplomatic studies, from Sir Harold Nicolson to Adam Watson and Geoff Berridge, have articulated the canonical understanding of diplomacy described in chapter 1. First, diplomacy is about relations between nation–states; second, it is concerned with matters of *haute politique*; and third, it was born in Renaissance Europe and straightaway achieved a transhistorical, or perhaps ahistorical, character that has persisted despite major change in the international system. Diplomacy, according to this traditional view, evolved along with the emergence of the nation–state and the idea of state sovereignty. The Treaties of Osnabrück and Münster, which constituted the Peace of Westphalia, in 1648 were themselves both a major product of the emergence of diplomacy as we know it and a significant building block in creating the nation–state system that reified and reinforced diplomatic practice. Those treaties, and others that followed it, were the core stuff of what diplomacy was supposed to be about: *haute politique*, or high politics, the dominance of the discourse of security over other political discourses. *Haute politique* conceives of sovereignty in a particular way: as referring to territory and borders, and about populations, ultimately even conquest and colonization. When *haute politique* considers economics, it conceives of economic issues only within the constructs of the security discourse. Is there access to enough oil and food for the army and the navy first, for the general public second? Is the power grid able to supply power to the heavy industries that can supply the armed forces?

But since the late 1980s, a newer group of scholars such as Donna Lee, Brian Hocking, Richard Langhorne, James Der Derian and Costas Constantinou have challenged positivist, 'classical' diplomatic theory, finding that the canonical understanding of diplomacy downplays, marginalizes, and omits very important, if not key components of contemporary diplomatic practice. Most importantly, the traditional canon of diplomacy downplays and marginalizes, when it does not omit altogether, the economic and the cultural at the expense of the security discourse at several different levels. First, the state-centric, rationalist focus on the high politics of the Westphalia system has always marginalized the economic and the social, in the same way that it has privileged the position of state actors in the international system over other types of actors, such as domestic interest groups or social classes, sub-national political units, or non-state actors like firms. This focus, which is part of the neorealist approach to international relations theory today, just barely makes allowance for the emergence and rôle of multilateral institutions and minimizes the importance of the rôle of non-state actors. In response to this approach, critics point to all the consular work, commercial diplomacy, export promotion and business facilitation that most governments have always carried out. From the Anglo-Portuguese Methuen Treaty in 1702 to the 1995 Treaty of Marrakech that created the WTO, not to mention the 1944 Bretton Woods Agreement that created the World Bank and the IMF, historically many of the most important diplomatic missions, the most crucial negotiations and the most significant bilateral and multilateral treaties signed have been about international trade.

Scholars of traditional diplomatic studies argue that governments and their diplomats have not viewed trade and economics as central to relations with other states. Instead, they argue, diplomats have regarded economics as a tool to gain political advantage, or to minimize threats, or to increase security. Many, if not most, traditional diplomats historically have disdained commercial diplomacy. Diplomats found negotiating trade agreements degrading and beneath their usually more noble station, and they have said so, often privately, occasionally even in public. Diplomats in the nineteenth and early twentieth centuries had the perception, often correctly, that accepting commercial posts in the foreign ministry would be damaging to the progression of their careers. William Ewart Gladstone, one of Britain's greatest prime ministers, openly scorned the haggling and hucksterism of commercial diplomacy, which he associated with tradespeople. Yet ironically Gladstone must be considered one of the greatest commercial diplomats of all time for signing the Cobden–Chevalier Anglo-French Commercial Treaty of 1860, a sort of proto-GATT that set off a wave of bilateral commercial treaty signings that lowered tariffs across Europe by over 50 per cent and changed the economic, political and social face of the European continent. Of course, if asked at the time why he was signing the treaty, Gladstone would have argued that it was to lower military tensions that had been building between England and France in the late 1850s.[2]

Historical sociologists give another explanation for this phenomenon: social class. Those who entered European and latterly North American diplomatic services from the seventeenth until well into the twentieth century tended to be from aristocratic families who derived their wealth and standing as *rentiers* of agricultural lands, through service to the crown or from finance. They regarded the rising commercial class that the solidification of the nation–state system had facilitated, and that in turn strengthened that system, as vulgar. They wanted as little to do with the bargaining and dealing of commerce as possible. British historian D. C. M. Platt described why diplomats at the British Foreign Office in 1870 were only too happy to abandon negotiated trade liberalization treaties in favour of a policy of unilateral free trade:

> Noblemen, bored, dispirited, and inexperienced in matters of commerce and finance, found in laissez-faire exactly the rationalization they were looking for; they could avoid a distasteful contact with the persons and problems of trade financiers, merely by referring, in good faith, to the traditions of non-intervention, Free Trade, and open competition. And it was true that *haute politique*, at their level and in the society with which they mixed, *was* far more interesting.[3]

The intellectual biases and interest preferences of postwar US academics, which tended to reflect the political, economic and cultural biases of the day, were instrumental in shaping the dominant paradigm for diplomatic studies, just as they were for the broader discipline of international relations. The global political economy was evolving and changing, and diplomacy itself changing functionally along with it. Yet at the same time diplomatic studies continued to articulate, reinforce and reify the traditional representations of who did diplomacy and what they did most. Scholars of diplomatic studies tended to focus on issues such as the division of Germany, the Cuban Missile Crisis, the SALT talks, the struggle over how many Soviet republics and which China to seat at the UN, President Richard Nixon's visit to China, and US–Soviet détente. Scholarship also focused on the negotiators who engaged in resolving Cold War conflicts. One of the most prominent of the negotiators of that age, US Secretary of State Henry Kissinger, wrote one of the defining works of the genre, *Diplomacy*.[4]

Yet throughout the Cold War period, the neorealist, bipolar security paradigm shared a bed with its estranged but much more all-encompassing *Doppelgänger*, the neoliberal international economy. The major theoretical approaches to understanding post-World War II international relations had to make sense of this uneasy relationship. Neorealism, with its theoretical focus on security, and neoliberalism, with its focus on international cooperation, had more in common as theories of international relations than it might have appeared. State-centrism and rationalist, empirical methodology were at the core of each. Both theoretical approaches separated the international from the domestic, the public from the private, politics from economics, and emphasized the former in each of these dichotomies. We can understand the emergence of neoliberalism in the 1970s not so much as changing traditional representations but as in fact reinforcing them, albeit in more nuanced, more subtle ways. Neoliberalism focuses on the emergence of multilateral institutions as facilitating prospects for cooperation between nation–states, as discussed in chapter 3. Traditional diplomatic studies has understood these institutions as venues for diplomacy between states, for communicating about and negotiating over particular issue areas. Understanding such institutions as facilitating cooperation would seem a good theoretical fit for updating the ways of explaining diplomacy as representation and communication between states to mediate between interests and minimize conflict. But neoliberalism also embodies within it a particular notion of international economics that presupposes the same separation of international from domestic, public from private, politics from economics. Neoliberalism makes its normative stance about how the international economy should be structured into a set of technocratic imperatives. It removes from the possibility of political contestation the international economic objectives of free trade in goods and services, free flows of capital and investment across borders, and the primacy of market pricing of goods and services. So neoliberalism facilitates the return of the focus of nation–state diplomats, and the scholars who study them, to issues of *haute politique*. Governments of states negotiate trade agreements for politics-as-security objectives. Neoliberalism ends up marginalizing all non-state diplomatic actors, even the multilateral institutions themselves, by viewing such institutions as impartial venues in which states interact.[5]

Donna Lee and David Hudson argue that the effect of what they call the positivist, rationalist paradigm on theorizing diplomacy is to render commercial diplomacy 'present-but-invisible'. Lee and Hudson point out that commercial diplomacy has always been at the core of diplomatic representation and communication since long before the emergence of the Renaissance city-states in the Italian peninsula. Trade missions have been taking place since ancient times. The working out of arrangements for payments across political boundaries and between different monetary systems has long been part of the core business of diplomatic relationships. Even since the emergence of modern diplomacy as understood by diplomatic studies, Lee and Hudson contend, commercial activities have occupied the majority of the time of diplomatic missions and the ministries behind them. They back this up by examining the actual historical records of diplomatic correspondence and transactions, as contrasted with the discursive preferences of the diplomats: the areas in which diplomats assert that their interests lie. Lee and Hudson argue for what they dub a 'political economy' understanding of diplomacy, arguing that the activity of commercial diplomacy by its nature integrates the domestic and the international, the private and the public, the economic and the political. Business leaders of global and local firms sit down with government officials to plan export promotion strategies; investment tours are organized; foreign economic policies are argued over politically between social groups with significantly different interests. For example, would a neoliberal Multilateral Agreement on Investment help or hurt workers in India and Canada? NGOs, the media and the general public in those countries, not thinking that the MAI would help them, organized opposition laterally across nation–state borders using the internet, with the result that nation–state and OECD diplomats negotiating that agreement in 1998 had to suspend their work.[6]

Lee and Hudson also note that that diplomacy is portrayed unreflexively as Eurocentric. This is not coincidental, but is part and parcel of the idea of diplomacy as a building block of the European nation–state system. It seats diplomacy within the frame of a particular culture and a particular historical period, even as it posits the actors, objectives and functions of diplomacy as timeless, as transhistorical or ahistorical. But to view diplomacy in this way excludes other cultures and the much broader historical sweep of interactions between cultures: the organized processes of representation and communication between cultures that have taken place across much of the world since ancient times. Kishan Rana's important volume *Inside Diplomacy* offers a compelling account of contemporary diplomatic practice in the context of a historical understanding of India's diplomacy that extends back at least as far as the third century BC.[7] Traditional diplomacy discourages the study of these interactions, because among other things it does not recognize pre-Westphalian governments as having equivalent standing to nation–states. Lee and Hudson suggest that it would be more useful, for example, to choose as a model of the emergence of a diplomatic system not the closed system, proto-Westphalian diplomacy of the city-states of the Italian peninsula in the fifteenth century, but rather the varied cultural and economic missions that for some time already had been exchanged between *La Serenissima* – the Venetian Republic – and the societies of the Levant and Asia.[8]

Costas Constantinou goes a step farther by challenging the notion that theorizing about diplomacy can be undertaken independently of diplomatic practice. Constantinou problematizes the whole idea of agency, arguing that diplomacy as a process is not only functional and structural but also by its nature intersubjective. Diplomatic subjects or actors do not exist prior to and independent of diplomacy, but are themselves constructed socially through the mutual recognition and interaction of diplomacy. When we talk about representation, we have to ask what is the actual work of diplomacy. Constantinou argues that we need to ask how representative action is personified in the representative, which requires an exploration of the politics of the accreditation process by which one is authorized to speak in the name of a sovereign subject. Constantinou proposes, as a metaphor, language itself as a sort of embassy, a diplomatic representative from the sender to the receiver, from the writer to the reader or the speaker to the hearer. The envoy, language, brings theory from the sender to a foreign place, which makes theory both diplomatic and politicized.[9]

Understanding diplomatic actors and the acts of representation in which they engage in this way has direct implications for how diplomacy is practised, according to Constantinou. Jacques Derrida, Constantinou points out, thinks of philosophical discourse as acts of embassy, in which presence, or Being, is transported. By being sent from the sender, presence or Being is represented to the receiver. Derrida contends that the diplomatic credentials of these envoys of theory are always subject to question, because they are not the sovereign itself, but only representatives of the sovereign. Hence diplomats should refuse to accredit envoys who claim the truth of their origin and the origin of their truth. When diplomats convey communications from their sovereign, the meanings of their messages are always open to interpretation. Diplomatic messages may not always be what they appear to be. Likewise diplomats may not hear what they want to hear, so they may interpret messages in such a way as to please their own sovereign.[10] When Iraqi diplomats communicated to their US and British counterparts in 2002 that Saddam Hussein's government did not possess weapons of mass destruction, some American and British diplomats did not believe them, whilst others of their colleagues did believe the Iraqis. It became a political decision for US and UK leaders which interpretation to accept and how to act upon it. The embassy of theory can still be valid, according to Constantinou, but only if we recognize it is a messenger of no sovereign authority. To be valid, diplomatic theory has to use the stratagems and discourses of diplomacy. Theory has to become the object of diplomacy itself; it always needs to be reflecting on the terms and categories that it is using. Constantinou's logic invites us to think about diplomatic practice as always constituting diplomatic theory to the extent that practice reflects upon itself, and to the extent that neither diplomats nor scholars of diplomacy assert diplomatic communication as authoritative and beyond interpretation.[11]

Ultimately the positivist and post-positivist approaches to theorizing about diplomacy differ both in terms of what they highlight in terms of diplomatic actors and practice, and in terms of how they think about the rôle of theory itself. Classical diplomatic studies has made important contributions to our understanding of contemporary diplomacy, as recounted in the preceding chapters, but only up to a point. Beyond that threshold, post-positivist theoretical approaches become essential for making sense of the evolution of diplomacy in the recent past and the challenges it faces in the near future.

Challenges for Practising (and Theorizing) Diplomacy Going Forward

In the first chapter of the book it was suggested that the study of contemporary diplomacy may offer the best way to understand contemporary global interaction in a complex world of nation–state and non-state actors, institutions and structures. The primary implication for diplomacy of an evolving global political economy in which nation–states are not less important, but have been joined by a range of types of non-state actors that wield considerable measures of power and influence in their own right, is that diplomacy will be evaluated less by who is doing it than by what they are doing and how they are doing it. In January 2009 global business media network CNBC reported a story on how pirates seizing commercial vessels in the Indian Ocean and holding their crews and cargoes for ransom engaged a spokesperson to communicate regularly to the media about issues concerning their undertaking. The pirate spokesperson reported such information as the number of pirates killed in armed conflict with naval forces seeking to recapture the ships. Although the pirate spokesperson was characterized by CNBC anchor Erin Burnett as 'public relations', with the quip 'there is no bad publicity', clearly it needs to be understood in the context of this book as another instance of diplomatic representation, and communication, of public diplomacy by a non-state actor, in this case a transnational criminal organization.[12] Again in keeping with Constantinou's argument, in the diplomacy of the age of a heterogeneous collection of post-Westphalian nation–states and other non-state actors, sovereignty is less important than power over outcomes. This is entirely an argument about effectiveness. A sub-national regional government that is able to negotiate to bring a major investment by a global energy firm into their region with the cooperation of an international environmental organization may be deemed to be more skilled at diplomacy than the relatively ineffectual federal government that is sovereign over the territory but whose economic development ministry played no rôle in making the deal. As Brian Hocking argued, traditional diplomatic institutions such as foreign ministries increasingly are likely to be bypassed in the real world of diplomatic practice to the extent that they attempt to hold onto their traditional rôle as gatekeepers for other government ministries that need to interact with their foreign counterparts. Only to the extent that they are willing to function as 'boundary spanners' that bring together and facilitate contacts between the many organs of a government and ministries of other governments (and representatives of non-state actors) will they retain a rôle at the core of diplomatic practice.

Hence, returning to the 'agent–structure' debate mentioned in the first chapter, diplomacy takes place in a world where agency is paramount: who acts as a diplomatic actor, how they engage in diplomacy and how well they do it. Structures interact with agents as constraints upon motivations and actions, but not as determinants in a mechanistic, positivist sense. Amongst structures that influence diplomacy, institutions are the most important: diplomatic institutions, institutions of governance, and institutions of the global market economy. Institutions arise, exist and evolve in history, so institutional choices condition the evolutionary paths that the institutions take and the choices that future actors have available to them. For example, by joining the World Trade Organization in 2001, China's government committed itself to the WTO's multilateral trade liberalization objectives and to the norms and practices of diplomatic representation and communication in the structure of the WTO. By doing so, the Beijing government made it much more difficult to change their minds and reject WTO objectives, norms and practices later, as the political cost of withdrawal from such an institution is much higher than the cost of never joining in the first place.

The first of the two broader philosophical questions raised in chapter 1 concerned how we are to distinguish between continuity and change in diplomacy. What has become evident from this investigation is that if we think of diplomacy as defined by its core functions of representation and communication, the essential continuity of diplomacy lies in that those core functions do not change significantly over time. Whenever diplomatic representation and communication is taking place, diplomacy is continuing, even if the types of actors doing it have proliferated and the channels and techniques for communicating have become more varied. Two significant changes are underway. First, power within the system has shifted and become more diffuse. The age of a small group of great powers managing the majority of diplomatic relationships is receding fast. Second, as the number of states and non-state actors has proliferated, the quantity of diplomatic representation and communication, negotiation and mediation of estrangements has increased significantly and is likely to continue to increase. For example, governments of the great powers, seeking to resolve the 2008 financial crisis, convened a summit meeting of the G20 grouping comprised of leaders of both great powers and large developing-country governments in November 2008. A more customary approach would have been simply to convene a meeting of the smaller and more exclusive diplomatic club of G7 major global financial powers. However, effective management of a global financial crisis of the 2008 variety required not only for the G7 to continue to meet on a regular basis, but also for regular meetings of the broader G20 grouping to become part of the operational structure of economic diplomacy. Without the full and active participation of emerging economic powers such as China, India and Brazil, the G7 alone would have found it difficult if not impossible to agree and implement global monetary and financial measures needed to stem financial panic that can move from country to country and from bank to bank in real time.

The second broad philosophical question concerned whether diplomacy is an emergent property of a truly global society. Our investigation lends support to the claim that such a society is indeed developing, and that its institutions and norms of operation are being and will continue to be driven by diplomatic representation and communication. At the broadest level, the importance of international or global issues relative to more localized questions on the political agendas of every polity worldwide continues to rise significantly. Global climate change, management of global resources such as water, energy and the seabeds, global trade, poverty, terrorism and its causes, and transnational organized crime are only some of the issue areas that are demanding a growing share of the attention of political leaders and the diplomats who work for them. Likewise, the trend towards a greater number of diplomatic actors and towards a growing number of types of diplomatic actors continues. One of the most significant implications of this trend is that diplomatic networks of representation and communication are becoming more complex, and at the same time 'thin'. Diplomats are being asked to represent their sovereigns to more and more actors using the same (or sometimes fewer) resources in terms of funding, staffing and mindshare of their superiors and the publics to whom they also are increasingly accountable. Hence diplomats are continuing to need to become more skilled at using new technologies and new media to communicate and to become more versatile in terms of where and to whom they communicate. Daryl Copeland has described this phenomenon as 'guerrilla diplomacy' in his eponymously titled volume, conjuring the image of a guerrilla diplomat travelling in the field, laptop in rucksack for email and blogging and wireless handheld device in hand for instant communication through social networking sites like Facebook and Twitter.[13]

As the forms and channels of diplomatic representation continue to be democratized and popularized in this global society, the need for diplomats to do more public diplomacy is likely to continue. New media forms, such as social networking websites and multiplayer internet games, are rising in importance as diplomats seek new ways to send and gather information through interaction with the global public. According to US Deputy Assistant Secretary of State for Public Diplomacy Colleen Graffy, using social networking sites such as Facebook and Twitter has become an important part of US public diplomacy strategy.[14] In the conflict between Israel and Hamas in Gaza, the Israeli government has used Twitter to communicate their position to the public, whilst al-Jazeera has used networks of postings on Twitter and Facebook to gather and report information about the conflict to their audience.[15] Similarly, the governments of Sweden and the European Union created virtual 'embassies' to represent themselves, their agendas and their interests in Second Life, a widely used global multiplayer game in which individuals inhabit and interact in a virtual world that they create collectively.

Going forward, the core diplomatic functions of representation and communication are likely to remain much the same. Yet the ongoing popularization of diplomatic representation and communication in global society suggests that the position of official diplomats is likely to continue to become less privileged. Increasingly, representation will be undertaken by private as well as public actors. There will come to be less of a perceived difference between official diplomats and other individuals who accomplish a given job of communicating or negotiating. This should not diminish the importance of official diplomacy and the personnel who carry it out. But the competition, as it were, should act as a spur to official diplomats to maintain and increase their effectiveness. The official rituals and protocol of diplomacy – the state dinner, the summit meeting, the multilateral negotiation – will continue to take place and to be recognizable. Over time, however, they are likely to count for less of the overall activity of diplomacy, as more of the ways in which people and institutions interact in global society will come to be understood as part of diplomacy's essence.

Notes

1 Introduction: Understanding Global Interactions Through Diplomacy

1 Maurice Keens-Soper, 'François de Caillères and Diplomatic Theory', *Historical Journal* 16(3), 1973, pp. 485–508.
2 G. R. Berridge, *Diplomacy: Theory and Practice*, 3rd edn, Basingstoke: Palgrave, 2005.
3 Paul Sharp, 'For Diplomacy: Representation and the Study of International Relations', *International Studies Review* 1(1), 1999, pp. 33–57.
4 Sir Harold Nicolson, *Diplomacy*, 3rd edn, Oxford: Oxford University Press, 1963, pp. 4–5.
5 Adam Watson, *Diplomacy: The Dialogue Between States*, London and New York: Routledge, 1991 (1982).
6 Sharp, 'For Diplomacy: Representation and the Study of International Relations'.
7 Organization for Security and Cooperation in Europe (OSCE), Signing of the Helsinki Final Act, http://www.osce.org/item/15661.html, accessed 11 December 2008.
8 Thomas C. Schelling, *Arms and Influence*, New Haven: Yale University Press, 1966, p. 1.
9 Christer Jönsson and Martin Hall, 'Communication: An Essential Aspect of Diplomacy', *International Studies Perspectives* 4(2), 2003, pp. 195–210.
10 Hedley Bull, *The Anarchical Society*, Basingstoke: Macmillan, 1977; Halvard Leira and Iver Neumann, 'Judges, merchants and envoys: the growth and development of the consular institution', paper presented to Clingendael conference on public diplomacy, The Hague, Netherlands, June 2007.
11 Douglas Von Korff, unpublished paper, Bennington College, 2007.
12 Geoffrey Wiseman, 'Pax Americana: Bumping into Diplomatic Culture', *International Studies Perspectives* 6(4), November 2005, pp. 409–30.
13 Raymond Saner and Lichia Yu, 'International Economic Diplomacy: Mutations in Post-modern Times', Discussion Papers in Diplomacy, no. 84, Netherlands Institute of International Relations (Clingendael), January 2003.
14 Barry Buzan, *From International to World Society? English School Theory and the Social Structure of Globalisation*, Cambridge: Cambridge University Press, 2004, pp. 228–70.
15 Geoffrey Allen Pigman and John Kotsopoulos, '"Do this one for me, George": Blair, Brown, Bono, Bush and the "Actor-ness" of the G8', *The Hague Journal of Diplomacy* 2, 2007, pp. 127–45.
16 Keith Hamilton and Richard Langhorne, *The Practice of Diplomacy*, Abingdon: Routledge, 1995.
17 James Der Derian, *On Diplomacy: A Genealogy of Western Estrangement*, Oxford: Basil Blackwell, 1987, p. 3.
18 David Marsh and Gerry Stoker, eds., *Theory and Methods in Political Science*, 2nd edn, Basingstoke: Palgrave Macmillan, 2002.

2 The Changing Landscape of Diplomatic Actors and Venues

1 Andrew F. Cooper, *Celebrity Diplomacy*, Boulder: Paradigm Publishers, 2008, pp. 47–8.
2 'Microsoft to invest Rs 2000 cr in India over 3 yrs', *The Times of India*, 15 November 2002.
3 James Der Derian, *On Diplomacy: A Genealogy of Western Estrangement*, Oxford: Basil Blackwell, 1987, pp. 105–16.
4 Der Derian, *On Diplomacy*, pp. 116–33.
5 Paul Sharp, 'For Diplomacy: Representation and the Study of International Relations', *International Studies Review* 1(1), 1999, pp. 33–57.
6 Garrett Mattingly, 'The First Resident Embassies: Mediaeval Italian Origins of Modern Diplomacy', *Speculum* 12(4), 1937, pp. 423–39; rptd as pp. 214–31 in Christer Jönsson and Richard Langhorne, eds., *Diplomacy*, vol. II, *History of Diplomacy*, London: Sage Publications, 2004.
7 Halvard Leira and Iver B. Neumann, 'The Emergence and Practices of the Oslo Diplomatic Corps', pp. 83–102 in Paul Sharp and Geoffrey Wiseman, eds., *The Diplomatic Corps as an Institution of International Society*, Basingstoke: Palgrave Macmillan, 2008.
8 Geoffrey Wiseman, 'Pax Americana: Bumping into Diplomatic Culture', *International Studies Perspectives* 6(4), November 2005, pp. 409–30.
9 Iver B. Neumann, 'The English School on Diplomacy', Discussion Papers in Diplomacy, no. 79, Netherlands Institute of International Relations (Clingendael), pp. 92–116 in Christer Jönsson and Richard Langhorne, eds., *Diplomacy*, vol. I, *Theory of Diplomacy*, London: Sage Publications, 2004.
10 Susan Strange, *States and Markets*, 2nd edn, London: Pinter Publishers, 1994.
11 Costas Constantinou, *On the Way to Diplomacy*, Minneapolis: University of Minnesota Press, 1996, pp. 31–2.
12 Geoffrey Allen Pigman, 'Hegemony and Trade Liberalization Policy: Britain and the Brussels Sugar Convention of 1902', *Review of International Studies* 23, April 1997, pp. 185–210.

3 Nation–state Governments, Sub-national and Local Governments

1 Joseph A. Camilleri and Jim Falk, 'Sovereignty in Theory and Practice', pp. 11–43 in Camilleri and Falk, eds., *The End of Sovereignty*, Aldershot: Edward Elgar, 1992; Michael Hardt and Antonio Negri, *Empire*, Cambridge, Mass.: Harvard University Press, 2000, pp. 3–202.
2 Costas Constantinou, *On the Way to Diplomacy*, Minneapolis: University of Minnesota Press, 1996, pp. 103–5.
3 Republic of Georgia Ministry of Foreign Affairs 2007 budget presentation, www.mfa. gov.ge/files/158_3357_647446_englisuri.ppt, accessed 15 December 2008.
4 James Der Derian, *On Diplomacy: A Genealogy of Western Estrangement*, Oxford: Basil Blackwell, 1987, pp. 8–29.
5 Brian Hocking, 'Privatizing Diplomacy?', *International Studies Perspectives* 5(2), May 2004, pp. 147–52.
6 Iver B. Neumann, '"A Speech That the Entire Ministry May Stand For," or: Why Diplomats Never Produce Anything New', *International Political Sociology* 1, 2007, pp. 183–200.
7 Brian Hocking, 'Introduction: Gatekeepers and Boundary Spanners: Thinking about Foreign Ministries in the European Union' and 'Conclusion', pp. 1–17 and 273–86 in Brian Hocking and David Spence, eds., *Foreign Ministries in the European Union*, Basingstoke: Palgrave, 2003.
8 Hocking, 'Introduction: Gatekeepers and Boundary Spanners' and 'Conclusion'.

9 Adam Watson, *Diplomacy: The Dialogue Between States*, London and New York: Routledge, 1991 (1982).

10 Hocking, 'Introduction: Gatekeepers and Boundary Spanners' and 'Conclusion'.

11 Frans W. Weinglas and Gonnie de Boer, 'Parliamentary Diplomacy', *The Hague Journal of Diplomacy* 2(1), 2007, pp. 93–9.

12 Noé Cornago, 'The Normalization of Sub-state Diplomacy', *The Hague Journal of Diplomacy*, 5(1), 2010.

4 Multilateral Institutions, Supranational Polities and Regional Bodies

1 Richard Langhorne, 'The Development of International Conferences, 1648–1830', *Review of International Studies* 11, 1982, pp. 61–92.

2 Richard Langhorne, 'Establishing International Organizations: The Concert and the League', *Diplomacy and Statecraft* 1(1), 1988, pp. 1–18; Andrew Williams, *Failed Imagination? New World Orders of the Twentieth Century*, Manchester: Manchester University Press, 1998, pp. 19–78.

3 Edward Newman, *A Crisis of Global Institutions? Multilateralism and International Security*, Abingdon: Routledge, 2007, p. 143.

4 Geoffrey Allen Pigman, 'Hegemony and Trade Liberalization Policy: Britain and the Brussels Sugar Convention of 1902', *Review of International Studies* 23, April 1997, pp. 185–210.

5 Williams, *Failed Imagination?*, pp. 212–36.

6 United Nations, www.un.org.

7 Mercosur is a preferential trading agreement between a group of South American countries.

8 M. J. Peterson, *The UN General Assembly*, Abingdon: Routledge, 2006, pp. 92, 119.

9 Edward C. Luck, *UN Security Council: Practice and Promise*, Abingdon: Routledge, 2006.

10 Peterson, *The UN General Assembly*.

11 Williams, *Failed Imagination?*, pp. 231–3.

12 James Raymond Vreeland, *The International Monetary Fund: Politics of Conditional Lending*, Abingdon: Routledge, 2007; Katherine Marshall, *The World Bank: From Reconstruction to Development to Equity*, Abingdon: Routledge, 2008.

13 Amrita Narlikar, *The World Trade Organization: A Very Short Introduction*, Oxford: Oxford University Press, 2005.

14 Hugo Dobson, *The Group of 7/8*, Abingdon: Routledge, 2007; Geoffrey Allen Pigman and John Kotsopoulos, '"Do this one for me, George"': Blair, Brown, Bono, Bush and the "Actor-ness" of the G8', *The Hague Journal of Diplomacy* 2, 2007, pp. 127–45.

15 Andrew Walter, 'Unravelling the Faustian Bargain: Non-state Actors and the Multilateral Agreement on Investment', pp. 150–68 in Daphné Josselin and William Wallace, eds., *Non-state Actors in World Politics*, Basingstoke: Palgrave, 2001.

16 Geoffrey Allen Pigman, *The World Economic Forum: A Multi-stakeholder Approach to Global Governance*, London: Routledge, 2006.

17 Dominic Kelly, 'Global Monitor: The International Chamber of Commerce', *New Political Economy* 10(2), 2005, pp. 259–71; International Chamber of Commerce, the World Business Organization, www.iccwbo.org, accessed 15 December 2008.

18 Council of the European Union, Homepage of Javier Solana, www.consilium.europa. eu/cms3_applications/applications/solana/index.asp?cmsid=246&lang=EN, accessed 16 December 2008.

19 Donna Lee, 'The Growing Influence of Business in U.K. Diplomacy', *International Studies Perspectives* 5(1), February 2004, pp. 50–4.

20 Vreeland, *The International Monetary Fund*, pp. 112–31.

21 Faizel Ismail, *Mainstreaming Development in the WTO*, Jaipur: CUTS / Friedrich Ebert Stiftung, 2007.

5 Global and Transnational Firms

1 Mark Landler, 'Seeking Business Allies, Clinton Connects With India's Billionaires', *New York Times*, 19 July 2009, p. A12.
2 News Corporation, Investor Relations, Corporate Profile, www.newscorp.com/investor/index.html, accessed 16 December 2008.
3 John Stopford and Susan Strange, *Rival States, Rival Firms*, Cambridge: Cambridge University Press, 1991.
4 David Campbell, *Writing Security*, revised edn, Minneapolis: University of Minnesota Press, 1998.
5 Carne Ross, *Independent Diplomat*, London: Hurst, 2007, p. 216.
6 Peter Zamborsky, 'Slovakia: Bargain Motors', *Economist Intelligence Unit – Business Eastern Europe* 23, 19 July 2004, http://people.brandeis.edu/~zamborsk/Article%20on%20investment%20incentives%20for%20Economist%20Group.html, accessed 20 July 2009.
7 Jade Miller, 'Soft Power and State–Firm Diplomacy: Congress and IT Corporate Activity in China', *International Studies Perspectives* 10(3), August 2009, pp. 285–302.
8 BBC News World Edition, 'US Firm Ditches Tax Dodge', 2 August 2002, http://news.bbc.co.uk/2/hi/business/2167602.stm, accessed 20 July 2009.
9 Miller, 'Soft Power and State–Firm Diplomacy'.
10 Donna Lee, 'The Growing Influence of Business in U.K. Diplomacy', *International Studies Perspectives* 5(1), February 2004, pp. 50–4.
11 Brian Hocking, 'Catalytic Diplomacy', pp. 21–42 in Jan Melissen, ed., *Innovation in Diplomatic Practice*, Basingstoke: Macmillan, 1999.
12 Susan Strange, *States and Markets*, 2nd edn, London: Pinter, 1994; Strange, *The Retreat of the State*, Cambridge: Cambridge University Press, 1996.
13 Jeffrey A. Garten, *The Big Ten*, New York: Basic Books, 1997.
14 Geoffrey Allen Pigman, 'The New Aerospace Diplomacy: Reconstructing Post-Cold War US–Russian Economic Relations', *Diplomacy and Statecraft* 15(4), December 2004, pp. 1–41.
15 Tammy Whitehouse, 'FASB May Adopt IFRS for Tax Accounting', *Compliance Week*, 28 May 2008, www.complianceweek.com/article/4161/fasb-may-adopt-ifrs-for-tax-accounting, accessed 18 December 2008.
16 Rob Wells and John Rega, 'Congress Rewrites U.S. Banking Laws', *Bloomberg.com*, 4 November 1999; F. Jean Wells, 'Banking and Finance Mergers and Consolidation: Policy Issues', CRS Report for Congress, 15 July 1998; Kathleen Day, 'Reinventing the Bank', *The Washington Post*, 31 October 1999.
17 'Citicorp and Travelers Group to Merge, Creating Citigroup: The Global Leader in Financial Services', Citigroup press release, 6 April 1998.
18 Geoffrey Allen Pigman, 'Citigroup, Microsoft and Global Firm–Host Country Relations: The Public–Private Interplay in U.S. Economic Diplomacy', paper presented to the International Studies Association 2000 Annual Conference, Los Angeles, 15–18 March 2000.
19 Richard B. McKenzie, *Trust on Trial*, Cambridge, Mass.: Perseus Publishing, 2000.

6 Civil Society Organizations and Eminent Person Diplomats

1 Andrew F. Cooper, *Celebrity Diplomacy*, Boulder: Paradigm Publishers, 2008, pp. 1–14.
2 David P. Forsythe and Barbara Ann J. Rieffer-Flanagan, *The International Committee of the Red Cross: A Neutral Humanitarian Actor*, Abingdon: Routledge, 2007, pp. 3–4.

3 Andrew F. Cooper and Brian Hocking, 'Governments, Non-governmental Organisations and the Re-calibration of Diplomacy', *Global Society* 14(3), 2000, pp. 361–76.

4 Richard Langhorne and William Wallace, 'Diplomacy towards the Twenty-first Century', pp. 16–22 in Brian Hocking, ed., *Foreign Ministries: Change and Adaptation*, Basingstoke: Macmillan, 1999.

5 James Der Derian, *On Diplomacy: A Genealogy of Western Estrangement*, Oxford: Basil Blackwell, 1987, pp. 134–67.

6 United Nations General Assembly, Report of the Secretary-General in response to the report of the Panel of Eminent Persons on United Nations – Civil Society Relations, 13 September 2004, A/59/354, p. 2.

7 Greenpeace website, www.greenpeace.org/international/about/faq/questions-about-greenpeace-in, accessed 23 June 2008.

8 Forsythe and Rieffer-Flanagan, *The International Committee of the Red Cross*, pp. 1–5.

9 Cooper, *Celebrity Diplomacy*, pp. 47–8.

10 Cooper, *Celebrity Diplomacy*, pp. 18–27.

11 UNICEF, UNICEF People, Goodwill Ambassadors, www.unicef.org/people/people_ambassadors.html, accessed 31 January 2008.

12 UNICEF People, Goodwill Ambassadors.

13 Cooper, *Celebrity Diplomacy*, pp. 36–69.

14 The Elders website, www.theelders.org, accessed 23 June 2008.

15 Fox News.com, 'Taliban Offers Military Support to Pakistan in Event of War With India', 2 December 2008, www.foxnews.com/story/0,2933,460646,00.html, accessed 24 December 2008.

16 Ayman al-Zawahiri, audio tape, November 2008, translated in *Free Republic*, 'Zawahiri Considers Obama Election a Victory for Al Qaeda, Warns Obama', 19 November 2008, www.freerepublic.com/focus/f-news/2134560/posts, accessed 24 December 2008.

17 An earlier but more detailed version of the case study appears in Geoffrey Allen Pigman and John Kotsopoulos, '"Do this one for me, George": Blair, Brown, Bono, Bush and the "Actor-ness" of the G-8', *The Hague Journal of Diplomacy* 2, 2007, pp. 127–45.

18 Cooper, *Celebrity Diplomacy*, pp. 36–8.

19 James Traub, 'The Statesman: Why, and How, Bono Matters.', *The New York Times Magazine*, 18 September 2005.

20 Cooper, *Celebrity Diplomacy*, p. 48.

21 The Commission for Africa, *Our Common Interest: An Argument*, London: Penguin Books, 2005.

22 Geraldine Bedell, *Make Poverty History: How You Can Help Defeat World Poverty in Seven Easy Steps*, London: Penguin Books, 2005.

23 Sebastian Mallaby, 'Trade and Aid: Stars Are Aligned', *Washington Post*, 21 November 2005.

24 Sir Bob Geldof made the remarks to Prime Minister Blair at the launch of the Africa Commission's report, March 2005. See 'Time is Ticking for Blair's Africa Plan', *The Times*, 11 March 2005.

25 Victoria V. Panova, 'Impressions of the 2005 Gleneagles Summit', G-8 Information Centre, Toronto, 18 July 2005.

26 See Chair's Summary, Gleneagles Summit, 8 July 2005, www.G-8.gov.uk/servlet/Front?pagename=OpenMarket/Xcelerate/ShowPage&c=Page&cid=1119518698846.

27 'G-8: Hope for Africa but Gloom over Climate', *The Guardian*, 9 July 2005; Cooper, *Celebrity Diplomacy*, p. 67.

28 'Reaction Polarized as G-8 Concludes', *Associated Press*, 9 July 2005; Cooper, *Celebrity Diplomacy*, pp. 63–7.

29 'Fresh Talks but Little Hope on Climate Change', *The Guardian*, 9 July 2005.

30 'Fresh Talks but Little Hope on Climate Change'.

7 Technological Change and Diplomatic Process

1 Iver B. Neumann, '"A Speech That the Entire Ministry May Stand For", or: Why Diplomats Never Produce Anything New', *International Political Sociology* 1, 2007, pp. 183–200.

2 David H. Dunn, 'The Lure of Summitry: International Dialogue at the Highest Level', pp. 137–69 in Christer Jönsson and Richard Langhorne, eds., *Diplomacy*, vol. III, London: Sage Publications, 2004; Erik Goldstein, 'The Politics of the State Visit', pp. 357–80 in Christer Jönsson and Richard Langhorne, eds., *Diplomacy*, vol. II, London: Sage Publications, 2004.

3 Jovan Kurbalija, 'Diplomacy in the Age of Information Technology', pp. 171–91 in Jan Melissen, ed., *Innovation in Diplomatic Practice*, Basingstoke: Macmillan, 1999.

4 John Stempel, 'Intelligence, Covert Action, and Ethics: Oxymoron or Necessity?', paper presented to International Studies Association Annual Conference, San Francisco, California, 2008.

5 Des Hammill, *The Treaty: Thoughts on the Treaty of Waitangi*, Wellington: First Edition, 2006; 'Waitangi Now; Living and Working with the Treaty Today', supplement to *The New Zealand Herald*, 3 February 2009.

8 Public Diplomacy

1 The first, second, fourth and fifth sections of this chapter draw upon research by Anthony Deos, for which the author is grateful. A more detailed discussion of the issues raised can be found in Geoffrey Allen Pigman and Anthony Deos, 'Consuls for Hire: Private Actors, Public Diplomacy', *Place Branding and Public Diplomacy* 4(1), 2008, pp. 85–96.

2 C. K. Webster, 'Must Diplomacy Be Secret?', *Christian Science Monitor*, 29 May 1934, p. WM 1.

3 Public Diplomacy Alumni Association, What is Public Diplomacy?, www.publicdiplomacy.org/1.htm, accessed 10 April 2008.

4 Kishan S. Rana, *The 21st Century Ambassador: Plenipotentiary to Chief Executive*, Malta and Geneva: DiploFoundation, 2004.

5 Joseph S. Nye, Jr, *Soft Power*, New York: Public Affairs (Perseus Books Group), 2004.

6 Jan Melissen, 'Theory and Practice', pp. 3–27 in Melissen, ed., *The New Public Diplomacy: Soft Power in International Relations*, Basingstoke: Palgrave Macmillan, 2005.

7 Eytan Gilboa, 'Public Diplomacy: The Missing Component in Israel's Foreign Policy', *Israel Affairs* 12(4), October 2006, pp. 715–47.

8 Randal Marlin, *Propaganda and the Ethics of Persuasion*, Toronto: Broadview Press, 2002, p. 22.

9 Merriam-Webster Dictionary (Online Dictionary) 2005, www.m-w.com/cgi-bin/dictionary?book=Dictionary&va=propagate&x=0&y=0, accessed 15 March 2006.

10 Edward Bernays, *Propaganda*, New York: IG Publishing, 1928, p. 9.

11 Bernays, *Propaganda*, p. 15.

12 Bernays, *Propaganda*, p. 15.

13 Bernays, *Propaganda*, p. 48.

14 Jacques Ellul, *Propaganda: the Formation of Men's Attitudes*, tr. Jean Lerner and Konrad Kellen, New York: Vintage Books, 1965.

15 Marlin, *Propaganda and the Ethics of Persuasion*, p. 22.

16 Karen S. Johnson-Cartee and Gary A. Copeland, *Strategic Political Communication: Rethinking Social Influence, Persuasion, and Propaganda*, ed. Robert E. Denton, Jr, Lanham, Md.: Rowman & Littlefield, 2004, p. 4.

17 *Business Week*, 'Charlotte Beers' Toughest Sell', 17 December 2001, www.businessweek.com/magazine/content/01_51/b3762098.htm, accessed 19 September 2008.

18 Rene A. Henry, Jr, *Marketing Public Relations: The HOWS that Make it Work*, Ames: Iowa State University Press, 1995, p. 29.

19 Shaun Riordan, 'Dialogue-based Public Diplomacy: A New Foreign Policy Paradigm?', pp. 180–95 in Melissen, ed., *The New Public Diplomacy*.

20 US Department of State, Announcement of Cal Ripken, Jr. as Special Sports Envoy, Secretary Condoleezza Rice Remarks with Under Secretary for Public Diplomacy and Public Affairs Karen Hughes, Washington, DC, 13 August 2007, www.state.gov/secretary/rm/2007/08/90860.htm, accessed 10 April 2008.

21 Kathy Fitzpatrick, 'Advancing the New Public Diplomacy: A Public Relations Perspective', *The Hague Journal of Diplomacy* 2(3), 2007, pp. 187–211.

22 Pierre C. Pahlavi, 'Evaluating Public Diplomacy Programmes', *The Hague Journal of Diplomacy* 2(3), 2007, pp. 255–81.

23 Nye, *Soft Power*, p. 106.

24 Albright was seeking funds to pay US arrears to the United Nations, whilst Helms was seeking to consolidate the Arms Control and Disarmament Agency, the US Agency for International Development (USAID) and the US Information Agency (USIA) under the Department of State. In the negotiation, only USAID had the leadership to resist the consolidation and retain some independence.

25 Nye, *Soft Power*, p. 113.

26 Peter van Ham, 'Power, Public Diplomacy, and the *Pax Americana*', p. 63 in Melissen, ed., *The New Public Diplomacy*.

27 'Brand U.S.A.', *Foreign Policy* 127, November/December 2001, p. 19.

28 Timothy Starks, 'Saudi Arabia Spent $14.6 Million on P.R.; King Will Host "Martyrs'" Kin', *New York Sun*, 30 December 2002, p. 1.

29 Sari Horwitz and Dan Eggen, 'FBI Searches Saudi Arabia's PR Firm', *The Washington Post*, 9 December 2004, p. A8.

30 Evan Potter, 'Branding Canada: The Renaissance of Canada's Commercial Diplomacy', *International Studies Perspectives* 5(1), February 2004, pp. 55–60.

31 Wally Olins, 'Making a National Brand', pp. 169–79 in Melissen, ed., *The New Public Diplomacy*.

32 Alia Ibrahim, 'A Divine Seal of Approval', *The Washington Post*, 19 November 2006, p. B3.

33 India Brand Equity Foundation, About Us, www.ibef.org/aboutus, accessed 15 December 2006.

34 Business for Diplomatic Action, Who We Are, Introduction, www.businessfordiplomaticaction.org/who/index.html, accessed 10 December 2006.

35 Remarks by Harris Diamond, CEO Weber Shandwick Worldwide, at University of Southern California Annenberg School for Communication, Los Angeles, 14 November 2005.

36 Diamond, 14 November 2005.

37 Business for Diplomatic Action, Learn, Overview; World Citizens Guide, History, www.worldcitizensguide.org, accessed 10 December 2006.

38 Paul Sharp, 'Making Sense of Citizen Diplomats', pp. 343–61 in Jönsson and Langhorne, eds., *Diplomacy*, vol. III, *Problems and Issues in Contemporary Diplomacy*, London: Sage.

39 *Business Week*, 'Charlotte Beers' Toughest Sell', 17 December 2001; Craig Hayden, 'Arguing Public Diplomacy: The Role of Argument Formations in U.S. Foreign Policy Rhetoric', *The Hague Journal of Diplomacy* 2(3), 2007, pp. 229–54.

40 Olins, 'Making a National Brand', pp. 169–79; Hayden, 'Arguing Public Diplomacy'.

41 John Jurgensen, 'Marketing of Image Conflicts with Perception as Aggressor', *Hartford Courant*, 19 March 2003; Hayden, 'Arguing Public Diplomacy'.

42 Hayden, 'Arguing Public Diplomacy'.
43 US Department of State, Biography, Karen Hughes, www.state.gov/r/pa/ei/biog/53692.htm, accessed 10 December 2006.
44 Hayden, 'Arguing Public Diplomacy'.
45 D. C. M. Platt, *Finance, Trade and Politics in British Foreign Policy, 1815–1914*, Oxford: Clarendon Press, 1968, especially p. xxv.
46 Interview with Harris Diamond, CEO, Weber Shandwick Worldwide, 3 January 2007.
47 Fitzpatrick, 'Advancing the New Public Diplomacy: A Public Relations Perspective'; Hayden, 'Arguing Public Diplomacy'.
48 Krishna Guha, 'Pakistan to Offer India Kashmir-free Project Deals', *Financial Times*, 30 January 2005, www.ft.com, accessed 30 January 2005; Tim Weber, 'Pakistan Pushes India on Pipeline', BBC News, www.bbc.co.uk, 31 January 2005, accessed 31 January 2005.
49 Weber, 'Pakistan Pushes India on Pipeline'.

9 Managing Economic Diplomacy

1 Donna Lee and David Hudson, 'The Old and New Significance of Political Economy in Diplomacy', *Review of International Studies* 30(3), June 2004, pp. 343–60.
2 D. C. M. Platt, *Finance, Trade and Politics in British Foreign Policy, 1815–1914*, Oxford: Clarendon Press, 1968.
3 Amrita Narlikar, *The World Trade Organization: A Very Short Introduction*, Oxford: Oxford University Press, 2005.
4 I. M. Destler, *American Trade Politics*, 4th edn, Washington: Institute for International Economics, 2005.
5 Narlikar, *The World Trade Organization*.
6 India Brand Equity Foundation, www.ibef.com.
7 World Trade Organization, Understanding the WTO: Cross-cutting and New Issues, Investment, competition, procurement, simpler procedures, www.wto.org/english/thewto_e/whati s_e/tif_e/bey3_e.htm, accessed 1 March 2008.
8 GlobalSecurity.org, Military, Venezuela Crisis of 1902, www.globalsecurity.org/military/ops/venezuela1902.htm, accessed 29 February 2008.
9 Narlikar, *The World Trade Organization*.
10 Andrew Walter, 'Unravelling the Faustian Bargain: Non-state Actors and the Multilateral Agreement on Investment', pp. 150–68 in Daphné Josselin and William Wallace, eds., *Non-state Actors in World Politics*, Basingstoke: Palgrave, 2001.
11 James Raymond Vreeland, *The International Monetary Fund: Politics of Conditional Lending*, Abingdon: Routledge, 2007.
12 Andrew Walter, *World Power and World Money*, New York: Palgrave Macmillan, 1991.
13 Hugo Dobson, *The Group of 7/8*, Abingdon: Routledge, 2007.
14 New York Federal Reserve Bank, 'Trading Foreign Exchange: A Changing Market in a Changing World', www.newyorkfed.org/education/addpub/usfxm/chap1.pdf, accessed 9 January 2009.
15 Reuters, 'Global Stock Values Top $50 Trln: Industry Data', 21 March 2007, www.reuters.com/article/idUSL2144839620070321, accessed 2 March 2008.
16 Maurice Obstfeld and Alan M. Taylor, *Global Capital Markets*, Cambridge: Cambridge University Press, p. 55.
17 International Monetary Fund, About the IMF, Anti-Money Laundering / Combating the Financing of Terrorism, Reference Materials, www.imf.org/external/np/leg/amlcft/eng/aml4.htm, accessed 7 March 2008.

18 The Wolfsberg Group, The Wolfsberg Statement against Corruption, www.wolfsberg-principles.com/statement_against_corruption.html#_ftn1, accessed 7 March 2008.
19 World Federation of Exchanges, Activities, www.world-exchanges.org/WFE/home.asp?action=activities, accessed 15 March 2008.
20 Ian Taylor and Karen Smith, *United Nations Conference on Trade and Development (UNCTAD)*, Abingdon: Routledge, 2007.
21 M. J. Peterson, *The UN General Assembly*, Abingdon: Routledge, 2006, pp. 139–40.
22 Dobson, *The Group of 7/8*.
23 Katherine Marshall, *The World Bank: From Reconstruction to Development to Equity*, Abingdon: Routledge, 2008, pp. 59–111.
24 Vreeland, *The International Monetary Fund*, pp. 5–36.
25 Club de Paris / Paris Club, www.clubdeparis.org/en/, accessed 3 August 2009.
26 Clinton Global Initiative, About CGI, www.clintonglobalinitiative.org/NETCOMMUNITY/Page.aspx?pid=2358&srcid=895, accessed 9 January 2009.

10 Managing Military and Security Diplomacy

1 Thomas C. Schelling, *Arms and Influence*, New Haven: Yale University Press, 1966, pp. 1–34.
2 Andrew Williams, *Failed Imagination? New World Orders of the Twentieth Century*, Manchester: Manchester University Press, 1998, pp. 50–78; Barry Buzan, *From International to World Society? English School Theory and the Social Structure of Globalisation*, Cambridge: Cambridge University Press, 2004, pp. 228–70.
3 Lars G. Löse, 'Communicative Action and the World of Diplomacy', pp. 179–200 in Karin M. Fierke and Knud Erik Jørgensen, eds., *Constructing International Relations: The Next Generation*, Armonk, NY: M. E. Sharpe, 2001.
4 Dana Priest, *The Mission: Waging War and Keeping Peace with America's Military*, New York: W.W. Norton, 2004, pp. 11–57.
5 Edward C. Luck, *UN Security Council: Practice and Promise*, Abingdon: Routledge, 2006.
6 Luck, *UN Security Council*.
7 Edward Newman, *A Crisis of Global Institutions? Multilateralism and International Security*, Abingdon: Routledge, 2007; Luck, *UN Security Council*.
8 Collective Security Treaty Organisation, www.dkb.gov.ru/, accessed 3 August 2009.
9 David J. Galbreath, *The Organization for Security and Co-operation in Europe*, Abingdon: Routledge, 2007.
10 Julian Lindley-French, *The North Atlantic Treaty Organization: The Enduring Alliance*, Abingdon: Routledge, 2007.
11 Lindley-French, *The North Atlantic Treaty Organization*.
12 For more on NATO see Julian Lindley-French, *The North Atlantic Treaty Organization*; also consult the North Atlantic Treaty Organization, www.nato.int.
13 Michael Graham Fry, Erik Goldstein and Richard Langhorne, eds., *Guide to International Relations and Diplomacy*, London: Continuum, 2002, pp. 485–87.
14 Fry, Goldstein and Langhorne, eds., *Guide to International Relations and Diplomacy*, pp. 487–90.
15 Fry, Goldstein and Langhorne, eds., *Guide to International Relations and Diplomacy*, pp. 508–9.
16 United Nations, Oceans and Law of the Sea, The United Nations Convention on the Law of the Sea, www.un.org/Depts/los/convention_agreements/convention_historical_perspective.htm, accessed 3 August 2009.
17 UN Framework Convention on Climate Change, Kyoto Protocol, http://unfccc.int/kyoto_protocol/items/2830.php, accessed 3 August 2009.

11 Managing Cultural Diplomacy

1 Erik Goldstein, 'The Politics of the State Visit', pp. 357–80 in Christer Jönsson and Richard Langhorne, eds., *Diplomacy*, vol. II, London: Sage Publications, 2004.

2 US Department of State, Ask the White House with Raymond P. Martinez, 8 May 2007, www.state.gov/s/cpr/news/84520.htm, accessed 15 March 2008.

3 Cynthia P. Schneider, 'Culture Communicates: US Diplomacy that Works', pp. 147–68 in Jan Melissen, ed., *The New Public Diplomacy: Soft Power in International Relations*, Basingstoke: Palgrave Macmillan, 2005.

4 Bay Fang, 'Musical Diplomacy Thaws U.S.–Korea Freeze', *The Baltimore Sun*, 26 February 2008, weblogs.baltimoresun.com/news/politics/blog/2008/02/music_diplomacy_thaws_usn_kore.html, accessed 16 March 2008.

5 Kishan S. Rana, *Inside Diplomacy*, revised paperback edn, New Delhi: Manas, 2002.

6 Geoffrey Allen Pigman, *The World Economic Forum: A Multi-stakeholder Approach to Global Governance*, London: Routledge, 2006.

7 Institute for International Education, opendoors 2007 Fast Facts, http://opendoors.iienetwork.org, accessed 4 April 2008.

8 H. E. Chehabi, 'Sport Diplomacy between the United States and Iran', *Diplomacy and Statecraft* 12(1), 2001, pp. 89–106.

9 'India Win Thriller', BBC News, 13 March 2004, http://news.bbc.co.uk/sport1/hi/cricket/other_international/3507532.stm, accessed 13 March 2004.

10 Karen Marcus, 'Ping-pong Melts Cold War Rifts', USC US–China Institute, reprinted from *USC Daily Trojan*, 27 September 2007, http://china.usc.edu/ShowArticle.aspx?articleID=814, accessed 4 April 2008.

11 FIFA, Mission, About FIFA, FIFA.com, http://www.fifa.com/aboutfifa/federation/mission.html, accessed 5 April 2008.

12 FIFA, Mission.

13 ICC, Mission Statement, About ICC, http://icc-cricket.yahoo.com/about-icc/mission-statement.html, accessed 5 April 2008.

14 The Olympic Truce, History, The Movement, www.Olympic.org, www.olympic.org/uk/organisation/missions/truce/truce_uk.asp, accessed 5 April 2008.

15 The Olympic Truce, History, The Movement.

16 Organization of the Islamic Conference, www.oic-oci.org/home.asp, accessed 22 July 2009.

17 John Cornwell, *Hitler's Pope*, New York: Viking Penguin, 1999.

12 Conclusions: Contemporary Diplomatic Practice and Theory Looking Ahead

1 Sir Ernest Satow, *A Diplomat in Japan*, Rutland, Vt.: Charles E. Tuttle, 1983.

2 P. K. O'Brien and Geoffrey Allen Pigman, 'Free Trade, British Hegemony and the International Economic Order in the Nineteenth Century', *Review of International Studies* 18, April 1992, pp. 89–113.

3 D. C. M. Platt, *Finance, Trade and Politics in British Foreign Policy 1815–1914*, Oxford: Clarendon Press, 1968, p. 374.

4 Henry Kissinger, *Diplomacy*, New York: Simon and Schuster, 1994.

5 Donna Lee and David Hudson, 'The Old and New Significance of Political Economy in Diplomacy', *Review of International Studies* 30(3), June 2004, pp. 343–60.

6 Lee and Hudson, 'The Old and New Significance of Political Economy in Diplomacy'.

7 Kishan S. Rana, *Inside Diplomacy*, New Delhi: Manas, 2002.

8 Lee and Hudson, 'The Old and New Significance of Political Economy in Diplomacy'.

9 Costas Constantinou, *On the Way to Diplomacy*, Minneapolis: University of Minnesota Press, 1996, pp. 31–62.

10 Constantinou, *On the Way to Diplomacy*, pp. 31–40.

11 Constantinou, *On the Way to Diplomacy*, pp. 31–40.

12 Erin Burnett, report on pirate spokesperson, CNBC, *Squawk on the Street*, 13 January 2009.

13 Daryl Copeland, *Guerrilla Diplomacy: Rethinking International Relations*, Boulder: Lynne Rienner, 2009.

14 Colleen P. Graffy, 'A Tweet in Foggy Bottom', *Washington Post*, 24 December 2008, p. A11, www.washingtonpost.com/wp-dyn/content/article/2008/12/23/AR2008122301999.html?referrer=emailarticle, accessed 13 January 2009.

15 Corey Flintoff, 'Gaza Conflict Plays out Online through Social Media', *NPR*, 7 January 2009, www.npr.org, accessed 8 January 2009.

Bibliography

Albright, Madeline, *Madam Secretary*. New York: Miramax Books, 2003.

al-Zawahiri, Ayman, audio tape, November 2008, translated in *Free Republic*, 'Zawahiri Considers Obama Election a Victory for Al Qaeda, Warns Obama', 19 November 2008, www.freerepublic.com/focus/f-news/2134560/posts, accessed 24 December 2008.

Anholt, Simon, *Competitive Identity: The New Brand Management for Nations, Cities and Regions*. Basingstoke: Palgrave Macmillan, 2007.

Axelrod, Robert, *The Evolution of Co-operation*. London: Penguin Books, 1990.

Bayne, Nicholas, and Stephen Woolcock, eds., *The New Economic Diplomacy*. London: Ashgate, 2003.

BBC News, 'India Win Thriller', 13 March 2004, http://news.bbc.co.uk/sport1/hi/cricket/other_international/3507532.stm, accessed 13 March 2004.

BBC News World Edition, 'US Firm Ditches Tax Dodge', 2 August 2002, http://news.bbc.co.uk/2/hi/business/2167602.stm, accessed 20 July 2009.

Bedell, Geraldine, *Make Poverty History: How You Can Help Defeat World Poverty in Seven Easy Steps*. London: Penguin Books, 2005.

Bernays, Edward, *Propaganda*. New York: IG Publishing, 1928.

Berridge, G. R., *Diplomacy: Theory and Practice*, 3rd edn. Basingstoke: Palgrave, 2005.

Bono with Michka Assayas, *Bono on Bono: Conversations with Michka Assayas*. London: Hodder & Stoughton, 2005.

Bull, Hedley, *The Anarchical Society*. Basingstoke: Macmillan, 1977.

Burnett, Erin, report on pirate spokesperson, CNBC, *Squawk on the Street*, 13 January 2009.

Business for Diplomatic Action, Who We Are, Introduction, www.businessfordiplomaticaction.org/who/index.html, accessed 10 December 2006.

Business Week, 'Charlotte Beers' Toughest Sell', 17 December 2001, www.businessweek.com/magazine/content/01_51/b3762098.htm, accessed 19 September 2008.

Buzan, Barry, *From International to World Society? English School Theory and the Social Structure of Globalisation*. Cambridge: Cambridge University Press, 2004.

Camilleri, Joseph A., and Jim Falk, *The End of Sovereignty*. Aldershot: Edward Elgar, 1992.

Campbell, David, *Writing Security*, revised edn. Minneapolis: University of Minnesota Press, 1998.

Chehabi, H. E., 'Sport Diplomacy between the United States and Iran', *Diplomacy and Statecraft* 12(1), 2001, pp. 89–106.

Clinton Global Initiative, About CGI, www.clintonglobalinitiative.org/ NETCOMMUNITY/Page.aspx?pid=2358&srcid=895, accessed 9 January 2009.

Commission for Africa, *Our Common Interest: An Argument*. London: Penguin, 2005.

Constantinou, Costas, *On the Way to Diplomacy*. Minneapolis: University of Minnesota Press, 1996.

Cooper, Andrew F., *Celebrity Diplomacy*. Boulder: Paradigm Publishers, 2008.

Cooper, Andrew F., and Brian Hocking, 'Governments, Non-governmental Organisations and the Re-calibration of Diplomacy', *Global Society* 14(3), 2000, pp. 361–76.

Copeland, Daryl, *Guerrilla Diplomacy: Rethinking International Relations*. Boulder: Lynne Rienner, 2009.

Cornago, Noé, 'The Normalization of Sub-state Diplomacy', *The Hague Journal of Diplomacy* 5(1), 2010.

Cornwell, John, *Hitler's Pope*. New York: Viking Penguin, 1999.

Council of the European Union, Homepage of Javier Solana, www.consilium. europa.eu/cms3_applications/applications/solana/index.asp?cmsid =246&lang=EN, accessed 16 December 2008.

Day, Kathleen, 'Reinventing the Bank', *The Washington Post*, 31 October 1999.

Der Derian, James, *On Diplomacy: A Genealogy of Western Estrangement*. Oxford: Basil Blackwell, 1987.

Der Derian, James, *Virtuous War: Mapping the Military-Industrial-Media-Entertainment Network*. Boulder: Westview Press, 2001.

Derrida, Jacques, *Of Grammatology*. Baltimore: Johns Hopkins University Press, 1997.

Destler, I. M., *American Trade Politics*, 4th edn. Washington: Institute for International Economics, 2005.

Diamond, Harris, CEO Weber Shandwick Worldwide, remarks at USC Annenberg School for Communication, Los Angeles, 14 November 2005.

Dobson, Hugo, *The Group of 7/8*. Abingdon: Routledge, 2007.

Dunn, David H., 'The Lure of Summitry: International Dialogue at the Highest Level', pp. 137–69 in Christer Jönsson and Richard Langhorne, eds., *Diplomacy*, vol. III. London: Sage Publications, 2004.

Dunn, David H., ed., *Diplomacy at the Highest Level: The Evolution of International Summitry*. London: Palgrave Macmillan, 1996.

Ellul, Jacques, *Propaganda: The Formation of Men's Attitudes*, tr. Jean Lerner and Konrad Kellen. New York: Vintage Books, 1965.

Fang, Bay, 'Musical Diplomacy Thaws U.S. – N. Korea Freeze', *The Baltimore Sun*, 26 February 2008, http://weblogs.baltimoresun.com/news/politics/blog/2008/02/music_diplomacy_thaws_usn_kore.html, accessed 16 March 2008.

Fierke, Karin M., and Knud Erik Jørgensen, eds., *Constructing International Relations: The Next Generation*. Armonk, NY: M.E. Sharpe, 2001.

FIFA, Mission, About FIFA, FIFA.com, www.fifa.com/aboutfifa/federation/mission.html, accessed 5 April 2008.

Fitzpatrick, Kathy, 'Advancing the New Public Diplomacy: A Public Relations Perspective', *The Hague Journal of Diplomacy* 2(3), 2007, pp. 187–211.

Flintoff, Corey, 'Gaza Conflict Plays out Online through Social Media', *NPR*, 7 January 2009, www.npr.org, accessed 8 January 2009.

Foreign Policy, 'Brand U.S.A.', 127, November/December 2001, p. 19.

Forsythe, David P., and Barbara Ann J. Rieffer-Flanagan, *The International Committee of the Red Cross: A Neutral Humanitarian Actor*. Abingdon: Routledge, 2007.

Fox News.com, 'Taliban Offers Military Support to Pakistan in Event of War with India', 2 December 2008, www.foxnews.com/story/0,2933,460646,00.html, accessed 24 December 2008.

Fry, Michael Graham, Erik Goldstein and Richard Langhorne, eds., *Guide to International Relations and Diplomacy*. London: Continuum, 2002.

Galbreath, David J., *The Organization for Security and Co-operation in Europe*. Abingdon: Routledge, 2007.

Garten, Jeffrey A., *The Big Ten*. New York: Basic Books, 1997.

Gilboa, Eytan, 'Public Diplomacy: The Missing Component in Israel's Foreign Policy', *Israel Affairs* 12(4), October 2006, pp. 715–47.

GlobalSecurity.org, Military, Venezuela Crisis of 1902, www.globalsecurity.org/military/ops/venezuela1902.htm, accessed 29 February 2008.

Goldstein, Erik, 'The Politics of the State Visit', pp. 357–80 in Christer Jönsson and Richard Langhorne, eds., *Diplomacy*, vol. II. London: Sage Publications, 2004.

Gordenker, Leon, *The UN Secretary General and Secretariat*. Abingdon: Routledge, 2005.

Graffy, Colleen P., 'A Tweet in Foggy Bottom', *Washington Post*, 24 December 2008, p. A11, www.washingtonpost.com/wp-dyn/content/article/2008/12/23/AR2008122301999.html?referrer=emailarticle, accessed 13 January 2009.

Graz, Jean-Christophe, 'How Powerful are Transnational Elite Clubs? The Social Myth of the World Economic Forum', *New Political Economy* 8(3), November 2003, pp. 321–40.

Greenpeace, www.greenpeace.org/international/about/faq/questions-about-greenpeace-in, accessed 23 June 2008.

Guha, Krishna, 'Pakistan to Offer India Kashmir-free Project Deals', *Financial Times*, 30 January 2005, www.ft.com, accessed 31 January 2005.

Habermas, Jürgen, *On the Pragmatics of Social Interaction*. Oxford: Basil Blackwell, 2003.

Hall, Rodney Bruce, 'The Discursive Demolition of the Asian Development Model', *International Studies Quarterly* 47(1), March 2003, pp. 71–99.

Hamilton, Keith, and Richard Langhorne, *The Practice of Diplomacy*. Abingdon: Routledge, 1995.

Hamm, Steve, *Bangalore Tiger: How Indian Tech Upstart Wipro is Rewriting the Rules of Global Competition*. New York: McGraw-Hill, 2007.

Hammill, Des, *The Treaty: Thoughts on the Treaty of Waitangi*. Wellington: First Edition, 2006.

Hardt, Michael, and Antonio Negri, *Empire*. Cambridge, Mass.: Harvard University Press, 2000.

Hayden, Craig, 'Arguing Public Diplomacy: The Role of Argument Formations in U.S. Foreign Policy Rhetoric', *The Hague Journal of Diplomacy* 2(3), 2007, pp. 229–54.

Henry, Rene A., Jr., *Marketing Public Relations: The Hows that Make it Work*. Ames: Iowa State University Press, 1995.

Hocking, Brian, 'Catalytic Diplomacy', pp. 21–42 in Jan Melissen, ed., *Innovation in Diplomatic Practice*. Basingstoke: Macmillan, 1999.

Hocking, Brian, 'Privatizing Diplomacy?', *International Studies Perspectives* 5(2), May 2004, pp. 147–52.

Hocking, Brian, ed., *Foreign Ministries: Change and Adaptation*. Basingstoke: Macmillan, 1999.

Hocking, Brian, and Steven McGuire, eds., *Trade Politics*, 2nd edn. London and New York: Routledge, 2004.

Hocking, Brian, and David Spence, eds., *Foreign Ministries in the European Union*. Basingstoke: Palgrave, 2003.

Horwitz, Sari, and Dan Eggen, 'FBI Searches Saudi Arabia's PR Firm', *Washington Post*, 9 December 2004, p. A8.

Ibrahim, Alia, 'A Divine Seal of Approval', *The Washington Post*, 19 November 2006, p. B3.

India Brand Equity Foundation, About Us, www.ibef.org/aboutus, accessed 15 December 2006.

Institute for International Education, opendoors 2007 Fast Facts, http://opendoors.iienetwork.org, accessed 4 April 2008.

International Chamber of Commerce, The World Business Organization, www.iccwbo.org, accessed 15 December 2008.

International Cricket Council, About ICC, Mission Statement, http://icc-cricket.yahoo.com/about-icc/mission-statement.html, accessed 5 April 2008.

International Monetary Fund, About the IMF, Anti-Money Laundering / Combating the Financing of Terrorism, Reference Materials, www.imf. org/external/np/leg/amlcft/eng/aml4.htm, accessed 7 March 2008.

Ismail, Faizel, *Mainstreaming Development in the WTO*. Jaipur: CUTS / Friedrich Ebert Stiftung, 2007.

Johnson-Cartee, Karen S., and Gary A. Copeland, *Strategic Political Communication: Rethinking Social Influence, Persuasion, and Propaganda*, ed. Robert E. Denton, Jr. Lanham, Md.: Rowman & Littlefield, 2004.

Jönsson, Christer, and Martin Hall, 'Communication: An Essential Aspect of Diplomacy', *International Studies Perspectives* 4(2), 2003, pp. 195–210.

Jönsson, Christer, and Richard Langhorne, eds., *Diplomacy*, vols. I–III. London: Sage Publications, 2004.

Josselin, Daphné, and William Wallace, *Non-state Actors in World Politics*. Basingstoke: Palgrave, 2001.

Jurgensen, John, 'Marketing of Image Conflicts with Perception as Aggressor', *Hartford Courant*, 19 March 2003.

Keens-Soper, Maurice, 'François de Caillères and Diplomatic Theory', *Historical Journal* 16(3), 1973, pp. 485–508.

Kelly, Dominic, 'Global Monitor: The International Chamber of Commerce', *New Political Economy* 10(2), 2005, pp. 259–71.

Kissinger, Henry, *Diplomacy*. New York: Simon and Schuster, 1994.

Kurbalija, Jovan, 'Diplomacy in the Age of Information Technology', pp. 171–91 in Jan Melissen, ed., *Innovation in Diplomatic Practice*. Basingstoke: Macmillan, 1999.

Langhorne, Richard, 'Establishing International Organizations: The Concert and the League', *Diplomacy and Statecraft* 1(1), 1988, pp. 1–18.

Langhorne, Richard, 'The Development of International Conferences, 1648–1830', *Review of International Studies* 11, 1982, pp. 61–92.

Langhorne, Richard, 'The Regulation of Diplomatic Practice: The Beginnings to the Vienna Convention on Diplomatic Practice, 1961', pp. 315–33 in Christer Jönsson and Richard Langhorne, eds., *Diplomacy*, vol. II. London: Sage Publications, 2004.

Langhorne, Richard, and William Wallace, 'Diplomacy towards the Twenty-first Century', pp. 16–22 in Brian Hocking, ed., *Foreign Ministries: Change and Adaptation*. Basingstoke: Macmillan, 1999.

Lee, Donna, 'The Growing Influence of Business in U.K. Diplomacy', *International Studies Perspectives* 5(1), February 2004, pp. 50–4.

Lee, Donna, and David Hudson, 'The Old and New Significance of Political Economy in Diplomacy', *Review of International Studies* 30(3), June 2004, pp. 343–60.

Leira, Halvard, and Iver B. Neumann, 'The Emergence and Practices of the Oslo Diplomatic Corps', pp. 83–103 in Paul Sharp and Geoffrey Wiseman, eds., *The Diplomatic Corps as an Institution of International Society*. Basingstoke: Palgrave Macmillan, 2008.

Lindley-French, Julian, *The North Atlantic Treaty Organization: The Enduring Alliance*. Abingdon: Routledge, 2007.

Löse, Lars G., 'Communicative Action and the World of Diplomacy', pp. 179–200 in Karin M. Fierke and Knud Erik Jørgensen, eds., *Constructing International Relations: The Next Generation*, Armonk, NY: M. E. Sharpe, 2001.

Luck, Edward C., *UN Security Council: Practice and Promise*. Abingdon: Routledge, 2006.

Marcus, Karen, 'Ping-pong Melts Cold War Rifts', USC US–China Institute, rptd from *USC Daily Trojan*, 27 September 2007, http://china.usc.edu/ShowArticle.aspx?articleID=814, accessed 4 April 2008.

Marlin, Randal, *Propaganda and the Ethics of Persuasion*. Toronto: Broadview Press, 2002.

Marsh, David, and Gerry Stoker, eds., *Theory and Methods in Political Science*, 2nd edn, Basingstoke: Palgrave Macmillan, 2002.

Marshall, Katherine, *The World Bank: From Reconstruction to Development to Equity*. Abingdon: Routledge, 2008.

Mattingly, Garrett, 'The First Resident Embassies: Mediaeval Italian Origins of Modern Diplomacy', *Speculum* 12(4), 1937, pp. 423–39; rptd as pp. 214–31 in Christer Jönsson and Richard Langhorne, eds., *Diplomacy*, vol. II, *History of Diplomacy*. London: Sage Publications, 2004.

Mallaby, Sebastian, 'Trade and Aid: Stars Are Aligned', *Washington Post*, 21 November 2005.

May, Christopher, *The World Intellectual Property Organization: Resurgence and the Development Agenda*. Abingdon: Routledge, 2007.

McKenzie, Richard B., *Trust on Trial*. Cambridge, Mass.: Perseus Publishing, 2000.

Melissen, Jan, 'Theory and Practice', pp. 3–27 in Melissen, ed., *The New Public Diplomacy: Soft Power in International Relations*. Basingstoke: Palgrave Macmillan, 2005.

Melissen, Jan, ed., *The New Public Diplomacy: Soft Power in International Relations*. Basingstoke: Palgrave Macmillan, 2005.

Miller, Jade, 'Soft Power and State–Firm Diplomacy: Congress and IT Corporate Activity in China', *International Studies Perspectives* 10(3), August 2009, pp. 285–302.

Nagl, John A., *Learning to Eat Soup with a Knife: Counterinsurgency Lessons from Malaya and Vietnam*. Chicago: University of Chicago Press, 2005.

Narlikar, Amrita, *The World Trade Organization: A Very Short Introduction*. Oxford: Oxford University Press, 2005.

Neumann, Iver B., 'The English School on Diplomacy', Discussion Papers in Diplomacy, no. 79, Netherlands Institute of International Relations (Clingendael); rptd as pp. 92–116 in Christer Jönsson and Richard Langhorne, eds., *Diplomacy*, vol. I, *Theory of Diplomacy*. London: Sage Publications, 2004.

Neumann, Iver B., ' "A Speech that the Entire Ministry May Stand For", or: Why Diplomats Never Produce Anything New', *International Political Sociology* 1, 2007, pp. 183–200.

New York Federal Reserve Bank, 'Trading Foreign Exchange: A Changing Market in a Changing World', www.newyorkfed.org/education/addpub/usfxm/chap1.pdf, accessed 9 January 2009.

Newman, Edward, *A Crisis of Global Institutions? Multilateralism and International Security*. Abingdon: Routledge, 2007.

News Corporation, Investor Relations, Corporate Profile, www.newscorp.com/investor/index.html, accessed 16 December 2008.

Nicolson, Sir Harold, *Diplomacy*, 3rd edn. Oxford: Oxford University Press, 1963.

Nye, Joseph S., Jr, *Soft Power: The Means to Success in World Politics*. New York: Public Affairs (Perseus Books Group), 2004.

O'Brien, P. K., and Geoffrey Allen Pigman, 'Free Trade, British Hegemony and the International Economic Order in the Nineteenth Century', *Review of International Studies* 18, April 1992, pp. 89–113.

Obstfeld, Maurice, and Alan M. Taylor, *Global Capital Markets*. Cambridge: Cambridge University Press.

Olins, Wally, 'Making a National Brand', pp. 169–79 in Jan Melissen, ed., *The New Public Diplomacy: Soft Power in International Relations*. Basingstoke: Palgrave Macmillan, 2005.

Organization for Security and Cooperation in Europe (OSCE), Signing of the Helsinki Final Act, www.osce.org/item/15661.html, accessed 11 December 2008.

Pahlavi, Pierre C., 'Evaluating Public Diplomacy Programmes', *The Hague Journal of Diplomacy* 2(3), 2007, pp. 255–81.

Panova, Victoria V., 'Impressions of the 2005 Gleneagles Summit', G-8 Information Centre, Toronto, 18 July 2005.

Peterson, M. J., *The UN General Assembly*. Abingdon: Routledge, 2006.

Pigman, Geoffrey Allen, 'A Multifunctional Case Study for Teaching International Political Economy: The World Economic Forum as Shar-pei or Wolf in Sheep's Clothing?', *International Studies Perspectives* 3(3), August 2002, pp. 291–309.

Pigman, Geoffrey Allen, 'Citigroup, Microsoft and Global Firm–Host Country Relations: The Public–Private Interplay in U.S. Economic Diplomacy', paper presented to the International Studies Association 2000 Annual Conference, Los Angeles, 15–18 March 2000.

Pigman, Geoffrey Allen, 'Hegemony and Trade Liberalization Policy: Britain and the Brussels Sugar Convention of 1902', *Review of International Studies* 23, April 1997, pp. 185–210.

Pigman, Geoffrey Allen, 'The New Aerospace Diplomacy: Reconstructing Post-Cold War US–Russian Economic Relations', *Diplomacy and Statecraft* 15(4), December 2004, pp. 1–41.

Pigman, Geoffrey Allen, *The World Economic Forum: A Multi-stakeholder Approach to Global Governance*. London: Routledge, 2006.

Pigman, Geoffrey Allen, and Anthony Deos, 'Consuls for Hire: Private Actors, Public Diplomacy', *Place Branding and Public Diplomacy* 4(1), 2008.

Pigman, Geoffrey Allen, and John Kotsopoulos, ' "Do this one for me, George": Blair, Brown, Bono, Bush and the "Actor-ness" of the G8', *The Hague Journal of Diplomacy* 2, 2007, pp. 127–45.

Platt, D. C. M., *Finance, Trade and Politics in British Foreign Policy, 1815–1914*. Oxford: Clarendon Press, 1968.

Potter, Evan, 'Branding Canada: The Renaissance of Canada's Commercial Diplomacy', *International Studies Perspectives* 5(1), February 2004, pp. 55–60.

Priest, Dana, *The Mission: Waging War and Keeping Peace with America's Military*. New York: W.W. Norton, 2004.

Public Diplomacy Alumni Association, What is Public Diplomacy, www.publicdiplomacy.org/1.htm, accessed 10 April 2008.

Rana, Kishan S., *Inside Diplomacy*, revised paperback edn. New Delhi: Manas, 2002.

Rana, Kishan S., *The 21st Century Ambassador: Plenipotentiary to Chief Executive*. Malta and Geneva: DiploFoundation, 2004.

Republic of Georgia Ministry of Foreign Affairs 2007 budget presentation, www.mfa.gov.ge/files/158_3357_647446_englisuri.ppt, accessed 15 December 2008.

Reuters, 'Global Stock Values Top $50 Trln: Industry Data', 21 March 2007, www.reuters.com/article/idUSL2144839620070321, accessed 2 March 2008.

Riordan, Shaun, 'Dialogue-based Public Diplomacy: A New Foreign Policy Paradigm?', pp. 180–95 in Jan Melissen, ed., *The New Public Diplomacy: Soft Power in International Relations*. Basingstoke: Palgrave Macmillan, 2005.

Ross, Carne, *Independent Diplomat*. London: Hurst, 2007.

Saner, Raymond, and Lichia Yu, 'International Economic Diplomacy: Mutations in Post-modern Times', Discussion Papers in Diplomacy, no. 84, Netherlands Institute of International Relations (Clingendael), January 2003.

Satow, Sir Ernest, *A Diplomat in Japan*. Rutland, Vt.: Charles E. Tuttle, 1983.

Schelling, Thomas C., *Arms and Influence*. New Haven: Yale University Press, 1966.

Schneider, Cynthia P., 'Culture Communicates: US Diplomacy that Works', pp. 147–68 in Jan Melissen, ed., *The New Public Diplomacy: Soft Power in International Relations*. Basingstoke: Palgrave Macmillan, 2005.

Sharp, Paul, 'For Diplomacy: Representation and the Study of International Relations', *International Studies Review* 1(1), 1999, pp. 33–57.

Sharp, Paul, 'Making Sense of Citizen Diplomats', pp. 343–61 in Christer Jönsson and Richard Langhorne, eds., *Diplomacy*, vol. III, *Problems and Issues in Contemporary Diplomacy*. London: Sage Publications, 2004.

Short, Clare, *An Honourable Deception?* London: Free Press, 2005.

Snow, Nancy, and Philip M. Taylor, eds., *The Routledge Handbook of Public Diplomacy*. Routledge: Abingdon, 2009.

Starks, Timothy, 'Saudi Arabia Spent $14.6 Million on P.R.: King Will Host "Martyrs'" Kin', *New York Sun*, 30 December 2002, p. 1.

Stempel, John, 'Intelligence, Covert Action, and Ethics: Oxymoron or Necessity?', paper presented to International Studies Association Annual Conference, San Francisco, 2008.

Stopford, John, and Susan Strange, *Rival States, Rival Firms*. Cambridge: Cambridge University Press, 1991.

Strange, Susan, *States and Markets*, 2nd edn. London: Pinter Publishers, 1994.

Strange, Susan, *The Retreat of the State*. Cambridge: Cambridge University Press, 1996.

Taylor, Ian, and Karen Smith, *United Nations Conference on Trade and Development (UNCTAD)*. Abingdon: Routledge, 2007.

Terriff, Terry, Stuart Croft, Lucy James and Patrick M. Morgan, *Security Studies Today*. Cambridge: Polity Press, 1999.

The Elders, www.theelders.org, accessed 23 June 2008.

The Olympic Truce, History, The Movement, www.Olympic.org, www.olympic.org/uk/organisation/missions/truce/truce_uk.asp, accessed 5 April 2008.

The Wolfsberg Group, The Wolfsberg Statement against Corruption, www.wolfsberg-principles.com/statement_against_corruption.html#_ftn1, accessed 7 March 2008.

'Time is Ticking for Blair's Africa Plan', *The Times*, 11 March 2005.

Traub, James, 'The Statesman: Why, and How, Bono Matters', *The New York Times Magazine*, 18 September 2005.

US Department of State, Announcement of Cal Ripken, Jr as Special Sports Envoy, Secretary Condoleezza Rice Remarks with Under Secretary for Public Diplomacy and Public Affairs Karen Hughes, Washington, DC, 13 August 2007, www.state.gov/secretary/rm/2007/08/90860.htm, accessed 10 April 2008.

US Department of State, Ask the White House with Raymond P. Martinez, 8 May 2007, www.state.gov/s/cpr/news/84520.htm, accessed 15 March 2008.

US Department of State, Biography, Karen Hughes, www.state.gov/r/pa/ei/biog/53692.htm, accessed 10 December 2006.

UNICEF, UNICEF People, Goodwill Ambassadors, www.unicef.org/people/people_ambassadors.html, accessed 31 January 2008.

United Nations General Assembly, Report of the Secretary-General in response to the report of the Panel of Eminent Persons on United Nations – Civil Society Relations, 13 September 2004, A/59/354.

van Ham, Peter, 'Power, Public Diplomacy, and the *Pax Americana*', pp. 47–66 in Jan Melissen, ed., *The New Public Diplomacy: Soft Power in International Relations*. Basingstoke: Palgrave Macmillan, 2005.

Vreeland, James Raymond, *The International Monetary Fund: Politics of Conditional Lending*. Abingdon: Routledge, 2007.

Walter, Andrew, 'Unravelling the Faustian Bargain: Non-state Actors and the Multilateral Agreement on Investment', pp. 150–68 in Daphné Josselin and William Wallace, eds., *Non-state Actors in World Politics*. Basingstoke: Palgrave, 2001.

Walter, Andrew, *World Power and World Money*. New York: Palgrave Macmillan, 1991.

Watson, Adam, *Diplomacy: The Dialogue Between States*. London and New York: Routledge, 1991 (1982).

Weber, Tim, 'Pakistan Pushes India on Pipeline', BBC News, www.bbc.co.uk, 31 January 2005, accessed 31 January 2005.

Webster, C. K., 'Must Diplomacy Be Secret?', *Christian Science Monitor*, 29 May 1934, p. WM 1.

Weinglas, Frans W., and Gonnie de Boer, 'Parliamentary Diplomacy', *The Hague Journal of Diplomacy* 2(1), 2007, pp. 93–9.

Wellman, David Joseph, *Sustainable Diplomacy: Ecology, Religion and Ethics in Muslim–Christian Relations*. Basingstoke: Palgrave Macmillan, 2004.

Wells, F. Jean, 'Banking and Finance Mergers and Consolidation: Policy Issues', CRS Report for Congress, 15 July 1998.

Wells, Rob, and John Rega, 'Congress Rewrites U.S. Banking Laws', *Bloomberg.com*, 4 November 1999.

Whitehouse, Tammy, 'FASB May Adopt IFRS for Tax Accounting', *Compliance Week*, 28 May 2008, www.complianceweek.com/article/4161/fasb-may-adopt-ifrs-for-tax-accounting, accessed 18 December 2008.

Williams, Andrew, *Failed Imagination? New World Orders of the Twentieth Century*. Manchester: Manchester University Press, 1998.

Wiseman, Geoffrey, 'Pax Americana: Bumping into Diplomatic Culture', *International Studies Perspectives* 6(4), November 2005, pp. 409–30.

Wittgenstein, Ludwig, *Philosophische Untersuchungen / Philosophical Investigations*, 3rd edn, tr. G. E. M. Anscombe. Oxford: Blackwell, 2001.

World Federation of Exchanges, Activities, www.world-exchanges.org/WFE/home.asp?action=activites, accessed 15 March 2008.

World Trade Organization, Understanding the WTO: Cross-cutting and New Issues: Investment, competition, procurement, simpler procedures, www.wto.org/english/thewto_e/whatis_e/tif_e/bey3_e.htm, accessed 1 March 2008.

Zamborsky, Peter, 'Slovakia: Bargain Motors', *Economist Intelligence Unit – Business Eastern Europe* 23, 19 July 2004, http://people.brandeis. edu/~zamborsk/Article%20on%20investment%20incentives%20for%20 Economist%20Group.html, accessed 20 July 2009.

Index

ABM (Anti-Ballistic Missile)
  Treaty 175
Afghanistan 9, 100, 166, 172, 196
Ahmadinejad, M. 27
AIDS (Acquired Immune Deficiency
  Syndrome) 17, 96, 102, 104;
  see also HIV
al-Qa'eda 90, 100–1, 124, 177
AML (anti-money laundering) 150–1
AFS (American Field Service) 190
Annan, K. 94
ANZUS (Australia, New Zealand,
  United States Security Treaty)
  166
APEC (Asia–Pacific Economic
  Cooperation) 49, 54, 81
Arab–Israeli War 164
ASEAN (Association of Southeast
  Asian Nations) 24, 49, 55, 143
AU (African Union) 24, 49, 55, 167
Australia 9, 23, 44, 71, 72, 166, 172

Bank Holding Company Act 85
Basel Committee on Banking
  Supervision 26, 35, 45, 56,
  149–51
BBC (British Broadcasting
  Corporation) 95, 112
BDA (Business for Diplomatic Action)
  130–2
Beers, C. 124, 128, 131–4
Belgium 27, 31, 42, 44, 52, 61
Berlin Wall, fall of 73–4

Bermuda 79
Bernanke, B. 64
Berridge, G. 3, 202
bilateral diplomacy 23–5, 50, 143,
  148, 153, 157, 192, 193
BIS (Bank for International
  Settlements) 52, 56, 64, 148–9
Blair, T. 64, 102–4, 197
Bono 17, 19, 90, 96, 98, 101–3
Bretton Woods 26, 52, 58–9, 63, 146,
  153, 203
Brown, G. 63, 102
Brussels Sugar Convention (1902) 22,
  25, 51
  Permanent Sugar Commission 25,
  51
Bruton, J. 29
Burma 37–8, 99–100
Bush, G. W. 1, 17–18, 101–3,128, 130,
  131–5, 174–5, 183
Bush, L. 183–4

Canada 44, 47, 59, 111, 147, 172,
  206
Caricom 24
Carter, J. 8, 19, 97–9, 174
Castro, F. 27
CFSP (Common Foreign and Security
  Policy) 43, 61
CGI (Clinton Global Initiative) 75,
  156
Charlemagne 12
Chavez, H. 27, 135

CII (Confederation of Indian Industry) 129, 143–4
CIS (Commonwealth of Independent States) 55, 162, 166–7
CSTO (Collective Security Treaty Organization) 160, 167
Citigroup 5, 12, 200
Citicorp–Travelers merger 83–7
climate change 11, 59, 61, 70, 102–4, 178–9, 210
Clinton, B. 1, 64, 75, 80–2, 84, 97, 130, 156
Clinton, H. 1–2, 70
CNN (Cable News Network) 1, 4, 112
Cold War 4, 32, 73–4, 82, 110, 116, 167–71, 173–4, 204; *see also* post-Cold War
Concert of Europe 25, 31, 50–1, 56, 161, 163, 173
Congress of Vienna (1815) 25, 50, 161
Constantinou, C. 14, 24, 202
Cooper, A. 91, 96, 101–2
Copeland, D. 211
Copeland, G. 123
CSCE (Conference on Security and Cooperation in Europe) 6, 167
Cuban Missile Crisis 110, 204

Darfur 9, 95, 99
Darling, A. 64
DATA (Debt, AIDS, Trade, Africa) 17, 90, 96, 102
de Gaulle, C. 27
Denmark 44, 71
Der Derian, J. 13, 19, 31, 92, 100, 119
Derrida, J. 207
Deutsche Bank 85
diplomatic corps (*corps diplomatique*) 20–1, 34, 133
diplomatic culture 21, 22, 26, 39, 45, 92, 99, 133, 177, 179

diplomatic protocol 10, 21, 182–3
diplomatic studies 3–4, 9–10, 202, 204–5
classical 37, 161, 169, 203, 208

EBRD (European Bank for Reconstruction and Development) 49, 55
Egypt 172
relations with Israel 7–8
Ellul, J. 123
ESDP (European Security and Defence Policy) 43, 61, 172
ESU (English Speaking Union) 181, 191
EU (European Union) 9, 11, 12, 24, 27, 28, 29, 33–4, 39–44, 49, 53–4, 61–2, 68, 71, 75, 76, 82, 118, 141, 148, 150–1, 156, 157, 167, 172, 187, 188–9, 190, 200, 211
DG Relex 40–1
PSC (Political and Security Committee) 43
see also CFSP; ESDP

Facebook 211
FAO (UN Food and Agriculture Organization) 57–8, 64
Federer, R. 97, 126
FIFA (Fédération Internationale de Football Association) 136, 193–4
First World War 3, 123, 173; *see also* post-First World War
FIS (Fédération Internationale du Ski) 194
Fitzpatrick, K. 126
France 19, 27, 28, 32, 42, 57, 59, 61, 95, 129, 147, 157, 163, 169, 174, 203

G7 (Group of Seven) 13, 26, 45, 49, 52, 59, 147–50, 210

G8 (Group of Eight) 13, 26, 29, 49, 52, 59, 68–9, 93–4, 96, 101–4, 148, 153–4
G20 (Group of 20) 29, 210
GAAP (Generally Accepted Accounting Principles) 80, 83, 152
Gates, B. 17–18, 75
  Bill and Melinda Gates Foundation 92
GATT (General Agreement on Tariffs and Trade) 26–8, 52, 58–9, 68, 140–1, 145, 153–4, 203
  TRIMs (Trade-Related Investment Measures) 145
Gazprom 5, 19
Germany 32, 33, 42, 43, 47, 51, 56, 59, 61, 71, 113, 122, 139, 143, 147, 157, 163, 165, 168, 170, 182, 190–1, 204
  Deutsche Bahn 105
Gladstone, W. 203
Glass–Steagall Act 84–5
globalization 50–1, 70, 84–5, 131, 142
  impact of technology 110
Gramm–Leach–Bliley Act 85–6
Greenpeace 11, 19, 88–90, 92, 94–5
Greenspan, A. 64, 81

Habermas, J. 101, 188
Hamilton, K. 13
haute politique 50–1, 169, 202, 204, 205
Hezbollah 129
HIPCs (Highly Indebted Poor Countries) 154–5
Hitler, A. 113, 196, 199
HIV (Human Immunodeficiency Virus) 92, 96, 104; *see also* AIDS
Hocking, B. 37, 39–41, 80, 91, 202, 209
Holy See 31–2, 198–9

HSBC (Hongkong and Shanghai Banking Corporation) 71, 78, 80, 85
Hudson, D. 205–6
Hussein, S. 4, 207

IADB (Inter-American Development Bank) 24, 55, 153
IAS (International Accounting Standards) 83, 152
IASB (International Accounting Standards Board) 151–2
IBEF (India Brand Equity Foundation) 129–30, 144
ICC (International Chamber of Commerce) 26, 29, 49, 53, 60, 67, 90
ICC (International Cricket Council) 193–4, 197
ICRC (International Committee of the Red Cross) 6, 11, 19, 28, 90, 91, 94–5, 105, 158
ICT (information and communications technologies) 34, 72, 109, 149
ILO (International Labour Organization) 28, 57–8
IMF (International Monetary Fund) 22, 24, 26, 29, 35, 49, 52, 58, 63–7, 146, 148, 153, 155, 158–9, 200, 203
India 17–18, 23, 32, 33, 70, 97, 101, 104, 129–30, 135, 143–4, 199, 206, 210
  relations with Pakistan 18, 101, 135, 192–3
  relations with US 186–7
International Atomic Energy Agency 35
International Relations 3, 4, 9, 13, 20, 22, 190, 201, 204
  English School 13, 22
  neorealist approach to 202

International Telecommunication
    Union 22, 26
IPU (Inter-Parliamentary Union) 46
Iran 27, 102, 180, 198, 199
Iraq 131, 132, 166, 207
    invasion of 2, 4, 61, 101
    war 126
IRB (International Rugby Board) 193
Ireland 29, 44, 182
    relations with UK 48
Israel 72, 129, 182, 187, 198
    Knesset 7
    relations with Egypt 7–8
    relations with Palestine 64, 164,
        211
ITF (International Tennis Federation)
    193–4

Jackson, J. 96, 97, 198
Japan 21, 32, 59, 71, 92, 95, 130, 147,
    148, 163, 172, 178, 182, 190, 193,
    201
Johnson-Cartee, K. 123

Kennedy, J. F. 110, 169
King, M. 64
Kissinger, H. 193, 204
Kosovo 9, 171, 172, 187
Kurbalija, J. 114

Lamy, P. 17
Langhorne, R. 13, 202
League of Nations 22, 25–8, 52, 56,
    117–18, 161, 163
Lebanon 96, 129
Lee, D. 202, 205–6
Lenin, V. 10
London 24, 61, 78, 84, 104
    Ken Livingstone 47
    London Stock Exchange 152
    terrorism 103
    Treaty of London (1831) 31, 51

Mandela, N. 19, 97–9
Marshall Plan 59, 189–90
Melissen, J. 122
Merkel, A. 64
Microsoft 6, 11, 17, 19, 71, 75, 79, 86,
    87, 92
Mitchell, G. 98
Molotov–Ribbentrop Pact 113,
    165
MSF (Médécins Sans Frontières) 22,
    90, 94–5, 105, 156
multilateral diplomacy 25–6, 28, 45,
    118, 147–9, 153, 163, 181
Mussolini, B. 198–9

NAFTA (North American Free Trade
    Agreement) 29, 49, 54–5, 63, 81,
    143
NATO (North Atlantic Treaty
    Organization) 11, 26–7, 29, 34,
    45, 46, 54–5, 111, 118, 162,
    167–73, 179
    ISAF (International Security
        Assistance Force) 172
    NAC (North Atlantic Council)
        168–9
    NACC (North Atlantic
        Consultative Council) 171
    NRC (NATO–Russia Council)
        172
    PfP (Partnership for Peace
        programme) 171
    PJC (Permanent Joint Council)
        171–2
Netherlands 44, 60, 71, 182, 185
Neumann, I. 110
New York City 24, 28, 78, 135,
    147
    Michael Bloomberg 47
    Rudolph Giuliani 47
    see also NYSE
Nicolson, H. 4–5, 202

Nixon, R. 169, 174, 183, 193, 204
Northern Ireland 48
    Good Friday Agreement 98
Nye, J. 122, 127
NYSE (New York Stock Exchange) 152

O'Neill, P. 17, 96, 102
OAS (Organization of American States) 54–5
Obama, B. 1–2, 98, 101, 134
OECD (Organization for Economic Cooperation and Development) 49, 52–3, 59–60, 63, 145, 206
    MAI (Multilateral Agreement on Investment) 53, 59–60, 81, 145, 206
Olins, W. 129
Olympic Games 48, 136, 191, 195–7
    IOC (International Olympic Committee) 47–8, 181, 195–7
OSCE (Organization for Security and Cooperation in Europe) 162, 167
OTM (organization employing terrorist methods) 177, 179

Pahlavi, P. 127
Pakistan 100–1, 135–6, 149
    relations with India 17–18, 101, 135, 192–3
Paulson, H. 64
People's Republic of China 6, 32, 56, 57, 78–80, 81, 103, 104, 125, 136, 148, 163, 174, 183, 190, 191, 193, 196, 204, 209, 210
    annexation of Tibet 199
post-Cold War 4, 5, 32, 57, 73, 116, 170–3, 175
post-First World War 18, 121, 161, 191

post-Second World War 6, 23, 32, 36, 44, 118, 121, 153, 157, 161, 165, 179, 190, 199, 201, 204
poverty 17, 59, 63, 90, 94–8, 101–5, 154–7, 178–9, 199, 210
propaganda 72, 122–3, 132
public diplomacy 7, 14, 32, 67, 72, 79, 90, 94–5, 101, 103, 109, 112–13, 121–37, 143, 173, 177, 181, 208, 211

Queen Elizabeth II 182–4, 191

Rana, K. 121, 206
Reagan, R. 111
Republic of China 32, 56, 176–7, 196
Republic of Georgia 33, 46, 176, 195–6
Rice, C. 101–2, 125–6, 133, 135
Royal Bank of Scotland 99, 200
Rubin, R. 64
Rushdie, S. 180, 199
Russia 9, 10, 23, 28, 32, 40, 57, 59, 64, 100, 116, 125, 148, 158–9, 163, 166, 171–2, 174–5
    relations with the US 81–2
    Revolution 92

SALT (Strategic Arms Limitation Treaty) 169, 174, 204
SCO (Shanghai Cooperation Organization) 29, 54–5, 167
Scotland 41, 47, 101
Second World War 26, 44, 58, 146; *see also* post-Second World War
September 11, 2001 attacks 2, 4, 128, 130, 131, 158
Slovakia 76–7
Somalia 95, 100
SORT (Strategic Offensive Reductions Treaty) 174

South Africa 39, 49, 78–80, 97, 99,
    136, 152, 190, 197
Soviet Union 6, 32, 73–4, 111, 111,
    116, 162–5, 169, 171, 174–5, 196,
    198, 204
  dissolution of 4, 23, 32, 166
Spence, D. 39–41
Stalin, J. 32, 113
START (Strategic Arms Reduction
    Treaty) 174
Strange, S. 23, 72, 80

TCO (transnational criminal
    organization) 89, 99–100, 105,
    149, 150, 177, 179, 208
The Elders 99
Tokyo 24
  Tokyo Stock Exchange 152
Toyota 5, 11, 19
trade liberalization 9, 17, 37–8, 51,
    65–6, 68, 81–2, 140–2, 145, 154,
    201, 204, 209
Treaty of Marrakech 35, 81, 140,
    145, 203
Treaty of Nice 43
Treaty of Versailles 13, 22, 25, 55,
    161
Tupac Amaru 21
Tutu, D. 97–9
Twitter 211

UK (United Kingdom of Great
    Britain and Northern Ireland)
    12, 32, 47, 48, 57, 59, 64, 71–2,
    84, 85, 102, 112, 119, 126, 130,
    147, 148, 151, 157, 182, 188, 190,
    197, 198, 200, 207
  relationship with Ireland 48
UN (United Nations) 6, 11, 19, 22,
    23, 24, 26–9, 35, 49, 52, 56–8,
    61, 68, 94, 97, 104, 118, 134,
    150–1, 157, 162–5, 176, 179–81,
    195

General Assembly 57, 94–5, 134–5,
    154, 194
  Security Council 56–7, 61–2, 162–5
  UN Charter 27, 35, 57, 163–5
UNCTAD (UN Council on Trade and
    Development) 57–8, 63, 153,
    154
UNDP (UN Development Program)
    57–8, 63, 153, 154
UNESCO (UN Educational, Scientific
    and Cultural Organization)
    57–8, 181
UNHCR (UN High Commissioner
    for Refugees) 97, 157
UNICEF (United Nations
    International Children's
    Emergency Fund) 97, 198
United States 1–2, 8, 10, 27, 32, 37,
    38–9, 45, 57, 61, 71–3, 80, 82–7,
    97–8, 101, 103, 112, 123–5,
    131–4, 143, 146–8, 151, 169, 172,
    174–83, 185, 188–91, 193, 200
USIA (US Information Agency) 127
USTR (Office of the United States
    Trade Representative) 38, 45,
    141

Vajpayee, A. B. 17–18
Van Ham, P. 127
Volcker, P. 147

Wal-Mart 71, 85
Wales 41, 47
Watson, A. 5, 40, 202
Westphalia, Treaties of 13
  Peace of 18, 202
  Westphalia system 19–22, 31–2,
    48, 117, 163, 202, 206, 208
Weill, S. 85
Wilson, W. 10, 121
World Bank 24, 26, 29, 35, 49, 52, 55,
    58, 63–4, 66–7, 153, 154, 158,
    203

World Economic Forum 17–19, 23,
    28, 29, 49, 52–53, 60, 63, 64, 67,
    69, 90–1, 93, 130, 135–6, 155,
    159, 176, 181, 186
  Global Competitiveness Report
    53
  Global Education Initiative 60
World Health Organization 35, 159
World Vision 22, 90

WSF (World Social Forum) 93–4
WTO (World Trade Organization) 6,
    9, 17, 25, 28, 29, 35, 49, 52, 58–9,
    61, 62, 63–9, 72, 81, 92, 94, 104,
    134, 139–45, 153, 203, 209
  Doha Development Round 9, 17,
    145, 201

YouTube 1–2

UNIVERSITY OF WINCHESTER
LIBRARY